STEPPING
STONES
SUCCESS

EXPERTS SHARE STRATEGIES
FOR MASTERING BUSINESS,
LIFE, & RELATIONSHIPS

Stepping Stones to Success
Copyright © 2011

Published in the United States by
INSIGHT PUBLISHING
Sevierville, Tennessee • www.insightpublishing.com
ISBN 978-1-60013-603-0

Cover Design: Emmy Shubert
Interior Format & Design: Chris Ott

January 2011

Wishing you fun-filled
success on this journey
called life.

Love
Light
Laughter

Helen pg263

A Message from the Publisher

There are many things I've come to understand throughout the many years I have been in this business. I've learned that it's never too late to grow and learn, to change course, to expand perspectives, and to admit I don't know everything.

Because I know it's important to learn from the experience of others, I reached out to many experts when putting this book project together and I gained some valuable information from them. The people I talked with have presented some insights that will expand your horizons and make you realize that you can be the key to your own success.

This book, *Stepping Stones to Success,* is your golden opportunity to profit from the knowledge of others. It will give you the facts you need to make important decisions about your future.

Interviewing these fascinating people was a unique learning experience for me. And I assure you that reading this book will be an exceptional learning experience for you.

—*David Wright*

The interviews presented in
Stepping Stones to Success
are conducted by

DAVID WRIGHT
President and Founder
ISN Works and Insight Publishing

TABLE OF CONTENTS

CHAPTER ONE

Living by Choice
An Interview with . . . **Camille Bulliard**

DAVID WRIGHT (WRIGHT)
Today we're talking with Camille Bulliard, Certified Professional Co-Active Coach and founder of Coaching for a Life in Balance. Camille offers a full complement of coaching and support services as "The Choice Coach." She helps Creative Professionals, Entrepreneurs, and CEOs create concrete steps to accelerate their careers and specifically transform their approach to business and life from a choice-centered approach. Former professional actress, Camille began her coach training in 2004 with The Coaches Training Institute, working with Creative Professionals in Hollywood, and has since grown to a bi-coastal practice.

An accomplished speaker and author, Camille also serves full-time as Assistant Professor of Theatre at the University of Louisiana at Lafayette.

Camille, welcome to *Stepping Stones to Success*.

I know you have heard many, many definitions of success, but how do *you* define success?

CAMILLE BULLIARD (BULLIARD)
I would define success as that feeling each one of us has when life is resonating with fullness. We are successful when we feel focused, purposeful, and secure or in control of the way life is unfolding. I believe a life filled with fulfillment is a successful life. Fulfillment is about being fully alive and living

in a state of the fullest expression of who we are. That can be a life filled with tremendous financial abundance and career success or a life pared down to complete simplicity or standing for what one firmly believes.

But a fulfilling life doesn't always mean that we're "feeling good." A fulfilling life that champions us to stand for what we believe could possibly mean that we've had to make some hard decisions about releasing people or circumstances from our lives *in order* to be fulfilled. So in living in the fullest expression of who we are can be filled with joy and happiness or sometimes downright fear, but it forces us to stand firmly on our own ground.

I believe the concept of fulfillment is an incredibly individual one. When we are living a life of fulfillment, we are most likely in alignment with our values, honoring them on a daily basis and making choices that honor them as well.

WRIGHT

When and how did you get into the coaching field?

BULLIARD

I first heard the term "life coach" while I was a student in graduate school studying theatre. A colleague returned from performing in a show after summer break and was speaking emphatically about how a life coach he met completely changed and organized his life. It was much different from the work he had experienced with a therapist.

Being very eager Master of Fine Arts (MFA) acting students, we were very interested in anything that would help us streamline our process of marketing ourselves—"getting ourselves out there"—and tools to deal with the challenges of time management and being overwhelmed, were heavily sought after. Even though many of us consulted with therapists here and there throughout the years, there was something really enticing about this approach. The process of working with someone in a way that was goal-oriented rather than solution-oriented, really spoke to me. I remember my friend saying to me, "You would love this woman! You need to call her. It will change your life!" And he believed it so completely, that the thought really stuck in my mind, but I wasn't yet moved to make the call.

A few years later, I had completed my graduate degree and made the move to New York City, then to Los Angeles, and was now managing a spa in Beverly Hills as my "day job," still pursuing an acting career.

Then two things began to happen:

First clue: The struggle to make time for auditions and acting classes while holding a full-time job became more and more challenging and less rewarding. The day job was sure to reward me with end-of-the-quarter bonuses if I put in the work, and the clients made me feel that I really made their day "special."

But the auditions began to feel like a lot of work that was going nowhere. I would prepare vigorously for a three-minute audition that, after all the prep work I had done, was left to vanish into thin air if I didn't get a call-back or get the job.

In contrast, the feeling of accomplishment while working at the spa was allowing me to realize that I was just as good at many other things *other than just acting.*

Every actor (especially right out of an MFA training program) feels and truly believes that he or she has something completely unique and powerful to offer the industry. But the opportunity to actually put those talents to use are so few and far between that my desire for the career was beginning to wane. I was also realizing that while working in the spa and wellness industry, I was really enjoying "taking care of" and "listening" to others—and I felt that I was making a difference.

I also began to realize that my study of "humanity" in my acting and theory classes was coming into excellent use because I was able to see issues and relationships and goals from many different perspectives, as if I were trying to pull apart, explore, and discover why "characters" were making the choices they were making in their lives. I also began to realize that I wasn't afraid to "step into" anything—that I could be present with anyone, about any issue or topic of discussion. I was intensely curious about them. I think my courage not only empowered me, but others as well because I was willing to be there with them about anything.

Another gift I attribute to my tremendous actor training was to be bold and take risks. So by default, I was becoming a sounding board, *acknowledging what others were experiencing.*

I then began to want more of the one-on-one time with people I was meeting and speaking with. Serendipitously, I had the opportunity to catch up with the colleague who mentioned the term "life coach" to me again. This time, though, something began to turn and simmer.

I took my grad school colleague's advice and called the coach he had met that summer. To my surprise, she was working in Los Angeles for a few weeks and had a complimentary session she was willing to offer me. *Great!* That session really opened my eyes and my heart and I knew this was something that I wanted more of, so I decided that I would learn more about the coaching field. I began doing research on coaching classes and training.

At this point, I had also begun working with a coach to find my own clarity in my life's direction using the various skills I had obtained. The coaching work was offering such clarity and momentum of change that I became a true believer. This level of supportive and objective relationship with a coach was a sure way to brainstorm, streamline, and create definitive action in one's life.

Second clue: A few months later, I was home one evening near New Year's Eve and was planning to continue narrowing down my research on coach training programs. I happened to open a copy of W magazine and there it was—a feature on one of the magazine's ten must-have items for the new year—a life coach! I was stunned and beyond inspired. Not only was this a "sign" for me (I believed) but this coach was listed as Hollywood's leading life coach and she was featured in a major publication (way cool, in my opinion).

I wasted no breath. I called the number immediately and left a message for an appointment with her. Being so inspired and excited, later that night I composed a very lengthy e-mail to her, explaining why I wanted to be a coach and how urgently I needed to speak with her.

We met within the next two weeks, and I have not looked back since. Eventually, I became her assistant while I was in my coach training program, while still juggling a day job; but the juggle became so much more enjoyable. I was learning so much. I truly felt that I was creating a niche for myself. I wanted to be a coach in the high-end, high-octane world of the entertainment industry, and I was on my way to making that happen. I would still be involved with actors and the world of creativity, magic, and lights, but I was making it happen on my agenda. It was completely empowering.

Still today, my coaching work finds its way into my classes as a university professor of an actor training program.

I come from the approach that the work of an actor is very much autobiographical; therefore, it is imperative for actors to know themselves and their instrument fully, as well as to be passionately curious about human behavior.

In service of that approach, my classes experience a great deal of work naming, acknowledging, and exploring the students' core values and ways of functioning within their own lives and relationships. I believe this deep, exploratory work gives actors in training a varied "self mirror" to look within as they begin to understand and deliver their work from a place of authentically, understanding their own life first, then translating that work to developing characters with depth.

WRIGHT

Who are your ideal clients?

BULLIARD

My ideal clients are creative professionals. But I actually have come to realize that absolutely everyone has a creative side available to them to assist in making changes, or at least a creative side that is yearning to be heard and released. I do work mostly with creative professionals, but my client base also includes entrepreneurs, CEOs, and sole proprietors. As a university professor, I also work with soon-to-be college graduates.

However, whatever background clients come from, we work within a co-creative container to achieve their goals. This co-creative approach means two things. Number one, that clients intrinsically have their own answers already present within themselves and are naturally creative, resourceful, and whole. Clients are in a place where they are ready for active collaboration to move forward in their life. Even though the approach is that clients have their own answers available to themselves, it is the job of the coach to uncover, encourage, and champion clients to trust and listen to those answers.

Number two, that the coach and client place their trust in the power of the coaching relationship to design and create, through a collaborative process, the client's wants, needs, and desires with the agenda always coming from the client.

For the executive, this approach can be incredibly refreshing, stimulating, and creative. For the college grad, it can offer a familiar conversation that he or she can grasp and get excited about.

Since the coactive approach can be applied to an array of professions and occupations, it is an integrative approach that includes the client's *whole life*. We experience circumstances from our personal lives in our professional lives and our professional lives, and ways of being often show up in our personal lives. So even though we may choose to focus on one area—career, relationship, health, finances, personal growth, etc.—each area has an influence on another. I believe that there is a sense of maturity in acknowledging that we are one person, living many varied aspects of our lives.

WRIGHT

What makes your coaching practice different from other coaching practices?

BULLIARD

Besides truly working from a co-creative place, meaning that there is always active collaboration and participation from both the coach and the client, my work centers around exploring and acknowledging the choices a client is making in his or her life. That is why I've come to call myself the Choice Coach.

I truly believe that we are at choice about absolutely everything we do, say, and think, in every moment of every day, from how we are going to embark on or execute something to how we choose to "show up" and "be" within a circumstance or relationship.

Clients come to coaching because they want something to be different, they want something to change. So we begin by looking at the choices they are making and what values are being supported or not supported by those choices—what needs to change. This helps the client feel more in control of how his or her life is happening. It's a huge acknowledgement to notice that life isn't turning out the way it is on the basis of "that's just how life happens." No—it's *not!* We're constantly choosing and making choices that bring those results to us, whether they are the things we want or not. So we need to get very specific about what we choose.

Some clients fear that this will be a lot of work to consciously monitor choices, but that's not the case. If the priority is to facilitate change and we are committed to seeing that through, then by being conscious of our choices, we are actually taking full ownership of our life—we are being present, intentional and responsible.

The choices we make on a daily basis either move us toward a fulfilling and balanced life or away from it. That's it.

WRIGHT

How would you describe your coaching style?

BULLIARD

I am a "choice-based" coach. I believe our lives are comprised of the choices we make, every single moment of every single day. We are always at choice, but consciously and deliberately choosing is vastly different from just wanting and hoping or even wishing. So I feel it is imperative to assist the client in getting very clear about what is important to him or her, so that whatever plan of action we create and implement is supported by the choices the client makes. Choosing is an action as well. Choosing is an internal process that affects outwardly how we show up in the world through our actions and attitudes.

> *"First comes thought; then organization of that thought into ideas and plans; then transformation of those plans into reality.*
> *The beginning, as you will observe, is in your imagination."*
> —Napoleon Hill

I begin that process in four "steppingstones" toward clarity of choice:

STEPPINGSTONE 1:

To begin, we work to get a sense or feeling of that "bigger life" vision that the client wants—the bigger agenda instead of just the small "to-do" steps. We do this through guided visualization and conversation, exploring the vision that has no boundaries or limitations around what the client could conceive of achieving, acquiring, or having.

STEPPINGSTONE 2:

Next, we clarify the client's core values—these are the key pieces that must be present in his or her life in order to live a fulfilled life. Our core values are who we *are*, not necessarily who we want to be or wish we would be, but who we are *today*.

Clarifying and defining clients' core values gives us an immediate road map, stating firmly what must be present in their lives for us to even consider moving toward fulfillment.

I feel that this step single-handedly individualizes the coaching for each client. This is about the client—figuring out what creates resonance and fulfillment in the client's life so we will create a path that supports *that*, rather than following a template for simply goal-setting. This is about reaching out to, connecting with, and having communion with the absolute deepest part of ourselves. It is highly individual.

The more clear we are about our values, the more organically and appropriate are our choices. After practicing, acknowledging, and clarifying values over time, we won't make choices that aren't in alignment with our values any longer. If we do, we will become immediately aware that we've made a choice that may move us away from fulfillment. We become highly aware almost instantly if this choice will move us closer to or further away from what we want. Then we get to choose: Do I want to move forward with this choice or not? Is it worth not honoring my values to bring this choice to fruition? Or is it worth stepping away from my values to bring this choice to fruition? The choice is ours, but now we are at least choosing consciously, not by default.

STEPPINGSTONE 3:

From this place, we have a clear path and understanding of what actions to take that are supportive of the client's values *and* bigger life vision, but we also have pieces that resonate with him or her individually.

Coaching is not a one-stop shop for just goal-setting, in my opinion. The coaching has to be created, catered, and molded for the individual. That is why it is imperative to "find out" who the client is at his or her core—the "self" that he or she wants to be without any judgments or limitations. Every client has a very unique image of what that "self" looks like as well as what action steps will be supportive of his or her psyche. Clients will also have the action steps they are truly committed to taking or willing to go out of their comfort zone to try.

STEPPINGSTONE 4:

Another piece that is unique to my approach is "Body Integrated Coaching"— deeply integrating the coach learning into the body. When discovery and learning from the coaching work is deeply anchored into the body, clients have another resource or structure for reminding themselves of the new choices they are making and for remembering the empowering feeling that accompanies those choices.

In this type of coaching, I focus on working with the self—the whole person—through the body by discovering, listening, and exploring sensations within the client's body. This somatic (mind/body) approach treats the body as an essential place of change, learning, and transformation. The body houses our history, our identity, and our strengths, creating a place where the body and the self are inseparable. It is remarkable to really understand and honor that the complete history of our lives exists within our bodies. This means that history, too, can be taken into account when creating new action because it is deeply imbedded in how we already take action and how we choose to be in relationships.

The intention is for clients to commit to new actions and ways of being that allow them to embody *new* skills and behaviors. This is very different from just having an action plan. It is a much bigger transformation than just achieving a goal. It offers sustainable change and learning to align actions with values, so goals are more fully realized through physical action to facilitate change.

For example, if I were working with Joe, an executive, on finding confidence and empowerment in his choices and leadership style, I would first take him through a guided visualization to a time where he remembers a very powerful moment in his life. We would dissect and explore the memory of that moment so that through his imagination and his mind's eye, he is experiencing that very "sweet" moment again by flooding his body with the feelings and sensations of the strength and confidence that were present.

I would then ask Joe in which part of his body did he "feel" that strength and confidence most. He may respond, "In my quadriceps. I felt like I was pulling up on them firmly, tapping into the strength of my legs."

Then we would complete the visualization and return to our coaching conversation. I will ask him to physically stand up, ground his feet firmly, and pull up or tighten those quadriceps to lock in the feelings of confidence and strength he experienced in his visualization. The act of "locking that feeling in" to the body and creating a sense of muscle memory is now something Joe can use anytime he needs to be reminded of where his strength and power lives in his body. Because it was always with him through the experience of his memory, he just needed to tap into it again and remind himself that it was there and give value to the experience that it will be of use to him.

This also gives the client the opportunity to experience moving away from the thinking mind to tapping into the visceral experience in the body. Focusing on "pulling up firmly on his quadriceps" in Joe's next presentation or board meeting will offer him a reminding supportive structure of his strength and confidence, giving him something physical to connect with rather than allowing any nervousness to overcome him.

This exercise keeps us on track, reminding us to remain in the body and out of the intellect, which can so often derail us with questioning or doubting ourselves using logic. Remember, our individual wants or needs may not be logical to anyone else but ourselves.

I also do this work a great deal with actors. I get them focused and dropped into the moment by taking inventory of the body and also connecting with the body as it is today. How is the body feeling today? What does it have to say? How will that support or not support your work?

I believe body-integrated coaching is a very powerful resource because when we can connect with something that is truly our own, our bodies (we own it!) can harness a great sense of control over our selves.

In our busy lives today, we have ample opportunity to get disconnected repeatedly, so body-integrated coaching gives us the chance to deeply connect and anchor a new thought or learning into the body.

A great deal of our lives is spent "looking outside" of ourselves and being exterior beings. This keeps us from changing and trusting who *we* are at our core. Many of us are looking for validation of our choices from "the outside" when the true barometer for whether a choice is appropriate for us or not lies within us.

For example, a great deal of our challenges with Attention Deficit Disorder is that the disorder keeps us from feeling sensation and breath and from being present in the moment; it creates a consciousness of selective unawareness. Instead, we need to be intentional and in the moment.

Once this process is understood and implemented, we can begin to consider that taking on a new way of approaching life by having conscious choice coupled with physical action, deciding, learning, and choosing to change doesn't happen solely through the intellect.

"You can't solve a problem with the same mindset that created it."
—Albert Einstein

It is wonderful to have an action plan to create the life we want, but if the work isn't integrated into the body and we haven't explored a different way of "being," then all we have is another list of goals—what will be different this time? How will we *be* different in our approach this time?

"The core competency of human being-ness is the development of witness consciousness."
—Bo Forbes, Yoga Therapist

It is important to point out that there is a difference between the things we "do" in our lives and the way we choose to "be" in our lives. Doing is about getting things done and directing our focus. Being is how we choose to show up—how we relate and interact with others.

The combination of the coaching work that is then deeply integrated into the body supports clients by *always* having a resource to tap into in an effort to remind them of what they value most. It also helps realign them with their goals by finding that the strength to remain on course literally comes from within.

WRIGHT

What do you think are the biggest obstacles people face in trying to become successful and reach their goals?

BULLIARD

I believe a major obstacle is lack of clarity about their vision for themselves as well as action steps to take that will truthfully support them individually, along with their vision.

In my experience, clients are overwhelmed and bombarded with so much "stuff" that fills up their lives, but most of the "stuff" is about *facilitating* life rather than *living* it. They are driven by circumstances rather than by the clarity of their choices—they are living their lives by default. Being out of balance shows up when we are driven by our circumstances. Fear arises from being out of balance and fear constricts our freedom of choice. When choice is gone, balance is gone and so is fulfillment.

WRIGHT

How do you know what you need to be successful?

BULLIARD

That is a purely individual question because what works for client A may not work for client B. However, having clarity of values and choice, then applying action is paramount to moving toward success. Doing what gives one a sense of feeling significant and having a purpose is a non-negotiable. Whatever those pieces are that will keep us committed and on purpose will serve us every time.

WRIGHT

Is it important to balance your success in your life? If so, how do you balance your success with your life?

BULLIARD

It is absolutely necessary to balance our success in our lives. The hope is that by having success in our lives, we've included balance as an integral component. We understand that success can't exist without balance.

When we are honoring our values, we are living in the success of living fulfillment. Likewise, when we are *consciously* making decisions that move us closer to or away from our values, we are also moving closer toward balance or away from it—we are always making slight adjustments to keep balance present.

I don't believe balance is a place to "reach"—we are always moving toward it or away from it with the decisions we make in our lives. Moving through this process forces us to be in the moment. When living consciously while making choices and decisions, we are making our life intentional.

When balance is not present in our lives, we are, instead, being driven by life rather than driving life and that can make us feel as though we have no control. But we *do* have control—we have a choice about absolutely everything. Just as we choose to maybe let the reins go a bit and be driven, we can also choose to take them back and decide where the path will take us and who we want to be on that journey. It brings it all back to being at choice.

WRIGHT

What is the message you want people to hear so they can learn from your success?

BULLIARD

I want people to understand three very important concepts: Have clarity of choice, patience, and trust within the process. However, trusting the process can be the most difficult component *if* you don't have the proper support around you. It is imperative that we create our team of support. If we want an area of our life to change, it is much more efficient and often easier with a team of support in place. A team not only offers support but can also offer different perspectives about how to approach a goal or task. Harnessing a good team allows us to focus more on what we do want and the actions that will keep us on the path.

Who are appropriate team members? Anyone who will support our vision. But it is important that the team members we choose are objective in order to keep the work about the work, without reminding us of the way things "used to be" or may have been approached in the past. Our objective team members allow us, and very often encourage us, to show up as the person we are closer to becoming and being.

In our society today, we are flooded with so many images, sounds, and sensations from so many different sources—media and the environments we spend our time in—that we become accustomed to having a thought, want, or need and expect it to manifest itself or come to fruition in the next moment.

Many of us have become conditioned to viewing life from the concept of reality television programming. For example, we all know the story of the beautiful young woman who joins the cast of a reality show, meets a guy, goes on three or four dates within the span of two weeks, and then has the most lavish proposal and wedding in the next two weeks, aired for millions to view. Now, this couple is expected to live out a passionate love life, forever. The issue here is that this just isn't based on reality. But because it is what we are conditioned to witnessing about how life can possibly unfold, we become disappointed when our own lives don't deliver the same results and speed for manifesting our thoughts, wants, or needs instantaneously.

There is a tendency to think that if something stimulates us visually or emotionally, we should expect it to manifest within the time frame of a thirty-minute episodic series, and that is not how our human instrument works—not if you want depth and longevity of the life of the experience. We've lost our patience with ourselves and our world.

Trusting the pace of the process and trusting that every circumstance or opportunity we are currently experiencing is contributing to the next step is vital. It is an integral component for remaining present and within the process. It is also important to trust that the process we are currently in is preparing us for what is next, so it is just as important to be here *as fully* as it will be once we reach that next step.

WRIGHT

Tell me, what is a "Choice Coach" and how are you different from other coaches?

BULLIARD

My approach is different because within my coaching work, the focus is on coactive creativity and collaboration between the client and the coach—the work is not necessarily systematic. This means that we are working in the moment with client's wants and needs individually so the choices we make are completely unique and individual about how to move forward, for that client.

When you are free to choose what supports *your wants*, *your values*, and *your goals*, there is complete freedom about choice and choosing. Holding this freedom as something that is powerful and applicable for a client is completely empowering and liberating because we are not trying to follow anyone else's path or template for success—we are creating the client's very own road map.

As a Choice Coach, I consistently remind and return a client to the perspective that we have a "choice" about what we do, so let's check in and see what feels right *for you*. What do your inner core values and being tell you is the right direction to move forward?

WRIGHT

Why are more people not in tune with their passion, if it is something all people possess?

BULLIARD

Webster's dictionary defines passion as: compelling emotion, a strong fondness, enthusiasm, or desire for something.

How does one translate that to having passion in their lives? Having passion is having such a commitment to something that no other "thing" gets in the way of being "with" or attaining the thing that one is passionate about. I don't think passion has to be this grandiose idea about something. It is simply the thing that you choose to be fully committed to, but also something that moves you deeply and emotionally on the inside.

So why would most be out of tune with their passion if it is all that people want? Fear and lack of clarity about how to pursue their vision, in addition to a lack of feeling confident that "whatever my passion is, is valid and socially acceptable and worth my energy and time."

When we are truthfully committed to something, no "thing" gets in our way from existing with it.

For example, it is how some people approach sports. Many will not allow any "thing" to get in the way of watching a favorite sports event. In fact, many will rearrange their lives to support the time for enjoying it. But this passion may get in the way of doing other things in life like tending to the lawn, doing additional research, organizing or taking meetings to close a deal, etc. But the strong underlying emotional resonance with sports connects them so deeply to a value they have that they are committed to it more than to other activities they could choose. An interesting thing is that if we can acknowledge and name that value that shows up so strongly around something that we are so passionate about, like sports, then we can also explore enlivening and aligning the less committed tasks to that same value, with that same passion and resonance.

When our values do not line up with a task at hand, then we are not as committed. Passion unfolds around what we intentionally spend our time with because it moves us emotionally, and what we spend our time with continues to build powerful, intense emotion.

Passion is the fire (the deep emotional connection) that allows us to propel ourselves forward. When we are passionate about something, we are willing to break the rules to achieve it—to make it happen at all cost. This is about aligning and standing up for your values. Passionate people seem to be driven by deep, powerful motives, displayed in business or life, a sense of self-worth, self-fulfillment, or self-satisfaction.

STEPS TO CONNECT WITH YOUR PASSION:
- BE COMMITTED—If you are trying to find your passion, name something that you are *truly* committed to. What is it about this "thing" that fills you up so much? Where else does this exist in your life? How do you want this to be more

fully available in your life? Small achievable steps—Create small, *enjoyable* steps that will help you further reach that goal.

- DEVELOP A TEAM OF SUPPORT—Work with mentors and role models who are objective.
- BE HONEST ABOUT WHAT ISN'T WORKING. Make changes where necessary and "clean it up."
- TIME ON TASK—Make connecting to your passion (or acknowledging the value of your passion) a daily commitment and notice how you show up differently when you are in a passionate place. How can you translate that way of "being" to an area of your life that needs more fuel for the fire?

WRIGHT

Would you say that when people follow their passion and excel at it, does the passion bring the success or does the success bring more passion?

BULLIARD

For the sake of longevity and continuity of living in fulfillment, being committed to and recognizing passion brings success. As mentioned previously, a life filled with fulfillment *is* a successful life—being fully alive, living in a state of the fullest expression of who you are, however *you* want it.

If you are fully plugged in to what you are passionate about on a continual basis, then all opportunity to execute and live fully in that state of being and living passion, will unfold. So what do you choose?

ABOUT THE AUTHOR

CAMILLE BULLIARD, Certified Professional Coactive Coach and founder of Coaching for a Life in Balance, offers a full complement of coaching and support services as "The Choice Coach." She helps Creative Professionals, Entrepreneurs, and CEOs create concrete steps to accelerate their careers and specifically transform their approach to business and life from a choice-centered approach. As a professional actress, Camille began her coach training in 2004 with The Coaches Training Institute, working with Creative Professionals in Hollywood, and has since grown to a bi-coastal practice.

An accomplished speaker and author, Camille also serves full-time as Assistant Professor of Theatre at the University of Louisiana at Lafayette.

CAMILLE BULLIARD
Coaching for a Life in Balance
5000 Ambassador Caffery Parkway
Province, Building 13
Lafayette, LA 70508
(310) 498-3410
www.camillebulliard.com

CHAPTER TWO

Innate Wisdom

An Interview with . . . **Marcella McMahon**

DAVID WRIGHT (WRIGHT)

Today we're talking with Marcella McMahon, Clinical Hypnotherapist and success coach who is dedicated to assisting individuals on their journey to success and fulfillment. McMahon, a national speaker, has been an entrepreneur since her youth and a business consultant since 1997, utilizing her intuitive skills to help businesses and individuals succeed.

Marcella, welcome to *Stepping Stones to Success.*

Marcella, define success.

MARCELLA MCMAHON (McMAHON)

Success is a very individual, subjective experience. It certainly can be thought of as a goal achieved. My earnest personal goals include loving deeply, assisting others, and making a difference in the world. There is more than enough success to go around. Giving our love, support, and encouragement to others on their journey to success never takes away from our own endeavors; in fact, it enriches us.

WRIGHT

What would you have wanted to know about life success when you were just beginning?

McMAHON

The short version of my steppingstones to success encompasses:

1. ALTRUISTIC BEHAVIOR AND CAMARADERIE—There is plenty of success to go around. We all need others on our journey.
2. INNATE WISDOM—We all have vast capabilities of wisdom available to us for free. All that is required is a few minutes of meditation a day.
3. SELF-TREATMENT—Honoring yourself, being thoughtful with your internal dialogue, and speaking your truth are keys to not only success, but true joy.
4. INTENTION DRIVES REALITY—Transformation begins in thought.
5. GOAL-SETTING—Taking one small step every day is important.
6. RELEASE FEAR—Fear is a negative emotion that holds us back from great success.

WRIGHT

Let's take each of those topics one by one. First, what do you mean by "altruistic behavior"?

McMAHON

Altruistic behavior is an unselfish deed that benefits the whole; it is selflessness. Do things without expecting anything in return. There is no limit to how many people may become successful. Someone else's achievement does not mean that there is one less chance for you to succeed. A flame does not dim its glow by sparking another candle—the more candles ignited, the brighter the light. I've found that the more I support others in their success, be it a co-worker, a friend, family member, or someone I don't even know, the more I am rewarded by this support. Of course, I don't support them to get something in return; I give altruistically. It is just something I've noticed as a side benefit.

I highly encourage others to find their bliss, I support their valiant efforts, and I uplift others as often as possible. Plus, it is really fun to see success all around me. It makes me continuously believe it is possible for me, as well. And since there is more than enough success opportunity for everyone, give it freely. It costs nothing.

There is a lovely book I highly recommend titled *Try Giving Yourself Away* by David Dunn. This favorite in my library offers ways we can give more of ourselves without dipping into a piggy-bank or feeling like someone is taking advantage of us. The book was written in the 1940s but the principles still apply today.

If everyone allowed themselves to be altruistically giving and not worry about what is in it for them, the world would be such an amazing and fun experience.

WRIGHT

You also mentioned Camaraderie. Intriguing. Why is camaraderie important for success?

McMAHON

We need each other. My great-grandfather used to say, "Life is too short to make all the mistakes—learn from mine." I am thankful to both him and my father, Bruce, for instilling these wise words in me. Life *is* too short. I find everyone to be my teacher—old or young, dolt or genius, kind or rude. In truth, we are all one. The more we can reach out to others, the faster we can learn.

My friend, Valerie, told me a story about getting an e-mail from a woman she managed. Years ago, Valerie had given the woman a small plaque that read:

> "Don't follow where the path may lead . . . go instead, where there is no path, and leave a trail."
> —Eli Fritz

The woman said the quote is something she lives her life by every day since receiving it. Valerie barely remembered the plaque or what it said, and was astonished that she'd had such a profound effect on someone's life.

I believe most people are unaware of the influence they have on others. Understanding how interconnected we truly are boosts the importance of how we treat each other.

A very nice side benefit to uplifting and instilling success in others is that we are more likely to achieve success for ourselves.

WRIGHT

Let's talk about the second steppingstone on your list, Innate Wisdom, where you say we all have vast capabilities of wisdom available to us for free.

McMAHON

Innate Wisdom is the truth within us. It is listening to our subconscious, highest-self, and greatest guidance. Often at first, it comes in the small, still moments between thoughts, and as we choose to work at listening and trusting our Innate Wisdom it comes to us easier and easier. It is up to each of us to learn and strengthen the connection to this internal guidance system.

As a clinical hypnotherapist, Innate Wisdom is absolutely one of my favorite subjects because through the trance state, which is the same as meditating and accessing our subconscious, we are strengthening our connection to this wisdom. This means you can learn to trust yourself and make better decisions.

Innate Wisdom is one of the most beneficial of all the steppingstones to success!

Meditation is the key to building your Innate Wisdom connection. The great thing is meditation is a natural state. The state of being during guided imagery is similar to meditation, contemplation, daydreaming, or hypnosis; some states are simply deeper than others. We move in and out of these natural states throughout the day. Quieting the logical mind gives way to various levels of relaxation from light to very deep and finally to sleep.

Think back to a time when you were driving in the car while daydreaming. On more than one occasion I thought, "Oh, did I just miss the exit?" only to realize that the exit is just coming up. This is a quite similar feeling to meditation or being in a hypnotic trance. You are in complete control of the car while your consciousness is daydreaming, yet if there was a problem you would immediately snap back to the physical world and correct the car. Even in the deepest hypnotic states, you are in complete control and at any moment you can bring your consciousness to the physical room; yet during the 'daydreaming' or trance you can gain access beyond the physical world.

WRIGHT

Tell me more about what you mean by "Innate Wisdom."

McMAHON

Innate Wisdom rests within each of us. It is our ability to tap into our highest-self to access all that is best for us. In other words, it is employing the vast wisdom of our subconscious, which most of us have forgotten exists. William James was on to something in 1908 when he said, "We are making use of only a small part of our possible mental and physical resources."

Many have given away their internal power of decision-making in lieu of trusting others' guidance. Instead, I recommend we turn within to access our Innate Wisdom through meditative practice or hypnosis and receive the guidance from self. This doesn't mean we should stop asking for the opinion of others, but it does mean that we need to check-in with our own guidance system before we get input elsewhere.

We have so much natural wisdom within us, yet we are not taught or encouraged to access it. Our schools teach us logic—the left side of our brain—but they fail us when it comes to using the right brain, which accesses this Innate Wisdom.

"The intuitive mind is a sacred gift and the rational mind is a faithful servant. We have created a society that honors the servant and has forgotten the gift."

— Albert Einstein

WRIGHT

How do we access this Innate Wisdom?

McMAHON

The most common method to accessing Innate Wisdom is through meditation. In meditation we can quiet the thinking mind and listen to our own internal guidance. The logic-based, thinking mind is the part that wants to narrate or criticize, whereas Innate Wisdom is that small, quiet voice that comes in faintly in the stillness between thinking.

Shutting down that inner narrator can take practice to master. Start by getting as comfortable as possible. For meditation, a recliner, comfy chair, or even lying down works well. I also find that when just learning to meditate, it is far easier to use a recording. The more you can allow yourself to relax, the greater success you will have long-term in accessing your own truths and building your Innate Wisdom muscle.

There are two types of meditation I use: active and passive. For both, I turn off the part of my mind that likes to question and describe everything that happens in the imagination. For passive meditation, the key is to just clear your mind and let information come to you.

In active meditation, before beginning, I focus on what I wish to accomplish. Often I write down a question before I begin an active meditative session. Then I relax the thinking mind and listen for the answers in those small silent periods. I find Innate Wisdom often comes in a slightly softer

21

internal voice or with a thought I know I did not think or with a sudden flash of a great deal of information.

At first your thinking mind often will rebel and want to continue narrating. What helps is giving it a job. I tell it simply to repeat a word: "Deeper" or "Relaxed" or "Truth." Have it say anything you find that works for you but try to keep your inner narrator quiet in the silence between each word repetition. By giving it a job, it tends to stop the desire to critique and put up roadblocks. With practice, simply focusing on your breathing will be enough to keep your awareness engaged.

Utilizing a hypnotherapist keeps you engaged and assists with directing the left brain or thinking mind, thereby allowing the right brain, the intuitive mind, to give accurate information. With self-hypnosis you have to flip between the right and left brain and this is a difficult task that takes practice. Within the thinking mind rests the ego. Ego doesn't allow much of your Innate Wisdom to come through. By quieting the thinking mind in meditation, you switch from ego and logic into the creative mind, which sends you into a higher state of consciousness. Having a live person engaging you will also keep you from going so deep that you fall asleep.

WRIGHT

Tell us more about meditation.

McMAHON

There are a vast number of techniques to use to access inner wisdom. In my early twenties, I managed a small staff and had trouble with one of the long-term employees who was normally very good. I could not figure what was going on with her. Suddenly, she began to come in late, and then she started lying to me. My staff knew that I would help them through any personal or business problem, as long as there was direct communication and honesty. One day she did not show up for work at all. All day I tried to call her. When I didn't hear from her, I decided to use meditation to understand the problem.

I sat down, got comfortable, and used my imagination to create her in my mind. I then started asking her to talk to me about her situation. I must admit, I had to wait for a long time before I could get my visualization of her to talk. This is where I had to be patient and keep the thinking mind busy, while not giving up. She described her struggle with a comment I made about her boyfriend's treatment of her; she was mad at me but could not tell me. After I allowed my image of her to finish talking, I told her that it was not him

I did not like but how he treated her and how she was worthy of better conduct. I also shared with her that I would not tolerate lying, but that I loved her and that we could work through it. Then, I asked her what I could do to help the situation. She said there was nothing I could do. I had no idea what that meant. I was shocked, because my logic and usual behavior would have me talk to her or write her a letter.

I wrote her a letter, despite her saying in meditation that there was nothing I could do, and came in early to put it on her desk only to find a resignation letter on my desk with her keys. Sadly, even though I tried to contact her numerous times, I never saw her again in person. Without that meditation, I would have never understood what had happened.

It is my goal to help people access their Innate Wisdom for themselves. We can do this on our own. This is a huge key, as we all can get the answers we seek to success through our own meditative time.

Utilizing meditation is not new to those who know success. As a matter of fact, the bestseller *Think and Grow Rich* by Napoleon Hill, written in 1937 states, "One of America's most successful and best known financiers followed the habit of closing his eyes for two or three minutes before making a decision. When asked why he did this, he replied, 'With my eyes closed, I am able to draw upon a source of superior intelligence.'"

WRIGHT

What meditation recommendations or techniques have you used to inspire greater success?

McMAHON

I find meditation to be helpful in finding answers to problems, methods of new direction, and wise guidance. My recommendation to clients is to meditate *daily,* even if for only five minutes. This daily practice offers far greater benefit than one hour once a week. If you can't reserve five minutes a day for yourself, your priorities are way out of whack.

Another technique I like to use to harness greater success comes from Napoleon Hill's suggestion in chapter fourteen of *Think and Grow Rich*, where he recommends imagining a council meeting and asking questions of the members at the conference table, allowing your imagination to guide you with answers to your most pressing questions. Here is a link to a free meditation I created: www.PowerToUplift.com/tgr, which was inspired by Hill's idea of creating your own council.

WRIGHT

Tell me more about that the council technique.

McMAHON

An imaginary council meeting uses our ability to use our creative mind and visualize. By visualize, I don't mean you have to see. For example, daydream your ultimate vacation spot. What are you doing? How does it feel? Can you see it? Visualizing is like recalling a dream, which can be just sensing rather than seeing in with our physical eyes. We all are born with the ability to stay quiet and use imagination.

Start the process by visualizing six or more people at a conference table you believe are wise or whom you would like to have as mentors. Some people don't actually see in meditation, so don't get caught up in that; you may just sense, hear, or feel their presence.

Now imagine people qualified to help with the particular problem. For instance, if you are working on a business problem, you may want to imagine Bill Gates and Oprah as a few of the people at your table. Likewise, if you have a spiritual problem, you could choose to visualize Jesus, Buddha, an angel or some other spiritual figure. When I am working on a leadership issue, I often choose people like Lincoln and Mother Teresa. Once I visualize or sense them, I ask any other appropriate members of my team to come forward and fill any empty seats; then I begin asking questions. The questions can be anything I wish to learn, grow, or solve. Then I sit back and listen.

WRIGHT

Does this really work?

McMAHON

I am often amazed at the answers I am given—things I would never have considered.

Years ago, as a business consultant, I was looking for a solution to help direct a client in how to best utilize his small advertising budget. I used this meditative technique and was astounded to have the council come up with faxing as the means to generate sales to his seminars. This was long before fax broadcasting was popular; as a matter of fact, I had never heard that term before. The advertising program was successful and his seminars were soon filled with paying attendees.

The meditation works not only for me but for almost everyone who uses the practice, which is probably one of the reasons *Think And Grow Rich* has been a best seller since the 1930s. Try the free audio file on my site and see for yourself.

WRIGHT

What other meditations work for success?

McMAHON

"The Power of Success through Divine Love" is a program I created from an article by Catherine Ponder. Ms. Ponder wrote a series of prosperity articles for *Good Business* wherein a successful businessman told of the most powerful of all energies—the power of love. I simulated an experiment involving a businessman who gathered a group of people interested in attuning to the energy of success. The first group began with live telephone-guided meditations. It soon evolved to a twelve-week meditation series that focused on the energy of divine love to solve life's problems and engage in success. The success manifested quickly for almost every member of the group. Some of the changes were small while others experienced major changes in their life success circumstances. The group never focused on the problem, but only on divine love to heal the situation. Love is the most powerful of all energies.

WRIGHT

Wow, that sounds amazing.

McMAHON

It has been a truly transformational experience. Many of the group shared stories of finding new jobs, healing broken relationships, and recognizing their life's purpose.

I was one of those people. My life has drastically changed since beginning The Power of Success through Divine Love. I had allowed my life to be less than it was intended. I had put my hypnotherapy business aside for two other companies I was running. About halfway into the series, I received wisdom related to my life purpose, which is to help heal others at a core level through hypnosis and meditation. This information catapulted me back into utilizing my hypnotherapy skills and transforming my life. I am happier now than I have ever been! In fact, the experience was so transformational, it inspired my meditation series: *Power of Success through Divine Love.*

WRIGHT

How does your third steppingstone, Self-Treatment, relate to success?

McMAHON

Self-treatment is a very large part of success. Honoring yourself, being kind to yourself, and speaking your truth are not only important to achieving success, but also to harnessing true joy. True inner joy helps one to lead a happier life and attract others into your life, which elevates your full being.

WRIGHT

It is like the Law of Attraction to some extent?

McMAHON

Yes! It is exactly that—the Law of Attraction. We attract to us what we are and thus the higher we raise our vibration to the level of joy, the more likely we are to surround ourselves with joyful people. This is very important in the success arena and often forgotten.

As humans, we are receptive to many things on an animalistic level, many things of which we are not even aware. On some level, everyone picks up on the vibrations of those surrounding them. For instance, when you walk into a room where two people have just had a fight, you can feel the tension. Those vibrations reach far. Negative emotions repel. I find clients who are keeping themselves from success just by their negativity. Yes, there is a master timing to the success of projects, but you must stay in joy, calm, love emotions, and focus on having fun, because this in turn will draw to you greater success.

Many people seek success but forget to pursue a truly happy and fulfilled life. By focusing your attention on treating yourself with love, you are also much more apt to attract others who treat you with the same kindness. Of course, money, power, and fame are good if used for a higher purpose, but only if you've achieved it with great joy will it result in a successful, fulfilled life.

WRIGHT

How do you suggest people make this important shift in self-treatment?

McMAHON

First and foremost, begin listening to the things you tell yourself. Listen to the words you use to describe yourself internally as well as what you say

26

aloud. I cannot stress enough how important it is to listen and become conscious of what you say to yourself.

I direct some clients to keep a journal of their internal dialogue. You may want to set an alarm every few hours and when it goes off, stop and listen to what you were saying to yourself about your body, attitude, money, job, and relationships. It should take less than a minute to write down. These few minutes of self-evaluation are intensely valuable. As you become more aware, it is much more likely that you will be able to make a shift thinking.

I no longer have to keep a thought journal—I just check in with my inner thoughts throughout the day. Even decades later, I still catch myself with limiting beliefs that need revising.

Someone once told me it takes one thousand times of stating a new belief to override the old. While I am not sure that number is accurate, I am sure that this is why affirmations are important to shifting internal dialogue. Daily affirmations retrain your mind in the areas you are negative.

I take whatever subject I feel needs mental adjusting and start writing sentences about how I wish to feel or behave. It is very important to keep all the statements positive. The mind dismisses negative words. For example, if I wrote, "I will not fall down," the subconscious mind hears, "I will not fall down," or simply "fall down" becomes the mantra rather than the desired effect of not falling. Instead you would want to say the actual desired outcome, something like, "I easily and effortlessly walk down all stairs." I also watch my feelings about the affirmation. If I find resistance, I revise the words until there is no conflict. For example, I wanted to lose weight and started writing "I am thin," but since I knew that was not the case, I was resistant to believing it. I then rewrote it as, "I am making changes daily to be the healthiest me possible." There are more articles on my blog about how to write affirmations.

Self-defeating, critical, or pessimistic internal dialogue is quite harmful. I don't think people realize how damaging it is. We live up to expectations and if our internal dialogue is negative, then how on Earth can we expect to be successful? Be kind to yourself.

In my late teens, a counselor shared with me this piece of wisdom. If there was a five-year-old child being spoken of or spoken to with the words you say to yourself, what would you do? I replied that I would protect the child and not allow anyone to say those things to him or her. The counselor then said, "Treat yourself as kindly as you would treat a five-year-old." This is perfect advice. Heed it and it will serve you well.

WRIGHT

You're right. We will often stand up for a child in ways that we don't stand up for ourselves. You also used the term "speaking your truth" with Self-Treatment. What do you mean by "speaking your truth"?

McMAHON

Equally as important as honoring self, being kind with internal dialogue is speaking your truth. Speaking your truth can be a scary endeavor. If it weren't for the fear we all would simply do it. The first step in the process is determining your truth, which takes awareness. Pay attention to the things that gnaw at you. Sometimes the fear is so overwhelming that we don't even listen to know how we really feel about a situation.

When I was a kindergartener, I came home crying. My mother asked what happened and I shared that our class frosted cupcakes that someone's mother brought and I didn't get to frost one.

Mom said, "Did you speak up and ask your teacher for what you needed?"

No, I hadn't asked. And Mom's pearl of wisdom was, "Well, if you don't ask for things, how will anyone ever know you need them?"

"Brick walls are there for a reason: they let us prove how badly we want things because the brick walls are there to stop the people who don't want it badly enough."

—Randy Pausch

If something bothers you, speak up for what you need. You don't have to be a demanding person to speak your truth. By speaking your truth, you in turn allow others the space to speak theirs.

Speaking your truth includes getting rid of the "shoulds" of life and allows you to say "no" to requests that are not in alignment with your time availability or heart's desire. Stop doing things out of obligation that do not serve your larger vision for your life.

Fears come from many sources, such as what others might think, how will we be perceived, or from remembered times when things did not work out as planned. Fear keeps us from speaking our truth. By pushing past our fears and facing them head on, we imprint new data onto the situation. Take a few more risks this week. Trust that you will be okay. You can even use meditation to connect with your truths -- your Innate Wisdom -- and ask for help in knowing you will be okay.

WRIGHT

I like your fifth steppingstone, Intention Drives Reality. I think I get where you are going on this one. Like the quote from Gandhi where thoughts become your destiny, right?

MCMAHON

Exactly! Transformation begins in our thoughts. I love that quote from Gandhi.

"Keep your thoughts positive, because your thoughts become your words. Keep your words positive, because your words become your behaviors. Keep your behaviors positive, because your behaviors become your habits. Keep your habits positive, because your habits become your values. Keep your values positive, because your values become your destiny."

—Gandhi

The quote shows the direct correlation of the progression from thoughts into destiny. And this too is why steppingstone three, Self Treatment, where we talked about the small voice within and what we tell ourselves, is so important. The thoughts we think do influence what we become.

Intention behind what we do is just as important, if not more important, than the action. Scientists have been studying intention for decades. Dr. Elisabeth Targ was granted 1.5 million dollars for an interesting study on intention and healing. In a double-blind study, she took twenty very ill patients (all with the same illness) and assigned ten to a control group. Experienced healers placed their attention on the other ten and sent intentions of healing out to them. That was it—they were not in contact, or for that matter, they weren't anywhere near the patient. The healers were simply sitting in their homes or offices sending intentions out into the universe.

Just like we know radio waves bounce through the atmosphere but we can't see them, so too are our intentions continuously being sent out into the atmosphere. The results were impressive. Four of the control group had died (the average mortality rate for the illness), while all of the patients who were sent intentions of healing were still alive. Targ then wondered if ordinary people could have an effect on illness. The subsequent study found results small but significant.

Numerous studies in intention have been compiled and I find it amazing how much our body sensory system picks up on the intentions, yet we may have no idea. For instance, the University of Washington selected couples for a study where one was the sender and one was the receiver. They wired them to an MRI machine to measure brain function. The sender was shown a flickering light and was instructed to transmit via thought what was being seen and the person's emotions about it. The study proved that recipients experienced increased blood oxygenation in the visual receptor area of the brain only when stimulated by the sender's intentions. Bastyr University repeated the study with those experienced in meditation and found much stronger connection between the senders and receivers. The receiver's brain reacted as if they were seeing what the sender was actually seeing.

Another study was done where the University of Edinburgh compared EEGs of closely bonded couples. When the sender was stimulated by a picture or small shock, the receiver's brain waves were in sync with the sender's experience, be it pain or pleasure.

Even plants pick up on our intentions. Cleve Backster did several experiments on plants using the equivalent of a lie detector machine. He placed the electrodes on the leaves and measured the plant's responses to various stimuli. I found fascinating the study where Backster had people file through the room with various intentions where a large plant was set up. One person was given a lighter and partially burned one of the leaves, which registered high on the detector. Even more interesting is that the study continued for weeks with various people flowing through the room. When the same person came back through the room, but this time without the lighter, the plant's reaction was the same!

Another interesting book is by Masaru Emoto titled *Messages in Water*. In it, Mr. Emoto shows the effects of intention on two sealed jars of uncooked rice. One jar is given the intention of love while the other is given thoughts of hate. The love jar stayed the same while the hate jar went rancid. If that is really what happens to rice under intense hate, imagine what we do to our friends, our children, or ourselves when we continuously send messages of hate.

Intentions matter. Many people do very nice things for each other but their intention behind it is negative. A negative example is thinking, "What's in it for me?" I would rather have someone not do something for me than have an underlying expectation. On the flip side, sometimes we are stern but the underlying intent is love. Intention matters.

WRIGHT

What does intention have to do with success?

McMAHON

Our body picks up on the intention of others even though we may not be aware of it. Our subconscious is sensitive to these signals. This means in life and in business, people will sense when the intent of the other person is either self-serving or kind. I find people who are truly successful, not just in business but in life, lead happy, fulfilled lives, and do things with the highest of intentions.

For me, doing things with good intention makes me happier. I am able to say no to things if my intention does not align. I find positive intentions naturally attract great people in my life as well as drawing many amazing opportunities – like the opportunity to be in this book.

WRIGHT

Your next steppingstone is about Goal-Setting. What have you experienced with goal-setting?

McMAHON

Goal-setting is a large part of my life. There are two very important components to goal-setting. The first is being clear on what you wish and the second involves actions you take to accomplish them. The latter is the more vital of the two.

Without goals and clear vision, we lack the direction to achieve what we really want. Get what you wish out of life by first deciding what you want. The goal must be clearly defined so that you may break it into small, bite-sized portions. By breaking it into small tasks, you are less likely to be overwhelmed by what it will take to get there and more likely to take action to achieve it.

There is an old story about two men, each in a boat, and they both want to visit a beautiful tropical island. One man has a map and takes time to set a course toward the island he has always wanted to visit. The second man doesn't have a map, therefore has no course set. They take off on the same day. One month later the first man has long arrived on his island and is having the time of his life while the second man has been aimlessly wandering the ocean, has run out of supplies, and has no idea what to do next. Which man would you rather be?

I use the Law of Attraction a great deal and have learned very important lessons about how I attract exactly what I am asking. The clearer I am, the more accurate the result is to what I really desire.

Each day we have the opportunity to realize there is one small steppingstone to success in front of us. I like to take the goal and break it down into daily or weekly tasks to help manage the course. Long-term goals are realized with one small step at a time. Just take one step every day and by the end of the month you will be in a totally different place than if you had just stood still.

In truth, the just-do-it attitude is often far more important than the planning. We can get sucked into planning and never achieve a thing. There are some projects for which I did not have a clear-cut plan, but every day I did something to work on achieving the goal because it gave me joy. Several of those projects turned out to provide immense value. For example, the initial *Power of Success through Divine Love* experiment was one of those ventures. I had no idea where it would lead, but I was really enjoying the weekly sessions of leading the group through meditation. In the end, the project was very healing for those involved, as well as for me personally. I just kept taking a small step each day or week with the project and soon it had a life of its own.

WRIGHT

Have you ever had a tough time completing a goal?

McMAHON

More than once!

WRIGHT

What advice would you give to those having trouble achieving their goals?

McMAHON

Be kind to yourself when you hit a roadblock or some other obstacle to your next steppingstone. At times, life can be difficult. We all hit obstructions during different periods. This often happens when we least desire it but they can be the most beneficial. So relax when things don't go your way, there just might be something better or some better timing coming for you.

Keep the joy even in the difficult waiting periods. It may be tough to find happiness, but if you stay in the vibration of joy, more and more good things will continue to come your way versus the alternative of getting frustrated, which creates a negative domino effect.

WRIGHT

Your final steppingstone is Releasing Fear. I am interested to hear what you have to say about fear.

McMAHON

Fear is a negative emotion and holds us back from success. Just like the discussion on intention and how its vibration is recognized in our bodies, fear has a vibration that is in the negative realm. This negative vibration repels not only people but good opportunities. The more we fear, the more we separate ourselves from true success.

Many of us are far greater than we believe or recognize ourselves to be. It can be scary to accept this as true and open ourselves up to the experience, but it can also be intensely rewarding.

My greatest advice to others is to let go of the fear and start taking risks; life is short. It is like jumping off a cliff with nothing only to find you can fly. You always could fly, you just didn't know it until you became brave enough (or desperate enough) to jump.

MARCELLA MCMAHON is a national speaker, author, and Clinical Hypnotherapist who lives in Northern California. She has been a business consultant for more than fifteen years and utilizes her intuitive skills to help businesses and individuals succeed. As an intuitive business consultant, she truly enjoys bolstering companies in finding the best methods of maneuvering through decision-making and producing creative strategies.

McMahon's life mission is to help individuals heal at a core level:

"The power to heal exists within you.
I am here to assist you in accessing your own healing power."

In addition to seeing clients on an individual basis and assisting businesses, she also teaches meditation, self-hypnosis, and personal empowerment techniques through speaking engagements, telephone appointments, and online classes.

Marcella McMahon is a Registered Certified Clinical Hypnotherapist with the *International Medical and Dental Hypnotherapy Association* and professionally trained in Past Life Regression Hypnosis by psychotherapist and author Brian Weiss, MD. McMahon of *Power of Success through Divine Love* is honored to have helped hundreds of people make transformative life changes.

MARCELLA MCMAHON
Power To Uplift, LLC
916.623.5438 or 888.576.3492
info@PowerToUplift.com
www.PowerToUplift.com
www.MarcellaMcMahon.com
http://blog.PowerToUplift.com

CHAPTER THREE

Envision Your Greatness
An Interview with . . . **Sarah Horton**

DAVID WRIGHT (WRIGHT)

Today we are talking with Sarah Horton who is an author and motivational speaker on Visionary Leadership, Entrepreneurship, and the Design Your Life-Business Process®. She is a personal and business coach, helping people thrive through life's challenges and transitions with authenticity and heart. Sarah's work centers on finding your unique and authentic voice. She has developed practical ways to bring the pursuit of happiness and freedom into the mainstream of life and the workplace. Sarah's rich background of life experience, travel, and education enables her to use different modalities to achieve exceptional results with all her clients.

Sarah's creative approach sparks ideas and solutions. Through the use of empathic listening and visionary guidance, clients identify success habits and manage their unique obstacles to growth while concurrently accessing their greatness, passion, and purpose. In the words of one of her many clients:

"Sarah, you held the space for us to really examine our inner selves and consciously articulate the values, dreams, vision, mission, wants, and desires that come from deep within our hearts. To consciously say, "This is who and what I am" and, "This is what is truly important to me," "This is what I need and want," and at

the same time be guided in the process of achieving those desires with practical down-to-earth planning.

Sarah, welcome to *Stepping Stones to Success.*

SARAH HORTON (HORTON)

Thank you David, I'm grateful for this opportunity to be here.

WRIGHT

Share with us some of your strategies for success in business.

HORTON

I would like to share a story to describe one of my first steppingstones to success. And this was a "Step UP."

After graduating from Boston University's School of Management with a BS in Marketing Communications, I began looking for work. My studies had been theoretical and I was interested in knowing how this all worked in the day-by-day setting of advertising and media. Companies were not recruiting women the way they were men. Most of the women were too busy getting work and moving on with their lives to notice. Most women were nurses or teachers. And, I was the only woman in the freshman class of management who was not a secretarial major. Since I was young and needed to get my real world experience, I answered an ad for secretary to the president of an advertising agency. This way, I could be a fly-on-the-wall and see how it all worked!

I was excited to get the interview and was up for this new adventure. I arrived in a suburban and newly constructed industrial park. I walked up one flight of stairs to the empty second floor foyer, followed the hallway down a long corridor to the end, turned a corner to find the only door. I opened the door into a huge, bright, sun-filled room with floor-to-ceiling windows on three sides. It was the open space of the entire second floor except for a desk, to my right, with a telephone on it. Behind the desk was an inner door.

Out of that door came a medium sized man who had blonde hair, huge blue eyes, and a wide smile. Sensing my wonder, he chuckled and motioned me toward the door into his office. There was a huge desk three times the size of the one I had just seen and an executive chair bigger than he was. He sat down and motioned me to sit in the chair positioned in front of the desk.

He looked at my resume, asked me some typical questions about my telephone and typing skills and asked me if I had any questions. Yes, I did.

"Why do you have that big empty floor out there with only one desk in it?" I asked.

"Oh," he replied, "that will be filled with people within the year." Then he asked if I wanted the job. It certainly didn't fit my traditional pictures, but something deep in me told me to say, "Yes."

Three weeks later, my boss asked me to go home and think about an advertising program for a bank he was going to pitch. I came in with suggestions such as, "You give us your green and we'll give you green" meaning that if you give us your deposits, we'll give you a huge indoor plant (instead of an iron or a mixer). Another was, "Our flowers for your dollars to brighten your life." Another was a public relations campaign for neighborhood improvements: if our clients' bank got x dollars in deposits, they would fund improvements to the parks and walkways. Local newspaper space was free for articles that talked about community improvements, and this was a "greening of America" campaign far ahead of its time. In Boston, "neighborhood" was a key word.

With his professional experience and my new ideas, he developed that into a print and broadcast media community outreach campaign. The two of us went into the bank, pitched the account, and they loved it. It was original, community-oriented, and *green!* (There was a time when banks were "community focused" and not multinational too-big-to-fail corporations.)

We left feeling so successful; yet, within minutes, I had a lump in my throat because I had undersold my skills in my first interview. On the drive home, my boss broke the silence when he told me to hire another receptionist because I was going to be too busy to be doing my old job. Taking a deep breath and clearing the lump, I took that opportunity to tell him the truth about my education—I really had a BS in marketing. Without skipping a beat he laughed and said, "Hire two secretaries and buy two more desks." Two years later, there were ten people and over $5 million in billings. Our agency was winning awards for our community service ad campaigns that soon spread to other regions of the United States.

I am grateful for *all* that this man taught me in those early years about trying new things and holding the vision. I learned some very important lessons:

- Use your creative imagination, develop and initiate programs that help people and the community;
- Details are the secret to the planning, execution, and the launch of an idea;
- Be accountable, show up, be honest;

- Focus on the end result—the practical skill of "holding the space (or picture of an idea in its end result) and allowing the process to fulfill the vision;
- Be in action as you create and be flexible to adjust toward the end result; it's never a straight line;
- Work in partnership or on a team to produce results larger and greater than any one person can do.
- Celebrate the stages of success and create momentum.

And we worked long hours that didn't seem long because we were having so much fun. The charismatic energy that surrounded our team was because we cared about our clients and the customers and we always included a community-building element in our campaigns. Working at this agency was a hands-on-MBA.

Later, I heard the term "visionary" referred to JFK, Martin Luther King, Edgar Mitchell, and I knew I had experienced a taste of magic. This was the first "visionary" and practical entrepreneurial experience I knew and it made me "Step UP" to my skills and abilities beyond background or education.

WRIGHT

What is vision? And how can it be a source of creativity?

HORTON

Vision is simply defined as "a picture or series of pictures of the future"— a view of how you want it to be, how you want the world to be, or how you want your life to be. This is where one starts—by simply dreaming and claiming it. Just as in my story above, there was a vision—an empty floor soon filled with people all working together toward community-oriented marketing programs that supported both the business objectives and a contribution to the community's healthy growth.

Do *you* have a vision for your future or for your business? What might it look like a week from now, a year from now, or five years from now? My clients start by answering the simple question: What do you want? Brainstorm with colleagues or family or friends to develop more of the picture. Draw on your unique traits and abilities, education and skills, and on your passions. Creativity ignites greatness. Write this down and eventually organize the pieces into a mini-business/life plan. You will have a start on the Design Your Life Business Process. (Visit www.steppingstonestosuccess.info for more information.)

WRIGHT

Who do you think are the visionaries now in this time of economic challenge?

HORTON

People who would be reading a book like this—people who have a picture, a dream, and a series of pictures for a specific part of society that needs renewal are visionaries-in-waiting. First, make a commitment to put your ideas into action; hold the vision for the end result. Then celebrate your accomplishments; feel your passion and greatness. Begin again with another part of the larger vision.

Many of the leaders we have today are operating from old success patterns and in systems that need to be reformed and re-energized. I believe that young people today have inside of them the creative genius to solve the issues and challenges of our society. If young, bright minds are given a chance to cultivate their ideas and express their new ways of doing things, accompanied by guidance and wisdom, the end results might be different and most likely better than what we have now.

The same minds that created the recent financial system failures through over-leverage and greed, draining the equity out of our assets, need a new way to think about things. We need *new* and *collaborative* reforms for our financial, health, transportation, and energy industries. We need *new and entrepreneurial* ways to think about business, possibly with an emphasis on collaboration, community values, worldview, sustainability, and generosity instead of greed. There is an opportunity for cross-cultural partnering to bring forth cooperation and use of our resources to benefit many and conserve more. It is necessary to make a shift in consciousness to be inclusive rather than exclusive. It is time for reform and time for a change.

WRIGHT

How can someone become a creative force in his or her own life?

HORTON

You were born with a *vision*. You were born with a unique and special set of talents, traits, and passions. Yes! You can create the you that you want to become—and are becoming—with the help of your creative imagination and by noticing exactly where you are now and what you want. Develop your unique skills, gather your resources, seek the people you need to meet, and attract to you the next steps for your own expression and contribution.

WRIGHT

How did you discover and develop your unique skills, which include empathetic listening and clairaudient abilities?

HORTON

The next steppingstone appeared out of nowhere! And didn't take the form I would have expected. This was a "Step IN."

Returning from the doctor with the diagnosis of breast cancer, I stood in front of the full length mirror and slowly undressed, letting my clothes drop to the floor piece by piece. I looked at my beautiful body. I tried to imagine what I might look like with only one breast. And scars. Fear, anger, and grief welled up inside of me. I said aloud, "How did I create this?" And I collapsed on the floor in tears.

I heard a firm, clear voice say, "You created this; you can uncreate this." I turned around, expecting to see someone standing there watching me. There was no one. I faced the mirror again and said out loud, "How? How can I uncreate this lump?"

The same clear voice said, "Take saunas, eat lemons, and drink pure water."

I listened. And then it occurred to me that I had nothing to lose and everything to gain. I got dressed, walked out the door, went to the store, and bought a bag of lemons, four gallons of water, and went home to take a hot sauna.

After three days of lemons, water, heat, sleep, and tears, I was in the sauna and the voice within began to guide me through a meditation. It was my voice, yet the voice was guiding me and it seemed to come from behind my heart rather than the front of my head. I began to use this meditation every time I got into the sauna. I imagined a ball of white light and directed that light from my heart into the lump and into my other organs. I continued to focus on this light as it moved through my body.

Later that day, I went to the typewriter and typed the question: "Who are you?" The voice behind my heart, which had now turned quiet and soft, answered. "I am the part of you that knows all, sees all, and is connected to all." It was a simple and sensible answer. And for the next several days I asked questions to my higher guidance and continued my silence, saunas, and listening to classical music. I asked questions about war, hunger, suffering, conflict, pain, and more. Answers came from a healing perspective and were filled with love. In the love, the energies of conflict and anger soon dissolved.

During one of my sauna sessions, around day nine, in my mind's eye I saw what looked like a brilliant ring of light with a dark circle in the middle, similar to a sun/moon eclipse—a black mass with light behind it. As I viewed this, it exploded into a million pieces and became a brilliant light inside my mind. In that instance, and without a thought, I knew the lump was gone. And yet, when I touched my breast, it was still there. Immediately, the soft gentle voice now spoke again, "The body is denser energy and it will take twenty-four to forty-eight hours to clear. Your focus now is 'to know that it is gone, to be vigilant with negative thoughts, trust, and have faith that it is gone.'" I "canceled" thoughts of doubt, despair, and judgment, and twenty-four hours later, the lump had completely disappeared, leaving sensitive nerve endings. I fell into gratitude and spent the next few days in a state of love, still wanting to be alone in my home, relishing this expanded awareness.

I returned to my doctor on the day of my appointment and questioned her. Why didn't she tell me I could heal the lump? What was wrong with her diagnosis that indicated surgery was the only answer? She went to medical school, why didn't she tell me about this option? She simply replied, "The lump is gone. Come back for a check-up in six months." I realized in that moment that I knew something she did not, even after all of her years of medical school and training. This was a precious gift—to touch the infinite self. My life was forever changed—a "Step IN." (For the gift of the channeled healing meditation, go to www.steppingstonesto success.info.)

WRIGHT

Listening to your authentic voice has given you an opportunity to help others.

HORTON

Yes, and it is a skill that can be used in practical ways—a skill that can be developed and practiced. Health, happiness, and wellness are a result of listening, knowing, and aligning with your true nature and purpose. So you see, not every steppingstone is an easy one. Some of the most significant learnings may involve emotional fear, release, and adversity.

Learning to listen to the authentic voice within is a skill that can be learned. Using our creativity and desires to ignite vision and greatness pulls us through tough times. Without desires and pictures of what we want, the future can be many possible futures—some we may want and some we don't want. If we combine that with trust in our talents, traits, we can create doorways to higher energy connections. The practice of "visioning" can create end results even beyond our imaginations. Some call these results "miracles."

WRIGHT

I see how you have applied this practice to your own life experiences.

HORTON

I deeply wanted a whole healthy body, one with both breasts. It was vanity and fear that fueled my will. I was in "dis-ease." I was willing to do what it took. It took trusting my inner voice—a voice that in that situation offered my conscious mind a different perspective. It offered one where I had to be willing to try something new—something different than what was being offered. I was educated, I was smart, and I chose to suspend judgment and try a new approach. I also had to visualize the "end result" of a strong, healthy, whole body. The result was that I experienced a feeling of love and greatness that came in to replace the vanity and fear.

WRIGHT

What suggestions do you have for our readers to begin their inquiry?

HORTON

I believe that this quest for self-knowledge is one reason people continue learning throughout life. It can take the form of seminars or university courses, coaching, mentoring, or professional certification programs. Make a choice to learn and move beyond your old habits and into new ideas. Some people use sports, yoga, hiking, or they train to run marathons, or go on silent retreats, or simply walk every day to their favorite place in nature. These experiences remind us to "go beyond" and "outside of the conditioned mind" and experience the greater and expanded self—the part of us that knows all, sees all, and is all—to get a glimpse into the greatness that we are. These are special moments in time to help us remember what is possible.

Just as we exercise the muscles in our body to keep toned, there are ways to exercise our minds. More and more scientific research is now available on the left and right brain, the linear and spatial dimensions of our thinking, intuitive trainings and explorations, scientific neurofeedback (NFB) applications, hypnosis, and neuro-linguistic programming (NLP), artist-way practices, and more. Finding *what works for you* is your adventure, just as my steppingstones were unique to me.

Write down a few names right now of people you admire. This may give you insight as to what you may want to do next. I encourage you to discover and notice what calls to you. Now, I love silence and meditation, and mountain and lake wilderness. However, when I started, if anyone had mentioned a silent retreat, I wouldn't have been able to do it. I had never experienced either of these methods of learning. Boston academia was my early model!

So I found mentors—people who I knew were practicing skills that I wanted to learn. I asked questions and I listened to my inner guidance. I asked for my highest options. I failed and made mistakes; but got right back up and kept going. I developed healthy eating habits and took care of my body so that it could support the clarity of mind and spirit that enlivened the way of life I wanted. I plan "nothing time" into my calendar—time to meditate. I have done many months of silence, walked on fire, explored the mountains and the oceans, scuba dived, high-dived, parachuted, hiked, biked, and swum miles. I've slept for weeks to rest my organs, and I've sailed many miles around many islands. Of course, I also worked full-time jobs but I have planned alternative uses of my time. And if I got laid off or had a break between commitments, I traveled because that is what I love to do—explore.

Currently, I downhill ski so I can touch the sacred space between Earth and sky at the tops of our beautiful mountains. I snowshoe, too, as it is a serene and quiet way to be in the beauty and experience of snow. I chose to live at 6,500 feet altitude at Lake Tahoe, so I have outer space around me that opens the inner space within.

What is it that you love? What takes your breath away? What fills you with love? What is it that releases your passion? And during that time, open to the inner spaces of your mind, your heart, and your incredible greatness.

WRIGHT

In your opinion, how can someone cultivate the connection to the aliveness in his or her own life?

HORTON

To answer this question, I have another fun story—a "Step Back."

When I was twenty-nine, my friends and I were sitting around the table talking about turning the big "three-zero." Turning thirty, as my friends had said, was terrible, over-the-hill, and not to be trusted. Complacency had set in. We argued about this for a couple of hours, and then I challenged them to consider what they wanted before they turned thirty. As a result, and in play, we made individual lists of ten things we wanted to do before we turned that unspeakable age of thirty. My own life was going rather well—I was a college graduate, already married, had a great job in advertising, and had recently built and designed my home, so the basics were covered and I was grateful.

I had to stretch my imagination to ask for other wants and desires. I put down items like: travel to Europe, clean water in the Charles River, have a big party with a band, sail to Nantucket, and be a photographer for National Geographic. (God, where did that come from?) Everyone burst out in laughter. And so did I. You have to understand that we did not know anything about the laws of manifesting, like the book, *The Secret,* teaches today. I was simply a "doer." If I wanted something, I just did it. I made everything— clothes, rugs, and even my own house. I had just bought a camera and my father had given me a subscription to National Geographic when I was a young girl. It still came to my house. The Charles River was so polluted that one could not swim or go in it without suffering health consequences. Science had the technology to clean it up and the Clean Water Act was in place. I didn't need to have a direct connection to knowing how it was going to happen. After all, this was a lark and it was just a list.

I put the list away and forgot about it. My daily life returned to work, home, and family. It was a good life.

Two years later, I found the folded list in the bottom of my jewelry box. I opened it up and sat down in a state of wonder and gratitude. I had just returned from canoeing the Mackenzie River with two other people, photographing and documenting the 2,565-mile shoreline for *National Geographic* and *Outside* magazines. I realized in that moment that I *had created that experience* by making that list two years before. Not only from being on the river for three months in the "land of the midnight sun," but by having *that* profound internal moment of realization did I get the power behind intention, making a list, or applying the rules of design to living my life. What an "a-ha" moment! I had consciously, created and designed my life—a Step Back to acknowledge what is asked for!

Yes, in the way we can design and sew a dress, design and build a house, we can create and design our life. And so I began to test my discovery, resulting in the "Design your Life-Business Process" that when these principles are applied to anyone's life, it brings clarity to the creative process and immediate results.

WRIGHT

Tell me what you learned being on the river for three months.

HORTON

It was over a year before I could put my experience into words because my consciousness had expanded and I didn't have words to match the experience. I had photographs when I first returned. Later, I was able to have a discussion with astronaut Edgar Mitchell who experienced going to the moon and the subsequent "integration" of a changed reality—a spiritual awakening.

How to describe what I experienced? Our natural wilderness provides the most profound and beautiful place to experience the gift of aliveness and solitude. Nature is rich in resources, and our bodies open to rejuvenate and regenerate. Every cell breathes and opens to a union with the energies of all living things. Freedom in our wilderness surrounds us with love and aesthetic beauty. It is a feast of colors and sounds that is vital to expand our vision—both inner and outer. This vast perspective shifts our beliefs and thought patterns—we expand and heal.

On the river, I became one with every living organism, including the rocks and minerals. I understood the wisdom of the great men and women who are dedicated stewards of our Earth—visionaries who set aside large tracts of land that cannot be developed and that are our national, state, and international wildlife park systems preserved for our present use and for the use of future generations.

On the Mackenzie River, which flows north to the Arctic Circle, is more than five hundred miles from civilization and there is no road access. I was never afraid, although respectful of the twelve-foot, sixteen-hundred-pound grizzly bears' habitat. I felt connected and safe when the wolves and other wild animals were curious and investigated our camp perimeters, which were mostly on islands. We traded butter and sugar with remote fishermen along the river for wild salmon and potatoes. The water was clean and clear—there was no industrial PCB run-off to think about. Eagles, hawks, osprey filled the clean air with their grace and magic. Sky, moon, and sun—the light was prismatic and ever-changing, re-energizing, frequencies transforming. A month of all light changed internal psychological cues. I was awake for thirty-six hours and slept for twelve—body rhythms kept a different time.

I returned healthier and fully alive from the river and the wilderness. From that point on I was dedicated to facilitate others to experiencing the gift of the wilderness and the Earth. For me, being surrounded by nature and held by the trees, rocks, mountains, flowers, lakes, grasses, clouds, weather, and

45

the natural environment is a profound connection like being with a lover or "other." When we have nature, space, and community, there is real wealth and abundance.

I became a guide to the wilderness—both an inner and outer guide—to assist others in exploration and discovery. The Expedition Program was a twenty-one-day retreat away from one's routine and familiar patterns.

I partnered with a talented explorer and adventurer trained by the British Special Service. The Expedition visited many of the known sacred places in the world. Our clients had remarkable experiences and discoveries. Thousands were touched by nature and reclaimed their connections through the work. They went on to fulfill their visions—actors, writers, doctors, entrepreneurs—making a difference. The Expedition included an action plan for life and in most cases, an entrepreneurial business idea and plan of action.

WRIGHT

So how do people begin? What strategy would you recommend?

HORTON

It's simple, really. There are many ways. I have shared what works for me, however, everyone has his or her own brilliance and attraction to what makes him or her feel connected. If you don't think you know, just look around you and notice what you like. Notice what you *love*.

At first, many of my clients find it difficult to take a "nothing day" to enhance their spirits and touch into their creative source. It is a requirement in my coaching programs. And for some, more than a day is needed to open. Coaching partnered with hypnosis, HypnoCoaching, has tools to accelerate this process. Take this opportunity to choose what *you* want, claim it, and if you have it already, appreciate and honor it.

Another way to begin is do what I ask my clients to do. I ask them to clear their minds by going through a process that ends with a list of wants and desires. Empty the mind. Feel beyond the physical and material to include emotional states, mental states, and worldview desires. When working with your wants and desires around relationships, use the following sentence: "My dream of my relationship with [name] is—"

Make your list of wants and desires right now to begin to access creative energies. People who *take action* and begin the *inner process* get results. Here, I am not asking you for "commitment," just to make a list of your wants and desires—a "Step *In*" to reveal what is there. Alignment with your true nature and purpose comes from within.

Choice brings freedom. Freedom of choice is primal and basic to our human nature in the United States. Freedom is a direct result of choice. The next steppingstone in this process would be prioritizing and choosing. After that, you may end up with twelve to twenty commitment statements. (Visit www.steppingstonestosuccess.info for further information.)

WRIGHT

Who were the mentors or teachers of life whom you found?

HORTON

My list of teachers begins when I was very young.

My family, of course. And many of my early elementary teachers because I loved school and it was really fun exploring early traits and skills for mainstream. As I matured and began to experience the pain in life, I wanted to unlearn some of my childhood conditioning as I mentioned above. I sought different teachers—academic and spiritual teachers and people who were making a difference in the world. I was exposed to these people living in Boston surrounded by colleges and universities. Robert Fritz PhD, a composer and musician who taught Dimensional Mind Approach, helped me understand my own healing experience and the integration of the creative mind and body. I learned to observe and access the witness state and from there, how to make choices that were the highest options.

Others include: Charles Kieffer, Visionary Leadership Institute (MIT), Peter Senge PhD, Marilyn Woodman PhD, Joseph Campbell PhD, and Richard E. Hughes PhD.

Other people who come to mind are right next to me in this book: Jack Canfield who I met in 1982 at the Health Optimizing Institute at UCSD. Jack met Mark Victor Hansen at a program I developed for The Mandala Society to bring together leading edge thinkers, healers, and leaders to expose medical professionals to alternative modalities. There, I met Edgar Mitchell, Apollo astronaut (Noetic Institute), Roselyn Brueyere, Moshe Feldenkrais, Norman Cousins PhD, Ida Rolf, Joseph Heller, Paul Brenner MD, John Travis MD, Harold Bloomfield MD, and Jeanne Houston PhD.

David Angus MacDonald and I developed and managed The Expedition. And, I worked in companies on teams that created educational entertainment. And later, Swami Chidvilassananda, Jack Kornfeld PhD, Deepak Chopra MD, T. Harv Eker, and many, many others who attended Peak Potentials seminars on health, financial management, entrepreneurship, relationship, and camps and celebrations of life. And the many people I met in the audience living everyday authentic lives.

WRIGHT

In summary, what else would you leave with our readers?

HORTON

Buckminster Fuller said, *"You never change things by fighting the existing reality. . . To change something . . . Build a new model that makes the existing model obsolete."*

John Lennon sang it well in the song he composed, "Imagine".

If you can daydream, if you can touch your heart, if you can open, if you can listen, then you can create. You can change. You can transform. You can call upon your visionary within—the genius that is inherent within you. Imagine, like a daydream, that you can dream your unique self. You can wake up your genius, and you can access the part of you that is connected to your *vision*. You take action and creativity ignites your greatness.

It is simple, really. Here are some initial steps you can take to open and relax into this always-available wisdom, vision, talent, and passion. Look at your calendar and pick a three-day period of time. Take healthy food, a journal, and go to where you can see for miles. Put your hand on your very own heart and ask it to speak to you. Listen, not to the voice in the front between your ears, but to the voice so soft and quiet from behind your heart. "Tell me what I need to know." Ask for information and your highest options to live the life you want. Then follow the instructions.

If you have trouble hearing your inner wisdom, then get coaching on developing this skill. Begin at your core and move from that center. Your true nature and purpose will evolve. And your inner wisdom and talents will blossom forth.

What is it that you love? What takes your breath away? What fills you with love? What is it that releases your passion? And during that time, open to the inner spaces of your mind, your heart, and your incredible greatness.

I support you in living your dream, connecting with the beauty all around, and stepping into your beautiful possibilities. And if you need some help along the way, my contact information is at the end of this chapter.

If you focus on your limitations, then you create more limitation. If you can notice your limitations and bilaterally focus on your vision, then you will create the vision. You will find a way through the obstacles to the end result. It may not be a straight line—maybe it will be a circular spiral. Celebration and gratitude along the way grounds the success and builds momentum. And begin again.

As mentioned, we are all unique and have different talents, interests, and callings. This is your opportunity to explore your own inner traits and talents. Resources that might help with your exploration are: *Traits of an Entrepreneur, Essential Skills for Entrepreneurs, Light Healing Meditation, Journey to your Future Self, Visionary Leadership Training.* Write to me directly for help on business development, speaking, training opportunities, and coaching programs for individuals, companies, and teams. I love to joint venture with others who may share the vision of wilderness, self-growth, lifelong learning, and community contribution.

In closing, give yourself the gift of the inner work necessary to *envision your greatness* and explore!

ABOUT THE AUTHOR

SARAH HORTON brings great depth and dimension from her successful career of over twenty years in business working in both the entrepreneurial and international corporate settings. Through the use of empathic listening and visionary guidance, clients identify success habits and manage their unique obstacles to growth while concurrently accessing their greatness, passion, and purpose. Testimonials attest that her clients experience *giant steps* toward their vision and financial freedom.

Currently, Sarah is an author, motivational speaker, seminar leader, Peak Potentials Certified SuccessTracs and Business Coach, Health Optimizing Institute Wellness Coach, and Vision Point Leadership Trainer working with entrepreneurs and in university and corporate settings, as well as Co-founder of the HypnoCoaching Certification Training recognized by Center for Hypnotherapy and National Guild of Hypnotists.

As a female pioneer at Boston University's School of Management, she graduated with honors and took her creativity to the advertising and marketing industry. Eventually, her love of photography and design led her to the Rhode Island School of Design for graduate work. Sarah has won numerous awards. As a Real Estate investor, she helped to "Landmark" Boston's historical St. Botolph Street neighborhood.

She has more than ten successful years in senior positions in marketing communications with an emphasis in consumer products and services, emphasizing branding, public relations, and social media, broadcast and print media, and online and Web development. Companies include Broderbund Software and The Learning Company leading the creative teams that published number one award-winning edutainment programs: *Where in the World is Carmen Sandiego, Family Tree Maker, Oregon Trail, Math Workshop, Amazing Writing Machine, Mavis Beacon, Dr. Seuss, and Charles Schultz licenses.*

Deeply inspired by natural wilderness areas, she is a published wilderness photographer and expedition leader to sacred sites in the Arctic, Northwest Territories, U.S. Mountain Regions, Hawaii, Great Britain Wilderness, Australia, Europe, Mexico, and India.

Sarah and her daughter, Annie, live at Lake Tahoe, recently designated a National Treasure and known as the "Jewel of the Sierra Mountains," located in Northern California/Nevada. She is involved in the community as an active clean water environmentalist, and past President of the Tahoe Nevada

American Association of University Women dedicated to community collaboration and fundraising for educational grants and scholarships.

SARAH HORTON
P.O. Box 4373
Incline Village, NV 89450
www.SteppingStonestoSuccess.info

CHAPTER FOUR

Find a Mentor and Believe in Your Dreams
An Interview with . . . **Jack Canfield**

DAVID WRIGHT (WRIGHT)

Today we are talking with Jack Canfield. You probably know him as the founder and co-creator of the *New York Times* number one bestselling *Chicken Soup for the Soul* book series. As of 2006 there are sixty-five titles and eighty million copies in print in over thirty-seven languages.

Jack's background includes a BA from Harvard, a master's from the University of Massachusetts, and an Honorary Doctorate from the University of Santa Monica. He has been a high school and university teacher, a workshop facilitator, a psychotherapist, and a leading authority in the area of self-esteem and personal development.

Jack Canfield, welcome to *Stepping Stones to Success*.

JACK CANFIELD (CANFIELD)

Thank you, David. It's great to be with you.

WRIGHT

When I talked with Mark Victor Hansen, he gave you full credit for coming up with the idea of the *Chicken Soup* series. Obviously it's made you an internationally known personality. Other than recognition, has the series changed you personally and if so, how?

CANFIELD

I would say that it has and I think in a couple of ways. Number one, I read stories all day long of people who've overcome what would feel like insurmountable obstacles. For example, we just did a book *Chicken Soup for the Unsinkable Soul.* There's a story in there about a single mother with three daughters. She contracted a disease and she had to have both of her hands and both of her feet amputated. She got prosthetic devices and was able to learn how to use them. She could cook, drive the car, brush her daughters' hair, get a job, etc. I read that and I thought, "God, what would I ever have to complain and whine and moan about?"

At one level it's just given me a great sense of gratitude and appreciation for everything I have and it has made me less irritable about the little things.

I think the other thing that's happened for me personally is my sphere of influence has changed. By that I mean I was asked, for example, some years ago to be the keynote speaker to the Women's Congressional Caucus. The Caucus is a group that includes all women in America who are members of Congress and who are state senators, governors, and lieutenant governors. I asked what they wanted me to talk about—what topic.

"Whatever you think we need to know to be better legislators," was the reply.

I thought, "Wow, they want me to tell them about what laws they should be making and what would make a better culture." Well, that wouldn't have happened if our books hadn't come out and I hadn't become famous. I think I get to play with people at a higher level and have more influence in the world. That's important to me because my life purpose is inspiring and empowering people to live their highest vision so the world works for everybody. I get to do that on a much bigger level than when I was just a high school teacher back in Chicago.

WRIGHT

I think one of the powerful components of that book series is that you can read a positive story in just a few minutes and come back and revisit it. I know my daughter has three of the books and she just reads them interchangeably. Sometimes I go in her bedroom and she'll be crying and reading one of them. Other times she'll be laughing, so they really are "chicken soup for the soul," aren't they?

CANFIELD

They really are. In fact we have four books in the *Teenage Soul* series now and a new one coming out at the end of this year. I have a son who's eleven and he has a twelve-year-old friend who's a girl. We have a new book called *Chicken Soup for the Teenage Soul and the Tough Stuff*. It's all about dealing with parents' divorces, teachers who don't understand you, boyfriends who drink and drive, and other issues pertinent to that age group.

I asked my son's friend, "Why do you like this book?" (It's our most popular book among teens right now.) She said, "You know, whenever I'm feeling down I read it and it makes me cry and I feel better. Some of the stories make me laugh and some of the stories make me feel more responsible for my life. But basically I just feel like I'm not alone."

One of the people I work with recently said that the books are like a support group between the covers of a book—you can read about other peoples' experiences and realize you're not the only one going through something.

WRIGHT

Jack, we're trying to encourage people in our audience to be better, to live better, and be more fulfilled by reading about the experiences of our writers. Is there anyone or anything in your life that has made a difference for you and helped you to become a better person?

CANFIELD

Yes, and we could do ten books just on that. I'm influenced by people all the time. If I were to go way back I'd have to say one of the key influences in my life was Jesse Jackson when he was still a minister in Chicago. I was teaching in an all black high school there and I went to Jesse Jackson's church with a friend one time. What happened for me was that I saw somebody with a vision. (This was before Martin Luther King was killed and Jesse was of the lieutenants in his organization.) I just saw people trying to make the world work better for a certain segment of the population. I was inspired by that kind of visionary belief that it's possible to make change.

Later on, John F. Kennedy was a hero of mine. I was very much inspired by him.

Another is a therapist by the name of Robert Resnick. He was my therapist for two years. He taught me a little formula: E + R = O. It stands for Events + Response = Outcome. He said, "If you don't like your outcomes quit blaming the events and start changing your responses." One of his favorite phrases was, "If the grass on the other side of the fence looks greener, start watering your own lawn more."

I think he helped me get off any kind of self-pity I might have had because I had parents who were alcoholics. It would have been very easy to blame them for problems I might have had. They weren't very successful or rich; I was surrounded by people who were and I felt like, "God, what if I'd had parents like they had? I could have been a lot better." He just got me off that whole notion and made me realize that the hand you were dealt is the hand you've got to play. Take responsibility for who you are and quit complaining and blaming others and get on with your life. That was a turning point for me.

I'd say the last person who really affected me big-time was a guy named W. Clement Stone who was a self-made multi-millionaire in Chicago. He taught me that success is not a four-letter word—it's nothing to be ashamed of—and you ought to go for it. He said, "The best thing you can do for the poor is not be one of them." Be a model for what it is to live a successful life. So I learned from him the principles of success and that's what I've been teaching now for more than thirty years.

WRIGHT

He was an entrepreneur in the insurance industry, wasn't he?

CANFIELD

He was. He had combined insurance. When I worked for him he was worth 600 million dollars and that was before the dot.com millionaires came along in Silicon Valley. He just knew more about success. He was a good friend of Napoleon Hill (author of *Think and Grow Rich)* and he was a fabulous mentor. I really learned a lot from him.

WRIGHT

I miss some of the men I listened to when I was a young salesman coming up and he was one of them. Napoleon Hill was another one as was Dr. Peale. All of their writings made me who I am today. I'm glad I had that opportunity.

CANFIELD

One speaker whose name you probably will remember, Charlie "Tremendous" Jones, says, "Who we are is a result of the books we read and the people we hang out with." I think that's so true and that's why I tell people, "If you want to have high self-esteem, hang out with people who have high self-esteem. If you want to be more spiritual, hang out with spiritual people." We're always telling our children, "Don't hang out with those kids." The reason we don't want them to is because we know how influential people are with each other. I think we need to give ourselves the same advice. Who are we hanging out with? We can hang out with them in books, cassette tapes, CDs, radio shows, and in person.

WRIGHT

One of my favorites was a fellow named Bill Gove from Florida. I talked with him about three or four years ago. He's retired now. His mind is still as quick as it ever was. I thought he was one of the greatest speakers I had ever heard.

What do you think makes up a great mentor? In other words, are there characteristics that mentors seem to have in common?

CANFIELD

I think there are two obvious ones. I think mentors have to have the time to do it and the willingness to do it. I also think they need to be people who are doing something you want to do. W. Clement Stone used to tell me, "If you want to be rich, hang out with rich people. Watch what they do, eat what they eat, dress the way they dress—try it on." He wasn't suggesting that you give up your authentic self, but he was pointing out that rich people probably have habits that you don't have and you should study them.

I always ask salespeople in an organization, "Who are the top two or three in your organization?" I tell them to start taking them out to lunch and dinner and for a drink and finding out what they do. Ask them, "What's your secret?" Nine times out of ten they'll be willing to tell you.

This goes back to what we said earlier about asking. I'll go into corporations and I'll say, "Who are the top ten people?" They'll all tell me and I'll say, "Did you ever ask them what they do different than you?"

"No," they'll reply.

"Why not?"

"Well, they might not want to tell me."

"How do you know? Did you ever ask them? All they can do is say no. You'll be no worse off than you are now."

So I think with mentors you just look at people who seem to be living the life you want to live and achieving the results you want to achieve.

What we say in our book is when that you approach a mentor they're probably busy and successful and so they haven't got a lot of time. Just ask, "Can I talk to you for ten minutes every month?" If I know it's only going to be ten minutes I'll probably say yes. The neat thing is if I like you I'll always give you more than ten minutes, but that ten minutes gets you in the door.

WRIGHT

In the future are there any more Jack Canfield books authored singularly?

CANFIELD

One of my books includes the formula I mentioned earlier: $E + R = O$. I just felt I wanted to get that out there because every time I give a speech and I talk about that the whole room gets so quiet you could hear a pin drop—I can tell people are really getting value.

Then I'm going to do a series of books on the principles of success. I've got about 150 of them that I've identified over the years. I have a book down the road I want to do that's called *No More Put-Downs,* which is a book probably aimed mostly at parents, teachers, and managers. There's a culture we have now of put-down humor. Whether it's *Married . . . with Children* or *All in the Family,* there's that characteristic of macho put-down humor. There's research now showing how bad it is for kids' self-esteem when the coaches do it, so I want to get that message out there as well.

WRIGHT

It's really not that funny, is it?

CANFIELD

No, we'll laugh it off because we don't want to look like we're a wimp but underneath we're hurt. The research now shows that you're better off breaking a child's bones than you are breaking his or her spirit. A bone will heal much more quickly than their emotional spirit will.

WRIGHT

I remember recently reading a survey where people listed the top five people who had influenced them. I've tried it on a couple of groups at church and in other places. In my case, and in the survey, approximately three out of the top five are always teachers. I wonder if that's going to be the same in the next decade.

CANFIELD

I think that's probably because as children we're at our most formative years. We actually spend more time with our teachers than we do with our parents. Research shows that the average parent only interacts verbally with each of their children only about eight and a half minutes a day. Yet at school they're interacting with their teachers for anywhere from six to eight hours depending on how long the school day is, including coaches, chorus directors, etc.

I think that in almost everybody's life there's been that one teacher who loved him or her as a human being—an individual—not just one of the many students the teacher was supposed to fill full of History and English. That teacher believed in you and inspired you.

Les Brown is one of the great motivational speakers in the world. If it hadn't been for one teacher who said, "I think you can do more than be in a special education class. I think you're the one," he'd probably still be cutting grass in the median strip of the highways in Florida instead of being a $35,000-a-talk speaker.

WRIGHT

I had a conversation one time with Les. He told me about this wonderful teacher who discovered Les was dyslexic. Everybody else called him dumb and this one lady just took him under her wing and had him tested. His entire life changed because of her interest in him.

CANFIELD

I'm on the board of advisors of the Dyslexic Awareness Resource Center here in Santa Barbara. The reason is because I taught high school and had a lot of kids who were called "at-risk"—kids who would end up in gangs and so forth.

What we found over and over was that about 78 percent of all the kids in the juvenile detention centers in Chicago were kids who had learning disabilities—primarily dyslexia—but there were others as well. They were never diagnosed and they weren't doing well in school so they'd drop out. As soon as a student drops out of school he or she becomes subject to the influence of gangs and other kinds of criminal and drug linked activities. If these kids had been diagnosed earlier we'd have been able to get rid of a large amount of the juvenile crime in America because there are a lot of really good programs that can teach dyslexics to read and excel in school.

WRIGHT

My wife is a teacher and she brings home stories that are heartbreaking about parents not being as concerned with their children as they used to be, or at least not as helpful as they used to be. Did you find that to be a problem when you were teaching?

CANFIELD

It depends on what kind of district you're in. If it's a poor district the parents could be on drugs, alcoholics, and basically just not available. If you're in a really high rent district the parents are not available because they're both working, coming home tired, they're jet-setters, or they're working late at the office because they're workaholics. Sometimes it just legitimately takes two paychecks to pay the rent anymore.

I find that the majority of parents care but often they don't know what to do. They don't know how to discipline their children. They don't know how to help them with their homework. They can't pass on skills that they never acquired themselves.

Unfortunately, the trend tends to be like a chain letter. The people with the least amount of skills tend to have the most number of children. The other thing is that you get crack babies (infants born addicted to crack cocaine because of the mother's addiction). As of this writing, in Los Angeles one out of every ten babies born is a crack baby.

WRIGHT

That's unbelievable.

CANFIELD

Yes, and another statistic is that by the time 50 percent of the kids are twelve years old they have started experimenting with alcohol. I see a lot of that in the Bible belt. The problem is not the big city, urban designer drugs, but alcoholism.

Another thing you get, unfortunately, is a lot of let's call it "familial violence"—kids getting beat up, parents who drink and then explode, child abuse, and sexual abuse. You see a lot of that.

WRIGHT

Most people are fascinated by these television shows about being a survivor. What has been the greatest comeback that you have made from adversity in your career or in your life?

CANFIELD

You know, it's funny, I don't think I've had a lot of major failures and setbacks where I had to start over. My life's been on an intentional curve. But I do have a lot of challenges. Mark and I are always setting goals that challenge us. We always say, "The purpose of setting a really big goal is not so that you can achieve it so much, but it's who you become in the process of achieving it." A friend of mine, Jim Rohn, says, "You want to set goals big enough so that in the process of achieving them you become someone worth being."

I think that to be a millionaire is nice but so what? People make the money and then they lose it. People get the big houses and then they burn down or Silicon Valley goes belly up and all of a sudden they don't have a big house anymore. But who you became in the process of learning how to be successful can never be taken away from you. So what we do is constantly put big challenges in front of us.

We have a book called *Chicken Soup for the Teacher's Soul*. (You'll have to make sure to get a copy for your wife.) I was a teacher and a teacher trainer for years. But because of the success of the *Chicken Soup* books I haven't been in the education world that much. I've got to go out and relearn how I market to that world. I met with a Superintendent of Schools. I met with a guy named Jason Dorsey who's one of the number one consultants in the world in that area. I found out who has the bestselling book in that area. I sat down with his wife for a day and talked about her marketing approaches.

I believe that if you face any kind of adversity, whether it's losing your job, your spouse dies, you get divorced, you're in an accident like Christopher Reeve and become paralyzed, or whatever, you simply do what you have to do. You find out who's already handled the problem and how did they've handled it. Then you get the support you need to get through it by their example. Whether it's a counselor in your church or you go on a retreat or you read the Bible, you do something that gives you the support you need to get to the other end.

You also have to know what the end is that you want to have. Do you want to be remarried? Do you just want to have a job and be a single mom? What is it? If you reach out and ask for support I think you'll get help. People really like to help other people. They're not always available because sometimes they're going through problems also; but there's always someone with a helping hand.

Often I think we let our pride get in the way. We let our stubbornness get in the way. We let our belief in how the world should interfere and get in our way instead of dealing with how the world is. When we get that out of the way then we can start doing that which we need to do to get where we need to go.

WRIGHT

If you could have a platform and tell our audience something you feel that would help or encourage them, what would you say?

CANFIELD

I'd say number one is to believe in yourself, believe in your dreams, and trust your feelings. I think too many people are trained wrong when they're little kids. For example, when kids are mad at their daddy they're told, "You're not mad at your Daddy."

They say, "Gee, I thought I was."

Or the kid says, "That's going to hurt," and the doctor says, "No it's not." Then they give you the shot and it hurts. They say, "See that didn't hurt, did it?" When that happened to you as a kid, you started to not trust yourself.

You may have asked your mom, "Are you upset?" and she says, "No," but she really was. So you stop learning to trust your perception.

I tell this story over and over. There are hundreds of people I've met who've come from upper class families where they make big incomes and the dad's a doctor. The kid wants to be a mechanic and work in an auto shop because that's what he loves. The family says, "That's beneath us. You can't do that." So the kid ends up being an anesthesiologist killing three people because he's not paying attention. What he really wants to do is tinker with cars.

I tell people you've got to trust your own feelings, your own motivations, what turns you on, what you want to do, what makes you feel good, and quit worrying about what other people say, think, and want for you. Decide what you want for yourself and then do what you need to do to go about getting it. It takes work.

I read a book a week minimum and at the end of the year I've read fifty-two books. We're talking about professional books—books on self-help, finances, psychology, parenting, and so forth. At the end of ten years I've read 520 books. That puts me in the top 1 percent of people knowing important information in this country. But most people are spending their time watching television.

When I went to work for W. Clement Stone, he told me, "I want you to cut out one hour a day of television."

"Okay," I said, "what do I do with it?"

"Read," he said.

He told me what kind of books to read. He said, "At the end of a year you'll have spent 365 hours reading. Divide that by a forty-hour work week and that's nine and a half weeks of education every year."

I thought, "Wow, that's two months." It was like going back to summer school.

As a result of his advice I have close to 8,000 books in my library. The reason I'm involved in this book project instead of someone else is that people like me, Jim Rohn, Les Brown, and you read a lot. We listen to tapes and we go to seminars. That's why we're the people with the information.

I always say that your raise becomes effective when you do. You'll become more effective as you gain more skills, more insight, and more knowledge.

WRIGHT

Jack, I have watched your career for a long time and your accomplishments are just outstanding. But your humanitarian efforts are really what impress me. I think that you're doing great things not only in California, but all over the country.

CANFIELD

It's true. In addition to all of the work we do, we pick one to three charities and we've given away over six million dollars in the last eight years, along with our publisher who matches every penny we give away. We've planted over a million trees in Yosemite National Park. We've bought hundreds of thousands of cataract operations in third world countries. We've contributed to the Red Cross, the Humane Society, and on it goes. It feels like a real blessing to be able to make that kind of a contribution to the world.

WRIGHT

Today we have been talking with Jack Canfield, founder and co-creator of the *Chicken Soup for the Soul* book series. Chicken Soup for the Soul reaches people well beyond the bookstore, with CD and DVD collections, company-sponsored samplers, greeting cards, children's entertainment products, pet food, flowers, and many other products in line with Chicken Soup for the Soul's purpose. Chicken Soup for the Soul is currently implementing a plan to expand into all media by working with television networks on several shows and developing a major Internet presence dedicated to life improvement, emotional support, and inspiration.

CANFIELD

Another book I've written is *The Success Principles*. In it I share sixty-four principles that other people and I have utilized to achieve great levels of success.

WRIGHT

I will stand in line to get one of those. Thank you so much being with us.

ABOUT THE AUTHOR

JACK CANFIELD is one of America's leading experts on developing self-esteem and peak performance. A dynamic and entertaining speaker, as well as a highly sought-after trainer, he has a wonderful ability to inform and inspire audiences toward developing their own human potential and personal effectiveness.

Jack Canfield is most well-known for the *Chicken Soup for the Soul* series, which he co-authored with Mark Victor Hansen, and for his audio programs about building high self-esteem. Jack is the founder of Self-Esteem Seminars, located in Santa Barbara, California, which trains entrepreneurs, educators, corporate leaders, and employees how to accelerate the achievement of their personal and professional goals. Jack is also founder of The Foundation for Self Esteem, located in Culver City, California, which provides self-esteem resources and training to social workers, welfare recipients, and human resource professionals.

Jack graduated from Harvard in 1966, received his ME degree at the University of Massachusetts in 1973, and earned an Honorary Doctorate from the University of Santa Monica. He has been a high school and university teacher, a workshop facilitator, a psychotherapist, and a leading authority in the area of self-esteem and personal development.

As a result of his work with prisoners, welfare recipients, and inner-city youth, Jack was appointed by the State Legislature to the California Task Force to Promote Self-Esteem and Personal and Social Responsibility. He also served on the Board of Trustees of the National Council for Self-Esteem.

JACK CANFIELD

The Jack Canfield Companies
P.O. Box 30880
Santa Barbara, CA 93130
Phone: 805.563.2935
Fax: 805.563.2945
www.jackcanfield.com

CHAPTER FIVE

Leading with Boots On: The Virtuous Cycle of Bootist Leadership®

An Interview with . . . **Anese Cavanaugh**

DAVID WRIGHT (WRIGHT)

Today we're talking with Anese Cavanaugh. Anese is the Founder of Dare to Engage, Inc., and the creator of "Bootism," a holistic approach to leadership, joy, and leading from the "inside out." Devoted to helping forward-thinking individuals, business leaders, and organizations agree upon and then achieve *their* definitions of success, she challenges clients to marry mindset, mission, energy, and action their way to build successful relationships, lead joyful and congruent lives, and deliver effective bottom line business and leadership results. Engaging with people during the last twenty years in the areas of leadership, relationship systems, "energy management," and performance and productivity, she calls her approach to living and leadership Bootist Leadership® for its blending of Eastern and Western philosophies with her personal passion for a great pair of boots, and the power of "putting your boots on" in life.

Anese, welcome to *Stepping Stones to Success*.

ANESE CAVANAUGH (CAVANAUGH)

Hi David, thank you.

WRIGHT

So what is Bootism, and what does it have to do with leadership?

CAVANAUGH

Well, Bootism's the name I gave my approach to living and leadership last year. There's a long story of how it came to be, but basically, it's based on the integration of the more Eastern holistic philosophies (e.g., joy, energy, intuition, people, self-care) of living, with the more Western philosophies (e.g., finances, outcomes, vision, strategy, business, leadership) of business. All of it is geared toward helping people live more authentic lives, lead in their own way, and in the process, create really great organizations, a strong foundation of trust (for self and others), and positive, collaborative relationships. While Western philosophy tends to focus on some of the more tangible parts of business, Bootism also looks at the less tangible, "softer" side of things that are essential to making all those big tangible pieces work well. You need both to succeed.

The way I lead and teach is that I tend to put an even bigger emphasis on the soft skills and the more interpersonal areas, because 1) that's where I'm naturally pulled and energized, 2) I truly believe they drive the people, who drive the business, and 3) I find that my clients get better results more quickly when they intentionally blend it all together. No matter what, even if you can't "see" it or "touch" it, the "soft stuff" is still there, emotionally and physically. It has a very big effect, so we work it! And when "East meets West," and you add in a splash of "12 Hugs & Cupcakes" (which I'll share later), and then consider that "putting your boots on" is an intentional act that transfers to leadership and "daring to engage," you now have a holistic approach to living that I call "Bootism."

I think one of the things I appreciate the most about this approach is the virtuous ongoing cycle that is created when you apply it. When the core areas of Bootism—the "tenets"—are truly in alignment with your personal values and who you are as an individual, your energy is better. When your energy is better, your leadership and relationships are better, and when these are better you get better results. When you get better results, you feel more aligned. When you feel more aligned, you have more energy. This is the virtuous cycle of Bootist Leadership.

WRIGHT

WRIGHT

So it's no relationship to Buddhism? I have to ask, how did you come up with the name?

CAVANAUGH

No, it's no relationship to Buddhism. Bootism is just a peculiar but meaningful little term that, in its odd way, was the answer to a question I'd been asking for years. I was just so close to it that I couldn't see the answer.

WRIGHT

So what was the question?

CAVANAUGH

Well, there were a couple of questions. The wrong one was, *"How do I brand myself and make my marketing really compelling?"* It got me nowhere. The right one was, *"What is the work I'm actually doing? And where do I feel my best?"* That one set me straight. I'd spent years torturing myself about how to define this work, and market it, and explain my sometimes quirky (but effective) perspectives on leadership, and I got into a place where I'd let myself subtly get sucked into doing it "right," which is a formula for unproductive stress.

I hated those formal networking introductions and meetings and "elevator speeches" because it never felt congruent for me. I always felt like I was in the "wrong place" and that there was a "right" way to do it, when, duh, it's really about just being real. But for me, being real would take a ten-minute connection with people to enable them to "get it." So it frustrated me to not have a better "handle" for folks. I needed help, so I bought into the "big business" marketing mentality where there was a "right way" and a formula for marketing, and a team of people to "make it look good," and a lot of e-mail broadcasts! And while they did their job, it still didn't feel great to me, so I opted out of all of it, and just started focusing on the work, which felt great.

And then one day, when I least expected it, out on a run with Ari Weinzweig after a day of meetings at Zingerman's, I started asking the deeper questions and doing a self-check on congruency in my own business and "marketing" and seeing more of where the "gaps" were. Weeks later, knowing about my affinity for jeans and boots, my methodology of blending so many different aspects (Eastern/Western philosophies), and my love for getting people hiking outdoors for this work, he joked that really I was just a "Bootist." And it just clicked. I realized that the work is different, it's unique, and it is, in fact, grounded in "boots." It wasn't going to have a traditional name or fit a traditional model or even have a "right way" to market it. So instead of struggling and trying to make it fit, and get everyone to understand it right off the bat, and make up all sorts of stuff that was keeping me in my own way, I decided to own it, name it, and run with it. And Bootism it's been ever since.

WRIGHT

It sounds like even the naming of the work was an act of Bootism. I've heard you talk about the best answers being *"in the body," "energy"* being key to everything, and the power of listening to and trusting your internal voice, to put it all into productive action. It's all actually a big part of your own methodology. How did that play out in this process?

CAVANAUGH

Bootism was something that I had to apply here because it required me to really get clear about how I felt, where my energy was in all this, and what did I truly want to do—my way? And then not only live it, but plug it into my business in a way that was energizing and joyful, and at the same time would have the effect I wanted it to. Not the "right" way, or the way someone else wanted, but in a way that was truly aligned with who I am. Before I let go of "getting it right" and ignoring my internal "knowing," I was off path. In retrospect, it wasn't horrible; it just wasn't humming along like I wanted it too. It didn't feel great. It felt "spiritually bumpy."

This experience gave me a new and really personal level of understanding as to why it's so important to stay conscious about the questions we ask ourselves, where we get help (consciously or subconsciously), and how intentional we are about creating what we want. You know, it's essential to be able to listen to your own internal voice, trust your own path and knowing, *and* then at the same time, ask for and be open to help from people who know you, understand your vision, and have your highest interest at heart. But, you have to be able to discern where their wisdom stops, and your internal wisdom and intuition take over.

I learned that I could have a great team of experts doing good things on my behalf, but ultimately, I had to trust my gut on what was aligned for me, and then be willing to say "no" when it was "off." Great life lessons! Oddly, this was just over some marketing and branding, but the effect was catalytic for seeing where else this was showing up in funny little ways. Where else was I not "listening" to myself? Where else was I trying to "do it right"? Where was I spiritually "off"? If it's "off" and you ignore it, it's likely to cost you a lot—in time, finance, energy, and spirit. This was stuff that I worked with clients on, on a regular basis, and here I had the gift of a front row seat for myself in my own life. A major gift!

WRIGHT

I think that one of the qualities of good leadership is being willing to know that you may be so in "it" that you can't see the forest through the trees, and then being willing to ask for help, get feedback, and know what fits and what doesn't. It's funny how help shows up sometimes.

CAVANAUGH

Yes! Totally agreed. First, we have to be open to help and feedback and to knowing that we don't know what we don't know. And the second part is that we have to balance that out with trusting our own internal knowing and knowing when to say it's right. I think these are lessons that we continue to get on a daily basis—painful sometimes in the moment, but worthwhile. And if we don't pay attention to them, we get suffering and struggle.

One of my mentors, Laura Whitworth, used to say to me, "Pain is inevitable, suffering is optional." When I find myself suffering or struggling with something, it usually means there's clarity to be created, a decision to be made, a stand to be taken, or help to be called for! Being intentional, but also open to how help shows up, is key.

WRIGHT

Something you've shared is that you at first tried to ditch your background in kinesiology, and working with the body, in your work with clients, and you couldn't do it, can you say more about that?

CAVANAUGH

Sure. My original training and work was in kinesiology and working with athletes and people who just wanted to improve their health and performance. When I started my coaching company about eight years ago, I tried to ditch the kinesiology and the energy and health component because I was *"moving on."* I tried to separate out leadership development and business coaching from the things I had done previously. I quickly realized I was very mistaken. I found that, for me, there was absolutely no way I could separate those pieces. The work on "energy leadership" alone was just too important and it generally isn't addressed in standard leadership coaching work. Effective energy leadership helps improve (or hinder) connection and performance on every level. I decided that these extra pieces I was coaching people on were actually essential, for their well-being and stamina, *and* their presence and effectiveness as a leader. My clients needed to address these things, in addition to the more tangible business issues, in order to make the work more effective and sustainable and their leadership better.

WRIGHT

Couldn't get away from the "body and energy" thing again, right? But I suppose knowing how strongly you believe in it, there's no way you could. You'd be "incongruent" then!

CAVANAUGH

Exactly—it would have been leaving a big piece of myself, my beliefs, and my passion out of my work, and that wouldn't have helped anyone. Ultimately it would have hindered my success with this work and within myself. So it's been an ongoing process. It's constantly evolving. It's come a long way since people would tell me "You can't do it. It won't work." I've noticed that the more I give myself full permission to swing out, the more effective the work is, the more fun I have, and the better results my clients get. . . so I just keep going. I actually made a pact with myself to stop comparing or aligning myself with others in ways that didn't serve, because it slowed me down so much.

I also noticed that the clearer I got on my own definition of success for myself personally and for the business, and the better I was at designing criteria and boundaries to support that definition, the better I got at explaining the work and who it was good for. It also opened up more time and energy to do more for myself, my family, and other things I really enjoy. Ironically, one of the hardest challenges in all of this was just naming it and explaining it, so I took care of that.

WRIGHT

So it sounds like focusing on the work, being present, sticking to what you know is true in your heart, and getting clear on your definition of success were all monumental in helping you not only refine your business and your message, but in managing your own energy as well! Are there other things that stand out for you that you helped you along the way?

CAVANAUGH

Definitely. First, I really leaned into my model to help me explore and navigate all the shifts. And I made really good friends with the following points that I personally consider essential to leadership success:

10 KEY POINTS FOR "STEPS TO SUCCESS" (WITH YOUR BOOTS ON!)

1. **Ask the right questions.** If you're stuck or feeling out of alignment, make sure that you're asking the right questions. Even better, get a trusted friend or colleague to ask them with you and push back constructively to help you.

2. **Listen to your internal voice**: Trust *yourself!* Stay on your path—check yourself constantly and pay attention to your body. Notice when things feel "good" in your gut, when things feel "off" or bad, and *where* those physical feelings live. The more you pay attention to this, the better you can use it as an internal resource. When you're not sure about a decision you need to make or the direction you should go with something, take the time to check your internal "congruency meter" or consult with a trusted resource to help you unfold what's true for you.

3. **Energy is everything**: 1) Make self-care a high priority at all times. Prioritize your self-care—emotionally and physically—so you have (*and maintain*) the energy you need to feel good and do great work, 2) be acutely aware of the way you manage your energy; "use" it wisely so that you maintain stamina and productivity, and 3) lead and be responsible for your energy. Pay attention to the energy you bring to your life and to all the people in it, in every moment. For example, pay attention to your attitude, your "vibe," your enthusiasm, any negativity or apathy you may bring to the table, and your general outlook. For example: Do you focus on what you want or what you don't want? Is the glass half empty or half full? Can you bring a whole room "down" with your presence? Or does your presence create excitement, connection, safety, and a "feel-good" feeling that makes others want to jump on board and do better work? Your energy *always* has an effect—what kind of an effect, is totally up to you.

4. **Do what is true for you**: Ditch the "should's," the "need to's," and the "wanna be's." Align your internal values and passion with your external actions in leadership so that you have more positive energy, greater inner peace, and ultimately get faster and better results. Know when to honor your own internal voice and guidance that says "Whoa! Back up! Left turn coming!" or "Ditch that picture!" When you don't honor yourself and if you don't stay true to your gut and what you really believe, it's not just a loss for you, it's a loss for those you lead.

5. **Notice your energy:** Where does it soar, hum, and dive? Make adjustments accordingly. It's likely that it soars, hums, and dives in relationship to how congruent and aligned you are on your path.

For example, when your energy is high, it's usually because you're doing something that honors your core values. You're focused on something that's bigger than you—a shared goal or a "cause" you believe in, or you're feeling grateful, or you're making a contribution to others, or you're focusing on what you want and setting clear intentions for it, or you're just doing something that makes you happy. It's many things! It would be good to start noticing this for yourself—when is *your* energy high? When our energy is low, it's commonly because we're simply just not paying attention to it or we're focusing on what's not working, on what we don't want, or on how hard things are.

6. **Clarify your mission, your vision, and your values, and tell yourself the truth**: Doing so helps you stay true to your path, which helps you create better problems and solutions, which helps you create better boundaries, which creates greater peace (and the ability to say "no" and "yes" fully!), which helps your energy stay positive and "life-giving," which helps (and calls) others to do the same. It's another Bootist "virtuous cycle"!

7. **Benchmark, learn, model, but don't "compare:"** There's a big difference between looking at what others do as a benchmark for something you'd like to do better, or to learn from, versus actually comparing yourself to them and holding yourself to standards that are really theirs and not yours. In my experience (with myself and clients), the latter is a losing game—no one wins. So benchmark, learn, and model in order to grow in your own work; but remember to stay true to yourself and what you really believe.

8. **Appreciate and honor your team as well as outside experts:** Delegate, share the load, and fully support them in the leading they're doing. Be open to the conversation, give thoughtful and productive feedback, do your due diligence, and stay true to your beliefs.

9. **Ruffled feathers? Say "Thank you!" (and even "May I have another?"):** If someone asks you a question or gives you feedback that "ruffles your feathers"—thank the person! He or she has just given you a gift. Feedback and questions that make us uncomfortable may be hard to hear, but they're often some of the best pointers to inconsistencies and where we're off track and can improve. (Hint: the fact that they "hit a nerve" is usually a sure sign that there's something amiss.)

10. **Don't panic if you find things out of alignment:** If you find spots of misalignment between your "walk" and your "talk" (what you say versus what you actually do) or between where you want to be and where you actually are, don't panic. We all have them. Forget beating yourself up for it. Learn from it, do a "power wash," get things lined up more effectively, and move on.

WRIGHT

These sound like good guidelines for engagement for anything. Living or leadership; but the way you talk, I don't see you hold them as different. So would you tell our readers some of the key pieces of Bootist leadership?

CAVANAUGH

I don't see them as different. I think that no matter your position or situation in life, you're leading. If you're not leading your life—actively leading it—who is? So I truly believe that these principles apply universally regardless of whether someone is "leading" in an organization or not. My model holds seven tenets that are the core beliefs of Bootism. Supporting each tenet are seven "heels and toes" that are actions and behaviors one can take to live the tenet. Readers can get the full model in *The Little Book of Bootism* (or even more details in the *Big Book,* which will be published in 2012.) For this chapter, I'll share the basic seven tenets.

1. **Tenet One**—*"True Vision: we're all on our own personal path; it's dynamic and evolving, it's yours, you lead it, you follow it."* This tenet is about creating a vision, and designing a path to support that vision (or goal), that is true to you so that you feel internally inspired and motivated leading it. When you feel internally inspired and convey that energy, others are more compelled to help you make it happen because they believe in you. Your leadership is congruent—it's what you say you want and where you say you're going and is in alignment with your actions and your energy. People feel that.

2. **Tenet Two:** *"Self-awareness is the key for determining who we are, what we want, and how we'll get there in a way that is true to us and brings forth our best self."* This tenet is about diving deep into personal values and other areas of self-awareness, so that you know who you are and what's truly important to you. It's also about really looking at the influence we have in our own lives and on the people in it—specifically how we affect those we lead. If we're not aware of these things, and we don't know what our values are, what drives us, what our strengths are, and what's important to us, and what we're actually demonstrating externally, then it's hard to know when we're congruent and incongruent with ourselves in different situations.

   If we're not paying attention to our effect on others, then it's hard to see why we are—or are not—getting the results we want. In both of these scenarios—whether it's for the affect I have on myself internally, and staying true to myself, or the influence I have on others externally—without paying keen attention to tenet two, it will be difficult to know what to do to bring that situation or feeling or relationship into a place of alignment. On the flip side, for example, when I have a higher level of self-awareness, I'm more easily able to identify what's up, and then course correct, bringing it all back to a more peaceful and productive place.

3. **Tenet Three:** *"Conscious energy, leadership, and vitality are the secret weapons to success."* This is all about tapping into your natural energy sources so that you feel good, have high vitality and stamina, and bring good energy to others. Because of my background and working with the body, intuition, self-care, and all these different pieces, I'm a huge fan of people using their energy intentionally and taking full responsibility for it, and for themselves as well, as for what kind of energy they bring to others every day. This helps them be more successful. I'll talk about this a little more in a bit as well.

4. **Tenet Four:** *"People make the world go 'round; the quality of our relationships and engagements significantly influences the quality of our leadership."* This is one that I think speaks for itself. It's all about relationships. If I improve the quality of my relationships, I feel better, I have more connection with those in my life, and we create better results together. My ability to effectively engage in relationships and to truly connect with people and have them feel seen and cared about by me, determines how effectively I'm going to be able to lead them—period.

5. **Tenet Five:** *"Intentional presence and mindset drives better results."* This is all about the "thinking" and the "being"! Whether we acknowledge it or not, we're always influencing the people around us. The better our mindset (the way we think about things, our attitude), the better our presence (mental, physical, and leadership), the better our energy, and the better the results we're going to get. These results may be on a huge project or in how we make others feel. Since we're always having an effect, there's a huge opportunity to be really intentional and consciously choose what sort of mindset, presence, and therefore energy we bring to our work, and in so doing, what kind of influence we're going to have. What we believe (our mindset) hugely affects what we do, which of course affects the results we get, so it's well worth paying attention to our mindset and what beliefs we bring to our work and relationships.

6. **Tenet Six:** *"Authentic systems, structures, and caring co-designed relationships, create the foundation for getting things done in a more rewarding and productive way."* This is about setting yourself up for success and "getting in front" of things with congruent systems. You can intentionally design your environment so it supports you (e.g., good working space, good energy in your home, and so on), as well as design systems up front with your peers (e.g., how you'll communicate, give feedback, check in, handle disagreements, and so on) so that everyone knows what he or she can count on. This has a tremendous affect on energy—saving it and enhancing it!

7. **Tenet Seven:** *"'Leadership' is a way of being and a mindset, and 'leading' is a verb."* This tenet is about really looking at the way you lead and making sure that your vision, values, beliefs, and all we've been talking about here are congruent with

your leadership. Ultimately, "leadership" is an attitude that you hold. It's the way that you come to your life and organization wherever you may be needed (e.g., on the front lines, in the back room, on the side, or wherever). If you come to your leadership not believing in the people or the organization or whatever you're leading or you're leading in a way that is out of alignment with your personal style or values (perhaps trying to "lead like someone else"), it's going to be painful, you're not going to be as effective, and your people are going to sense it—fast.

SEVEN KEY THINGS THAT CAN HELP YOU AS AN EFFECTIVE, CONGRUENT LEADER:

1. you have to have the wanting, attitude and ownership of "being a leader,"
2. your true self, style, and values have to be there,
3. your "walk" has to match your "talk,"
4. you need authentic connection and trust with people,
5. there's got to be something (a mission, shared vision, shared purpose, etc.) bigger than you to lead "in service of" (the mindset of servant leadership does wonders here),
6. you need a commitment to ongoing self-reflection and continuous personal growth, and finally,
7. you need the basic skills to lead and evoke leadership in others.

If we can connect in our own way with these seven things, we can create a scenario of internal motivation and authentic and effective leadership to create action and results.

Tenet seven focuses on congruent leadership and making sure that not only do clients practice their own style of leadership, but that they have the skills necessary to get the best leadership results and connect with their teams more effectively.

So those are the seven tenets at their core. The whole Bootist Leadership Model is designed to help people address these tenets to get their energy humming, and to make their leadership more effective, their lives more congruent, their relationships more connected, and their results better all the way around. Applied consistently and intentionally, shifts happen. It's a lot to remember, so I always invite people to look at it through four core lenses. If you pay attention to these and keep them at consistently high levels, you'll have the essence down and great results will follow:

- **Energy:** Nurture, manage, lead, and own it so that it stays positive and productive almost all the time.

- **Leadership:** Do it, check your mindset, get out there, go. If you're not leading you, who is? And if you can't lead yourself, how will you be able to lead others?

- **Relationships:** Pay attention to them, nurture them, collaborate in them, and engage them pro-actively so that you have great support, good insight, and mutually rewarding days.

- **Congruency:** Be incredibly aware of what your beliefs and values are. Listen to your internal voice, check what's congruent and true for you—and what's not—and stay on the path so that everything flows better, feels better, and creates better results in every aspect of your life.

WRIGHT

What does someone get from practicing Bootist Leadership? What do you notice from your clients?

CAVANAUGH

The first thing I notice for them is relief. At the core, we're talking about being congruent and we're talking about being very aware and managing your energy and leading your energy and using it. When people start to do this work, they get in touch with where they are on their path, and they work the tenets I just shared, they then feel a sense of relief. All of a sudden they realize that they don't have to do things "right" and they don't have to follow the path that somebody else thinks they should be following. Rather, they challenge themselves to look at what they're doing, who they are, where they are, what they want, and if they are, in fact, on the right path that's true to themselves—a path they really passionately believe in and want from the heart.

I also notice that many of the problems clients had that were stressing them out before they would do this work, started to go away. Many of those problems start to go away because often they were actually problems that went with a different path or other peoples' problems (or even perceived problems) that they took on when they embarked on a path they really didn't believe in. So now, problems they have are better ones because they're actually tied to them being on their true path. When you're on a path that's congruent with who you are and what you believe, the "problems or challenges" that come up are much easier to get through because your energy is clearer. It's also more compelling to work through your new problems because they're the right kind! Yet another virtuous cycle!

Ultimately, this all leads to more rewarding engagement with their lives, richer relationships, more effective leadership, a better quality of work, better bottom line business results, and greater trust and focus on the things that are truly most meaningful. They learn a lot about themselves and about what makes them tick, all the while putting it to good use—from day one.

As a bonus, this kind of work is contagious as the virtuous cycle continues. When people are working in ways that are congruent with who they are and leading from a place of alignment, they know it, and their team feels it. When their team knows it, the team trusts them more. The team is going to be more engaged and will do a better job. Everybody wins.

WRIGHT

So how does the idea of energy management fit into or play a key role in Bootism?

CAVANAUGH

To me it's at the core of everything. There are multiple ways I look at energy. First, I should say that I refer to all the ways I look at energy as "energy" in general, but there are several layers. Let me talk about three of them here.

First, there's "personal vitality and stamina," there is energy management, and then there is energy leadership. Personal vitality and stamina is how you personally take care of yourself (physically and emotionally) to make sure you're the best instrument of change possible. In order to set yourself up for success, lead most effectively, and ultimately feel good and achieve your desired outcomes, there are things you can do that are within your control. For example, how much exercise I get, what I put in my body for fuel, what kinds of boundaries I create for self-care, how I come to my relationships, what I tolerate, etc., are all part of creating positive physical and emotional vitality.

Then there is "energy management," which is looking at how you're actually using your energy throughout the day so that you can be as productive as possible and focused on the right things for you. It's about how you're actually moving through your day, what you're inviting from others, and just being very consistent about that. I actually tell clients to manage energy instead of trying to manage time because if they can do that, the time they actually need for something seems to become more efficient!

It boils down to being responsible for and intentional about how, where, and with whom you're going to expend your energy. This includes checking your mindset (attitude/the way you see things, etc.) so that it supports you. Energy leadership is about being totally responsible for the energy (also known as the vibration) you bring to others. No kidding. We're bringing energy in every moment of every day—it's up to us to decide what sort of energy we want to bring. Energy (in all the areas mentioned here), combined with mindset, vision, and action, is the most powerful combination of "forces" I've come across for creating effective leadership and better bottom line results. No matter how you slice it, energy is right there through all of it.

WRIGHT

Anese, what do you say to people about stress? That's a lot of energy to manage—yourself, your day, your effect on others, and the bottom line! What about the stress that goes with all that?

CAVANAUGH

The thing with energy is that when we're feeling stressed out about what's going on, it usually means we're taking on other people's energy. When we take on other peoples' energy, we're not staying fully present with ourselves, we're actually getting away from staying grounded within ourselves and are starting to slide into "being or working in their business."

So if I'm stressed out about something, it often means that I'm not managing my own energy, I'm not holding my own space, and so I start to take on other people's energy. It's a slippery slope. What ends up happening is that it can become overwhelming. If I'm going to lead or if I'm going to work with a team or work with a client, I'm not as clear, my resource state is diminished, and I probably won't make very good decisions.

Now let's flip it. If I see this going on, I can stop and reboot in the moment, and bring myself present (Tenet 5: Mindset & Presence). I can get back into my own energy and business and decide what to do. From there, if I'm really good about staying present and truly leading my energy and keeping my "space" clear, I'll be a more effective and engaged leader, parent, coach, friend, and so on! (Not to mention how much clearer and better I'll feel!)

WRIGHT

That's interesting; it definitely puts this all in a different perspective for me. Speaking of which, what do "12 hugs, cupcakes, and boots" have to do with leadership? I've been leading now for forty years and I've never heard of it.

CAVANAUGH

My guess is you probably have "12 hugs, cupcakes, and boots" all over the place in your life, and just haven't thought of it this way! Twelve hugs, cupcakes, and boots are some of my favorite things about Bootism—it makes me smile just saying it. The tenets are important, they provide really great structure and I think can be very helpful to move through for creating congruency and solutions for just about any issue. But the thing is that it's all about boots, twelve hugs, and cupcakes. I've come to realize that this is part of the "secret sauce" people have mentioned in our work together throughout the years but have been hard pressed to put a handle or label on it.

The "12 hugs" are about good relationships and connections. The "cupcakes" are about finding joy in all aspects of one's life. The "boots" are about positive, congruent leadership.

What I've come up with over time as I've played with this is that a "hug" can take many forms. It can be literal, it can be figurative, it can be virtual. It can be a really good, meaningful conversation where each person feels heard and seen and better for having it, even if it's only a minute long! It takes little to do it, it's quick, and it can be simple. It can be as short as just acknowledging someone for thirty seconds—truly listening and caring, saying thank you, recognizing their contributions, or even their positive energy. It can make all the difference in your company! And it's free! No need to spend millions on an "engagement initiative." This is a place where every single person, every single leader, can have a positive influence on those around him or her—now. It makes a difference and has a ripple effect all the way up and down the line!

WRIGHT

Wow. I like the literal or figurative; there's something in there for everyone, and when you put it like that, it really is easier than we make it out to be in our busy worlds. What about cupcakes and boots?

CAVANAUGH

I've got a four year old, she's really into "12 hugs," and she had some of her little classmates doing this thing with 12 hugs. She'd walk in and say, *"Have you had your 12 hugs today?"* and it was really cute. And then when I'd be going out of town, we'd do hugs for each day I'd be gone, so sometimes it was like forty-eight hugs in advance. I was writing a paper about "hugs" and she informs me *"Whoa, mom, it's not just about the hugs, it's cupcakes too."* So we started looking at cupcakes and what that means in our life.

And the thing with cupcakes is that that's the thing that I do with Izzie (or my son, Jake) that gives us that special time together. It takes a half hour, and it's an opportunity to stop and actually engage with them and make some cupcakes (or color or work a puzzle). It's one of those things that it would be so easy to say, *"I don't have the time, I've got a million other things to do, we'll just buy the cupcakes from the store,"* but there is that connection, that bonding that we feel that has become our special little space.

If you take that concept and put it into the rest of your life, it's looking at where you have that special space and what things you have in your life that are really easy to put on the back burner because there is not the time to do them. I see this a lot with people in taking care of themselves, eating well, working out, taking a day off, taking an afternoon off, getting that special chair or book or a massage or going to the zoo. These things are all cupcakes. They're special and, while it's easy to cut them out to save time, the irony is that having them in your life creates more energy, more joy, and more connection with the people around you. The time takes care of itself.

After hugs and cupcakes comes "boots." It's about "putting on your boots" and making things happen in your life or organization, and doing it from the mindset of leadership in a way that is true for you. Marching in those boots from a place of alignment and truth, doing what needs to be done in service of moving forward, daring to engage, it's all about just getting in there and making things happen. Truck through the mud if you've got to truck through the mud, and truck up the hills, wade in your waders, or dance in your boots, whatever. Put your own boots on, whatever those boots may be for you, and get in there and lead. That element is the boots. The boots are all about personal power and self-leadership and making things happen. It's not waiting for someone else to put on their boots—you want it (whatever "it" may be for you). Put *your* boots on—your real and authentic boots—and go get "it."

WRIGHT

"Hugs, cupcakes, and boots"—I get it. It's the "soft stuff" we've talked about, but really essential. So why do you think this philosophy resonates for people?

CAVANAUGH

I think it's different because the name in itself invites people to think about what their "boots" are and what Bootism means to them personally. It's not a "color by numbers/these are the right answers" movement or about doing it "right" or being "balanced" in ways that other people think you should be. It's just the opposite. Bootism invites people to do it their way, and then honor their own "Bootist Practice," whatever that may be. The core of it has to come from them, their path, what they want, listening to their internal voice, etc. When you invite someone to do that, a path starts in their own gut, in their soul. Bootism encourages people to become even more of who they are. They become stronger in their "being," more aware, and they lead more effectively. It's a non-traditional approach, but actually a very simple way of looking at leadership.

The thing about Bootism is that I'm not telling anybody how to do it or what it should mean for them. I'm giving people a place to look and to explore what's true for themselves. In fact, I'm not even concerned that they call it Bootism as much as that they benefit from the principles. The name gives us a "handle," but it's the effect that counts.

Part of what clients hire me for is to just challenge them around congruency. I help them be congruent in their lives and leadership, and in many cases I help them define what their criteria for being congruent actually is. So they get to unfold this criteria and what's important to them, and set their own vision and personal "code" and agreements for congruency, which is all based on their vision and values and the work done in the model. Then they have their very own vision that's true to who they actually are and an action plan to get there. Because they've done the work and unfolded it themselves (with me as a muse/champion/coach/teacher and fellow Bootist versus a "teller of what their path should be"), they own it and use it. That's much more fun and sustainable. Add the energy piece in there, and the whole things just begins to feel great.

WRIGHT

I think parenting is an interesting analogy you use for finding congruency. How does Bootism tie into parenting?

CAVANAUGH

I believe that one of the best things we can do as parents is to be true and honest and who we are, all while being in service to our "kids." I know personally I've had my own work to do around parenting, and applying my own "boots approach" has been helpful.

My way of parenting is very different than my mother's or my mother-in-law's, or the way of many of my girlfriends. It has been incredibly different. It took me a long time to make peace with that because I wanted to do it "right."

But I'll tell you, once I made peace with that and actually started to do it in a way that was authentic for me, a lot of the stress melted away. I felt more aligned and I think I'm a better parent now because of it. My kids don't get the dissonant energy of my trying to do something that's not congruent for me, which is a good thing. When we can do this, whether parenting our kids or leading our organizations, it makes us better "parents" because it's easier to connect from that place of knowing and self-trust than doing it "right" in a way that doesn't fit. We get happier results.

WRIGHT

Happier results—that sounds like a goal worth pursuing whether you're a parent or a leader in business or whatever your role! So we've talked about quite a lot today, Anese. What do you want people to get out of this chapter?

CAVANAUGH

I think about the name of this chapter, and the book as a whole, and it makes me think about this word "success" and what it actually means. It's a big word. So there are a couple of things I hope the reader walks away with.

First, I think it's so important to take a step back and look at what your definition of success really is. See if it's congruent with who you are and what you really believe, and that it reflects your heart's desire. Is it aligned with your values? Is it truly what you want? Does it feel good to be going after it? It's really important to look at what your definition of success is, so that you make sure you're going in the right direction and you're measuring yourself by using the right benchmarks. Really look at what success means to you personally.

The other thing I'd like folks to understand is congruency and energy and leading. Pick your path, put your boots on; your best leadership and life are literally a boot, a hug, and cupcake away. If you find yourself "struggling" with something, thank the struggle for the gift, and use it to identify where you might be out of alignment or off your path. So the invitation is to really take a look at what that definition is, to really step up, take the reins, and lead it.

If readers want to use some of the concepts that are in this chapter, if they want to look at those tenets, if they want to look at them from a personal or a business standpoint and really start to play with them in a way that resonates, and question what some of those things might be for them, go for it! Do the work, let it unfold, get on a congruent path to get where you want to be, and go. I believe that this is where the ability to create our desired influence in this world, in our organizations, and in our lives, lies.

WRIGHT

Well what a great conversation. This is something special and those Seven Tenets are really great. I've been taking copious notes here. I really appreciate all this time you've taken to answer these questions for me today. I did really learn a lot and I am sure that our readers will have a lot to think about after they read this chapter.

Anese, thank you so much for being with us today on *Stepping Stones to Success*.

CAVANAUGH

My pleasure! Thanks so much for the opportunity to share!

ABOUT THE AUTHOR

ANESE CAVANAUGH, President of Dare To Engage, Inc., Founder of Bootist Leadership®, muse, speaker, and author, gets people "in their boots" while learning with and coaching high achievers, leading her own business, and being "mom" to two. Using energy, mindset, mission, and action as cornerstones of her "Bootist" philosophy, she helps forward-thinking individuals and organizations create positive energy, successful relationships, congruent leadership, and joyful results wherever they go.

For more about Anese or the Dare To Engage Programs, to access her blog, or to receive a complimentary copy of her latest publication, go to www.DareToEngage.com or call 1.877.994.DARE (3273).

ANESE CAVANAUGH

3031 Stanford Ranch Rd.
Suite 2507
Rocklin, CA 95765
877-994-DARE (3273)
anese@daretoengage.com
www.LeadingWithBootsOn.com
www.DareToEngage.com

CHAPTER SIX

Essence Leadership:
Energizing Systems from the Inside Out

An Interview with . . . **David Larson**

DAVID WRIGHT (WRIGHT)

Today we're talking with David Larson, MS, LP, CPCC. He is a licensed psychologist, certified life coach, and leadership trainer. He is founder of the Institute for Wellness, and co-owner of Triumph Leadership Training, the developers of Essence Leadership. David and his business partner, Kate Sholonski, offer programs to train executives, managers, organizations, and teams in Essence Leadership across the United States. David is also author of the popular e-course, *How to Stop Your Anxiety Now!*, sold in fifty-nine countries worldwide. He has produced a relaxation CD called *Serenity* to ground people in positive performance, and he hosts a television talk show on family and wellness issues in Minnesota.

David, welcome to *Stepping Stones to Success!*

DAVID LARSON (LARSON)

Thank you, David, nice to be here.

WRIGHT

What is the essence of Essence Leadership?

LARSON

Essence Leadership begins with the premise that there is a leader in everyone. It may be untapped or underdeveloped, but we believe that the leader is there, and we want to draw out that leader.

Furthermore we believe that every leader is unique. What we want to do is find the uniqueness of each individual because that's where we believe his or her real power is.

Our approach to surface this essence leader begins by dealing with the whole person in our workshops. Essence Leadership training goes beyond the *doing* of the leader to the *being* of the leader. We recognize that a person is not just a sum of his or her actions. We acknowledge there is an energy—a *being*—behind those actions.

Essence Leadership is designed to call forth the best in people by focusing on who they are as a foundation for what they do. We harvest the goodness of people, and we emphasize their uniqueness and their individuality.

For example, I recall one leader who has a very quiet way of being—a rather gentle man. Seeing his gentleness, you might overlook his power. But when you look at his essence you see that his quiet way of being is actually one of his greater strengths. One of the great gifts he brings is his ability to create safety, which promotes trust and brings out the best in his team. He's an example that leaders don't have to be loud or forceful to be effective. In his calm reflective way, he will see what others may overlook.

There are certain roles and tasks that are well served by outgoing, gregarious people, and other responsibilities that are better suited for more contemplative individuals. We want to help each leader we work with to identify and own *his or her* unique gifts, which may be disregarded or get overshadowed in some busy organizations.

One workshop participant I'm thinking of, for example (much to the amazement of both his bosses and his subordinates) transformed from a detached, demanding manager to a more sensitive and open leader. This reduced not only stress for himself, but for those who worked around him. Those responsible to him found him more approachable, easier to get along with, and were drawn out to be more cooperative with him because he was less domineering. It's easy to see why this would bring about greater performance from his subordinates, synergy with his team, and productivity in his workgroup.

When people are leading with essence there is ease, rather than the stress of trying to fit into a mold of someone else's style that would be unnatural for him or her. Essence Leaders are better able to recognize their most powerful ways of being as well as the unique gifts of their workers, and support what each team member does best instead of trying to force everyone to do things his or her own way.

Essence Leaders have different ways of holding people accountable based on individuality. They know who responds to e-mail feedback or a text message, for example, as opposed those who respond best to their supervisor stopping in to visit.

People perform best, David, when they believe they have something great to offer, and know that others see it too.

And we're seeing that turnover is significantly reduced when people are seen and appreciated.

In short, Essence Leaders first claim the best in themselves. Secondly, they know how to acknowledge those they lead for the unique value they're bringing to the job. Those who work for Essence Leaders are appreciated as people. There is a level of awareness and respect that cuts through the superficial. This leads to more cooperative relationships on the team, and greater productivity in each division or department.

WRIGHT

How does the Essence Leadership training differ from trainings that are already out there?

LARSON

A lot of trainings, as you know, David, are didactic in nature, teaching people to do things in a certain way—usually someone else's way. There can be a lot of value in that. Having outlines and specific instructions and handouts can be very helpful. However, our emphasis, behind all of the specifics, the "particles" as we sometimes call them, is about helping people find their own most powerful way to do something.

Essence Leaders believe in the positive potential in people. For example, Essence Leaders know that when a worker's performance is subpar, it's not time to blame or criticize that person, but rather to become curious to find out what is being expected of that worker that's not coming naturally to him or her, or what is needed for that person to succeed.

Essence Leaders understand that people are currently doing their best, so how could you criticize them for doing their best? If my workers are not performing up to speed, as an Essence Leader I'm asking myself, "What is it that they need from me so they can bring their best forward?"

The secret to our trainings is that they are designed and presented experientially. Participants are not just receiving intellectual information—they *feel* the difference in their bodies; consequently they integrate their learning and own it.

For example, we don't just talk about levels of communication. In our workshops, participants actually experience what it's like to be heard as opposed to when they are not heard. In our training, leaders try out different approaches in expressing themselves to find out what works for them, not just what they have heard works for others. They leave with clarity about what will work for them from experience, not just because someone said so.

Because of the experiential nature of the training, attendees also get to hear and learn from other participants' immediate and fresh perspectives, on top of the learning they receive from the trainers.

Our participants have a real sense of growing together. They are drawn out of their heads into their hearts. They let down their guard so they can really be with one another at a very human level.

We create experiences where light bulbs turn on from the inside. Part of what excites me as a trainer is seeing people's eyes light up with a new awareness that perhaps they never realized before. We're not asking them to buy something we're saying. We want them to have experiences in which they uncover and underscore what really works for them. Being in our workshops goes way beyond absorbing information to encountering an awakening from within.

I'll share the example of Judy, currently the editor of a newspaper, who quit her job at a software company after embracing rather than hiding the part of her personality she called her "Imp." This was the playful self within her, which once she identified and claimed, unleashed her creativity that had been kept in box labeled "traditional professional."

The "traditional professional" role wasn't fun for her, and she didn't do as well playing that game—the one for which she had the most formal training. She found coming from her Essence more liberating, and became an "untraditional professional." She was much more fun to work with, and she earned respect from her peers and subordinates as an authentic human being. People were attracted to her and followed her because she was real. Her production and the production of her team went way up when she led from her Essence.

WRIGHT

That's interesting. Say more about what the impact is on the workplace following this training?

LARSON

The impact on each person is that when people feel good about who they are, they're more conscientious and more attentive. Their affect on others is therefore more positive.

They are happier workers, they stay longer, and are more productive. They help in the functioning of the team flow. There is a reenergizing in the workplace that generates more energy and stimulates creative solutions.

A concrete example of that might be something like this: When we were working with one group of managers, they not only formed deepened connections with themselves and others, but also to commitments around living out their essences in their respective departments. After we left them, they spontaneously created a monthly meeting where they could support each other to stay centered in their essences—in their positive power. They really had each other's back and were mutually supportive of each other.

WRIGHT

That's very inspiring. Say more about how else the training affects relationships among the staff.

LARSON

Essence Leadership trainees tend to be more cooperative with each other because they're not only coming from their own essence, but are also looking for the essence in their workers. They know that if they can bring out the best in their employees, then that's what's going to make for the greatest production.

Essence Leadership is not ego-based in attitude, so there is no need for backbiting or ego-driven actions because those who understand and practice Essence Leadership do not have to prove themselves. They rest rather confidently in the knowledge of their own strengths, and they're happy to acknowledge the beauty of their varied strengths observed and acknowledged in their coworkers as well.

Now another interesting thing, David, is that since one person's essence is never threatened by another person's essence, Essence Leaders are not threatened by the creativity of others. They recognize with appreciation what those who are different from them bring to the workplace. It eliminates unhealthy comparison and the stifling judgment that occurs in many organizations. No longer am I worried if I am good enough. I know inside I'm good enough; this is why I don't need to tear down or compete negatively against co-workers.

What happens time and time again, David, is that when leaders lead from essence, they learn to see the positive potential in those they work with, which fosters much more cooperation and synergy—the key to exceptional performance of a team.

WRIGHT

What do you mean by "ego" and why is leading from ego detrimental in the workplace?

LARSON

Recently one worker we know was fired for forgetting to turn in her thermometer at the end of her shift. We found out her whole department was run by threats, both stated threats and implied threats. They knew they would lose their jobs if they didn't follow every rule to a T and that sort of thing.

Fear is a hallmark of ego leadership. Ego leaders tend to believe that fear is a good motivator. Sometimes we call this process "scaring people into conformity." This contrasts with Essence Leadership, which can be characterized as more like placing a rose in a cup of warm water so that it gently opens up and releases its beauty.

Ego leaders tend to be afraid that they will look bad, that they won't be making enough this quarter, that their team members won't be respecting them and so on. We discovered that when leaders lead from ego, a fear is driving it. What we want to do is eliminate that fear. Fear tends to breed desperation, exaggerated self-appraisal, and blaming others.

Ego based leadership has a tendency to put down and to motivate through manipulation, and we don't feel that this is the most effective way to lead. What we're looking for is rather than leading from an apprehension that something isn't going to turn out right, people can lead from a place of calm, peace, and positive expectancy in their workers, which, of course, brings out their best to yield the most satisfactory result.

Another thing we find about ego leaders, David, is that they often hold back showing their humanness. Sometimes this is because they've been trained to keep an emotional distance. At other times I think it's because they believe they can't be as powerful with people if they share their vulnerability. They think that in order to effectively get things done they need to hold back their true selves. Rather than be authentic, they may tend to "act" like a leader rather than just "be" a leader and be more human.

Another way to tell if we're leading from ego or essence is how it feels. For example, ego leaders either tend to either feel anxious or puffed up with their own importance. Essence Leaders, by contrast, tend to feel excited rather than anxious, and enjoy the mutual power shared by themselves and their workers. Ego leaders tend to be more tense and have a guarded way of relating. You might say they are more "combustible" rather than having fun and fostering cooperation. Therefore, leading from ego breeds lack of trust and anxiety in other team members.

A final evidence of ego leadership shows up in not responding to the personal lives of workers. One who leads from ego many not think it's relevant if a team member's dog died or if their child is sick or if a family member has a drinking problem. One who leads from Essence knows the importance of understanding such dynamics in the lives of their workers. They know that if a person's mother is dying of cancer or their husband lost their job or if their child was arrested for shoplifting or suspended from school, that these things impact a person's performance. In these instances, compassionate responses are not only the right choices, but also pay off big in terms of performance, longevity on the job, and keeping morale high in an organization.

Often ego leaders are not even aware of the fear that's driving them, so we create a safe atmosphere in which they see how they're self-sabotaging. Then we help them find their own essence where they don't have to be afraid. When they lock into their own essence and lead from their power, it eliminates the unhealthy aspects of competition and dissipates fear, allowing workers to be their best, and then the entire staff relaxes around them.

WRIGHT

Will you say more about what you mean by your tagline "energizing systems from the inside out"?

LARSON

Sure. We focus on changing leaders from the inside first, so that they can make more effective, powerful changes in their workplace. We focus on helping leaders get to know themselves more deeply, and excel at their strengths. We find that when leaders focus on changing themselves first, it gives implicit permission for other employees to look at themselves first as well in making changes they need to make. This is exactly what managers want—their workers to look at and change themselves. So it's a lot about setting an example of, "I'm willing to change myself and I invite you to join me on that path of changing ourselves so we can be the best that we can be."

Let's take an example of someone who comes late to a meeting. Now, if I'm thinking from the outside, as the boss I might be judging the person's behavior, right? I might see him or her as irresponsible, or doesn't care. I might be asking myself what is wrong that he or she couldn't show up on time? I may judge the action rather than understanding the dynamics behind the action. So my own fear is about the negative consequences of how that person not showing up on time might threaten my own performance or security, or that of my division.

But those who lead from the inside out know that their workers are more than their actions, and there are good reasons for any failures or mistakes. Furthermore, they see a mistake as something to learn from. They can remember what John Madden said, "There are no mistakes, only feedback. Failures are steppingstones, not stumbling blocks."

Everything is grist for the mill. Anything that happens is a blessing, a chance to learn something new, a chance to practice compassion, a chance to be challenged, to dig deeper into our creativity in order to find solutions we didn't know were possible.

Here is the interesting thing too, David—the leadership goes both ways. Just like we began this discussion with the idea that there is a leader in every person, subordinates in an organization will feel the impact of their boss owning his or her own power without being manipulative. The employees will likely act the same way when they're called forth.

For example, suppose my boss is having a bad day and spewing negativity. Rather than blame or criticize her for not acting kindly, or react in my own anger, I might start looking for the reasons she is yelling or overreacting. Maybe she had a near accident on the way into work or maybe she is being pressured in some way by her own superiors. Bosses may have their own personal problems such as a recent fight with their spouse or an injury to their child. Everyone we know is being challenged by something.

So being an Essence Leader means I see things from the point of view of those with whom I work, and rather than just being focused on what I need them to do, I can respond to them in a compassionate way—to "walk a mile in their moccasins," so to speak—and look for ways I can be understanding of their situation.

WRIGHT

What is needed so that this training will stick and be kept alive for participants?

LARSON

Well, as simple as it may sound, attending creates a great beginning. Kate and I are not satisfied with superficial trainings. The experiences that people have must be deep enough to change them—to move them from the inside. Again, this goes way beyond head learning to body/spirit learning. On top of that, we help design ways to follow up and hold each other accountable so that they remain inspired to keep it alive.

We generally do this training in two or three phases during a twelve- to eighteen-month period. This gives participants a chance to layer in and gain a deeper understanding of the concepts over time. It allows them to practice what they're learning in their real life workspaces and relationships. Then they can bring their challenges back to us and we can help them fine-tune what they're missing and strengthen skills that need more support.

Then we recommend adding subsequent conference calls to each training. Questions can be answered, victories can be celebrated, and work relationships can continue to be strengthened through reconnection, remembering, and reinforced support. It also provides encouragement to stay connected with not only the revolutionary principles they've learned, but also with the people who keep them grounded in their learning.

We also recommend the follow-up individual coaching calls. These can be rather magnificent because they help us focus in on each individual and what he or she needs over time. We find that giving our clients individual attention accelerates their personal transformation.

So it's coaching calls, phone conference support, group coaching, additional trainings to build on previous trainings, and designing meetings that provide in-house support as they move forward into the future—all of these things are extremely helpful.

WRIGHT

Let's talk for a minute about authentic leadership. What does authentic leadership mean to you, and how do you bring it out in your participants?

LARSON

Oh, that's a great question. Authentic leadership for us means leading from ease, from compassion and caring in a relationship of trust and respect for oneself as well as those being led. Authentic leading is not contrived—it's natural. It's leading from a solid sense of self-awareness of personal gifts. It's leading without "trying." Authentic leadership is present when people are connected with who they are, and understand that trusting who they are is important and helpful and powerful. There is no need to compare or tear down one another's way of leading or being; it's based on the assumption of equality and the belief in the magnificence of team members.

So authentic leadership for us, again, is not ego driven, but it's spirit driven. There is no fear or need to control. Authentic leadership leads from the heart rather than from a need to look good. A leader's self-esteem is not tied into his or her leading, and so the leader doesn't have to manipulate. Authentic leaders can instead make decisions independent of their own personal interest to what is best for the company and the employees.

The way we bring this about is by creating an environment of safety in the training. The training atmosphere is free of judgments, which allows participants to be themselves, allowing them be seen for who they really are. We really don't pound out leaders, David, we provide an environment that nurtures and grows leaders.

We design fun experiences to help people enjoy their training and remember it. Learning is made real in what we do. Participants remember what they learn because they experience their own power right in the training. Trainees are not just being presented with concepts, but participate in the building blocks of true leadership.

WRIGHT

What other benefits do you see occurring for participants who take your Essence Leadership program?

LARSON

Well, joyful employees make better workers than uninspired ones. Happy employees produce greater output, with higher quality, and with less stress.

The elements of joy, happiness, contentment, and peace that are present in an Essence Leader are going to be present across the board, too, which means participants in our workshops take home tools that work in their families and in the organizations they are involved in outside of work such as church or civic groups. The bottom line is we're making people leaders of their lives, not just in their office.

WRIGHT

So how would you summarize the tenets of your Essence Leadership Model?

LARSON

It's an inclusive model, David, where everyone is recognized for his or her individual gifts and skills. In Essence Leadership, the "being" drives the "doing," not the other way around. It involves fostering and appreciating the authenticity of people, empowering them rather than powering over them, and creating learning from personal, inner awareness. It's whole person oriented, experiential, and "in the bones." We create change from the inside out. The Essence Leadership model is interactive and fun. We believe people learn best when they're relaxed and feeling good about themselves. This program creates that kind of learning.

WRIGHT

Sounds exciting! I really appreciate all this time you've spent with me, David. This has been very enlightening for me and I'm sure it will be for our readers.

LARSON

Thank you, David.

WRIGHT

Today we've been talking with David Larson, licensed psychologist, certified life coach, and leadership trainer. David offers programs to train managers, organizations, and teams in what we have learned today is the Essence Leadership Model. I have learned a lot about it, and I'm willing to take a shot at the concept of Essence Leadership—it sounds good to me, David.

Thank you so much for being with us today on *Stepping Stones to Success!*

LARSON

Thank you. It's been my pleasure.

ABOUT THE AUTHOR

DAVID LARSON is a life fulfillment coach, psychologist, and workshop leader. His specialty is uncovering the untapped potential in his clients for optimum performance in their work, as well as meaningful, lasting fulfillment in who they are.

David developed the *Institute for Wellness* in 1987 for the training of excellence in service and personal development. David helps turn fear-based reactions into compassion-based responses through highlighting the strengths, uniqueness, and oneness of all human beings.

He joins Kate Sholonski *in Triumph Leadership Training* programs to bring productivity and joy to the workplace, transforming desires into action, confusion into clarity, separation into unity, conflict into understanding, and hope into reality.

David is known for his ability to help people capitalize on personal growth quickly. His easy-going, insight-generating style enables each client to see his or her own magnificence and perform at the top of his or her game.

David is an alumnus of Augsburg College in Minneapolis, Minnesota, and did his post-graduate work at TCU in Fort Worth, Texas.

A specialist in the management of anxiety and panic, David is the author of the popular anti-anxiety e-book course, *How To Stop Your Anxiety Now!*

His recently produced relaxation training CD, *Serenity: Guided Imagery for Health and Life*, provides meditations for balance and clarity of mind for his students and clients.

As talk show host for KSMQ-TV's *Family Connections* and *Health Connections* programs, he brings significant wellness issues to the airwaves.

As a motivational and inspirational speaker, his personal passion is providing experiences to audiences of all sizes to achieve exceptional connectedness in relationships and peace through full acceptance of self and others. Through providing personal coaching, counseling, workshops, and professional trainings, David brings each individual and system he works with to a level of functioning not previously thought possible. His business clients include leaders from both national and international entities.

DAVID LARSON, MS, CPCC, LP
Institute for Wellness
Triumph Leadership Training
244 W. Clark St.
Albert Lea, MN 56007
507-373-7913
davidlarsonleadership@gmail.com
www.callthecoach.com

CHAPTER SEVEN

Follow the Miracle Road
An Interview with . . . **Kate Michels**

DAVID WRIGHT (WRIGHT)

Today we're talking with Kate Michels. Kate is a popular, renowned and established veteran practitioner, trainer, and instructor in the field of self-help and life coaching. Personally and professionally committed to life-coaching tools since being introduced to some of the great masters of the movement in high school, such as Milton Erickson, her commitment to everyone living up to their full potential reaches from pregnant women and their newborn infants to those who have committed crimes and are serving time in prison.

Creator, designer, facilitator, and chief instructor of Core Alignment Coaching, she is a best-selling author in several books. She is a sought-out motivational speaker, a "Wake Up Woman," representative of the Summer of Peace, Center Point's LPIP Answer Woman, an "amazing dreamer," and a successful Real Estate broker in Portland, Oregon. Kate is also a wife, mother, daughter, sister, and grandmother. Her commitment to the principle that everyone is whole, perfect, creative, resourceful, and making the best decisions with the information they currently have, leads to her continued pursuit of gathering information. She has experienced lasting results with everything from bi-polar, anxiety issues, eating disorders, sleep issues, and just the normal struggles of everyday living.

Kate, welcome to *Stepping Stones to Success*.

KATE MICHELS (MICHELS)

Thank you it's good to be here.

WRIGHT

So you support people in having success in their lives through a process called Core Alignment. What exactly is Core Alignment?

MICHELS

Core Alignment is a reality check where we realign ourselves with what is true, what is present, and what is real. From there people begin to move in the direction they want to go and achieve successes rather easily.

What I say is, throughout life we experience incidents and accidents. From these incidents and accidents we have feelings; from the feelings we have thoughts; and from those thoughts we create beliefs. We then run around with these beliefs and gather evidence that support them. So throughout life we make decisions based on beliefs that have nothing to do with the present or the reality.

Core Alignment is a principle that realigns our beliefs with our truths. This realignment gets us rolling easily down the roads of our life.

WRIGHT

This sounds like a principle that will influence people's entire life, is that right?

MICHELS

Yes it does, it affects their whole life, all of their relationships—especially relationships within themselves. As people realign with what occurred in the past, they are more aware of the present and more adept at creating our future.

WRIGHT

So this alignment process creates the ability to take steps toward success?

MICHELS

Yes it does. I use five steps. They are:

STEP ONE:	Know who you are and what you want.
STEP TWO:	Ask for what you want.
STEP THREE:	Show up to get what you have asked for.
STEP FOUR:	Keep your word.
STEP FIVE:	Have a natural attitude of gratitude.

WRIGHT

So the first is to know what you want. How does one go about knowing what they want?

MICHELS

Well, one of the processes from Core Alignment is the "Wizard of Oz Process." It's similar to the movie, *The Wizard of Oz*. Like Dorothy, all of us are experiencing the incidents and accidents in life that send us spinning much like the tornado in the movie. We think we know what we want and we run away looking for it, as Dorothy did. We go on this incredible journey, struggling, battling, and trying to figure out what we really want. When we finally get to the end of our journey, most of us often look around and say, "Wow, I already had what I really wanted. If I'd only known who I was, I would have realized that it was right here all along." It often is as simple as clicking our heels together, claiming who we are, and standing in what is true. The search within brings realignment, the truth, and the answer to what we want. This becomes a synch when the dust from the spinning settles.

WRIGHT

So the next step you mentioned is asking—asking who and how?

MICHELS

Along Dorothy's journey in Oz, she asked everyone she met how she could reach her goal. At the very beginning (before the tornado) when she was confused, she asked her uncle, she asked the friend who was taking care of the pigs, she asked her aunt, she asked everyone she could think of. Then, when she found herself in the Land of Oz, she asked Glenda, the good witch, she asked the Scarecrow, she asked everyone, wherever she went, "Can you help me get what I want?" Ultimately, it came right down to her having to ask herself.

The way we ask is through honesty, sharing ourselves with those we meet, being willing to open up, trusting, and taking risks. Knowing our truth as we stand in alignment, we ask ourselves and others for what we know we want and it shows up everywhere along the journey and also within everyone we meet.

WRIGHT

Then the next step that you mentioned is showing up to get it. What do you mean when you say "showing up"?

MICHELS

This is a really big one. Often, just showing up makes all the difference. It might mean something as simple as going where you say you're going to go. On the other hand, I also mean more showing up as the true you aligned and more in your present life, showing up with all of the gifts you have and recognizing all you are capable of doing.

In the example of *The Wizard of Oz*, all of these characters could have had all the things they wanted if they had been willing to really show up with who they were and aware of all they had to offer. In fact, they did have everything they wanted when they showed up with all they were created to be. Their essence and their purpose showed brightly to others, only they missed it.

The Scarecrow was striving to have a brain. When he actually showed up, he showed up as the smartest character along the way. The Cowardly Lion was actually the bravest, but he didn't show up as being truly brave. The Tin Man had the biggest heart, but he wouldn't show up as having the biggest heart. Dorothy, on the other hand, was someone who was totally committed to her family, totally committed to her values, and when she finally showed up, she was capable of getting what she wanted.

As characters in our lives, we really want to show up as who we really are, give what we really have to offer, and honestly acknowledge and share our gifts with others.

WRIGHT

Sounds like to me it's the action step, you've got to do it to be it.

MICHELS

It *is* an action step and all of these steps are action steps. They are action steps on the road to miracles. They all come from knowing our core; they all come from our standing in our truth and knowing deep down inside who we are, where we are going, and what we really want.

WRIGHT

So the next step is keeping one's word. That sounds like a big one. Will you tell our readers something more about keeping one's word?

MICHELS

Yes. When I say "keeping one's word," I mean more than just doing what you say you're going to do. It means being willing to take risks and being willing to go the extra mile.

When Dorothy met with the Wizard of Oz and he said, "When you come back, bring me the wicked witch's broom," she was willing to go out, keep her word, and bring back the broom. It was big—bigger than any fear she had ever faced before, yet she went, kept her word, and did what she set out to do.

Many of us would say to the wizard, "Wait a second. You're supposed to do this, you're supposed to do that." Instead, Dorothy went out and did what she said she was going to do—she kept her word and realized that she had the brains, the heart, and the courage to do what she needed to do to get what she wanted. Keeping your word means to know your word, keep your word, and to be your word. Take the actions—keep going on the road that will get you what you want.

WRIGHT

Do you think it's hard for people to keep their word in this culture?

MICHELS

I think it's really hard to keep our word on a daily, consistent basis, and yet if we don't, we miss out on the miracles that come from showing up. It is harder to not keep our word and have to pick up the pieces that this causes for us and for those around us. When we spin less and less in our life by aligning with our values, it is easier than we thinks to keep our word. With life in alignment, keeping our word assists us in showing up with all we have to give, to know our value, and, the value of all we have to give. The resistance to showing up decreases every day when we keep our word and show up truly aligned. The road becomes smoother and easier to travel on.

WRIGHT

So the fifth step, as you say, is a natural attitude of gratitude. How does one do this step, or is it just something that happens?

MICHELS

I say it's a natural attitude of gratitude—it occurs naturally. For example, natural athletes may show up looking as though they have this ability. They must have been born with it because it appears so easy. They were born with the ability to be themselves, they chose to commit to a specific skill, they practiced that skill, and as they practiced that skill, it became more and more natural to them. It occurs naturally.

With our natural attitude of gratitude we choose it and practice it. The more we practice it, the more natural it becomes. The best way to practice a natural attitude of gratitude is to practice during those times when being grateful wouldn't come naturally—when there are trials and tribulations and when we're face-to-face with "the Wicked Witch of the West." When we're face-to-face with our greatest fear, that's when we become grateful for our natural abilities, our natural gifts, and the strengths and attributes of those around us. Again, it is like athletes—without continual effort of showing up and keeping their word, this natural skill would not be fully developed. Even when the score is low, athletes keep playing the game, showing up, keeping their word, asking for the ball, and being who they truly are.

WRIGHT

Isn't it hard to see gratitude or to be grateful when you're going through some sort of a tribulation? It's somewhat fuzzy, isn't it?

MICHELS

Yes, it might be a bit fuzzy, yet when you look around at the people who are there with you, you can begin to stand again in that attitude of gratitude. When we look around, things begin to clear and we see who we are, we can stand in gratitude easily.

When Dorothy was up in the tower at the most dangerous time of her journey, she looked into the crystal globe and saw Auntie Em. She knew what she wanted more than anything—"I want to be home. I want to be with my family. I'm so grateful for you." That is what gave her strength to go on.

Our gratitude is what will give us the ability to stand up, to move on, and to "make it through the poppy fields when we fall asleep." It keeps us going and it gives us courage. It gives us our heart, it gives us our mind, and it moves us. This is why it's the fifth step. It is also the first step, and an action step along the way that is required constantly.

WRIGHT

So how do people stay focused on their success in the midst of things changing or, as you mentioned earlier, during the spinning?

MICHELS

This is a good question. Right now there are so many people who are, as I said, caught up in the tornado of what is happening in their lives. They feel like they've lost control and are or have been victims to what is happening around them. Recognizing reality—the reality of the past and the present—creates alignment. The knowledge that they have a choice to stand in their strength, to stand on their truth, to stand in their core, will give them the stability to make the journey that is ahead to gather the people who will come with them and gather the strengths inside of them—their heart, their courage, and their mind—to move forward and to ultimately reach the goal.

Everything is changing. The one thing we know that is constant is change, and if we have that natural attitude of gratitude about change, then even when things are spinning, we look forward to what is ahead. The landing after the tornado brought Dorothy to the Land of Oz—the land of her purpose—and it put in her true value and put her ruby slippers on her feet. These ruby slippers gave her more power then she'd ever had before. Without that spin—without the running away, without the tornado—she would not have ever known how truly grateful she was to be who she was and where she was. She would never have known what she wanted, how to ask for it, that she could really show up, keep her word, and all that she was grateful for.

WRIGHT

So Core Alignment and the steps to success are more than goal-setting principles. What would you say they are for you and for others?

MICHELS

Core alignment is realigning with our purpose, it's realigning with our essence, it's realigning with all of the characters and all of the voices inside us. It's knowing what we have to do, what we are capable of doing, what we are willing to do, what we want to do, and what we are here to do. It is being in alignment with our true self.

WRIGHT

So what's in the future for you? What are you going to do using this Core Alignment concept? How do you see yourself changing folks?

MICHELS

I stand, myself, on the principle of recognizing that miracles happen every day, and, as people know who they really are, they will be able to stand in their truth. When they stand in their truth and when their core is aligned, they will also be standing for miracles happening every day, and the world will be changing one day at a time.

My mission right now is to see everyone grateful for the life they've had, for the choices they've made, for the incidents and accidents that have occurred in their lives and that have brought them to where they are now. This will take them to where they are going. I want everyone to wear the ruby slippers that they can click together at any time to take them where they really want to go.

WRIGHT

I have one last question. The other day, when I asked someone about coaching and who needs it, the person asked me who I thought the greatest golfer on the circuit is today. My reply was Tiger Woods. This person asked me, "Do you know that he has a coach?" The point was that everybody needs a coach. Do you think all people need a coach and can be better by having someone help them, or will mentors do?

MICHELS

Going to go back again to the analogy of The Wizard of Oz, I'll use the example of Dorothy and Glenda, the Good Witch. Glenda is a perfect example of what a life coach is. She showed up and she reminded Dorothy of who she was and what she wanted. She asked Dorothy, "How do you get it?"—she never told her how to do it. At the very end of the movie, when Dorothy called on Glenda one more time, Glenda said, "I'm always here for you." Dorothy said to Glenda, "How do I get home now?" Glenda said to her, "You have always had the answer—you have always had the ability inside of you, it's always been up to you."

A coach shines the light on who a person is. When people see themselves, they see that inside of them is the answer and that they have the ability to go wherever they want, and to do whatever they want to do. We will all realize that all we need to do is ask, be, and we will have everything.

WRIGHT

Very interesting. These core principles and these steps sound like they might work; at least I think I'm going to try them. This has been a great conversation and I have certainly learned a lot. I appreciate all the time you've taken to answer these questions. I think our readers are going to find this very interesting and perhaps life-changing.

MICHELS

Thank you.

WRIGHT

Today we've been talking with Kate Michels, a popular veteran practitioner, trainer, and instructor in the field of self-help and life coaching. Creator, designer, facilitator, and Chief Instructor of Core Alignment Coaching, she is a best-selling author of several books and a sought-after motivational speaker.

Kate, thank you so much for being with us today on *Stepping Stones to Success*.

MICHELS

Thank you.

ABOUT THE AUTHOR

KATE MICHELS is a popular, renowned, and established veteran practitioner, trainer, and instructor in the field of self-help and life coaching. Personally and professionally committed to life-freeing tools since being introduced to some of the great masters of the movement in high school, such as Milton Erickson, her commitment to everyone living up to their full potential reaches from pregnant women and their newborn infants to those who have committed murder and are serving time in prison.

Creator, designer, facilitator, and chief instructor of Core Alignment Coaching, she is a best-selling author of several books. She is a sought-out motivational speaker, a "Wake Up Woman," representative of the Summer of Peace, Center Point's LPIP Answer Woman, an "amazing dreamer," and a successful Real Estate broker in Portland, Oregon. Kate is also a wife, mother, daughter, sister, and grandmother. Her commitment to the principle that everyone is whole, perfect, creative, resourceful, and making the best decisions with the information they currently have, leads to her continued pursuit of gathering information. She has experienced lasting results with everything from bi-polar anxiety issues, eating disorders, sleep issues, and just the normal struggles of everyday living.

KATE MICHELS
www.CoreAlignmentCoaching.com
CastleBuildingCoaching@yahoo.com

CHAPTER EIGHT

There is no "I" in Success!

An Interview with . . . **Laura Burke**

DAVID WRIGHT (WRIGHT)

Today we're talking to Laura Lynn Burke. Laura is known to wear a multitude of hats—she has gone from Avon Lady to CEO. Her story is quite simple; through partnering and power networking she is able to build strong alliances that help develop her businesses. Her career started in Real Estate as an investor and Real Estate agent. She intertwined her Real Estate experience into the mortgage arena, becoming a loan officer. As a loan officer, Laura originated in excess of $35 million of residential mortgage transactions in one year.

She is now CEO and Founder of Footprints International, d/b/a/ The Mortgage Institute, a training and consulting company. Burke is the director of operations and lead instructor for the Illinois Tax Training Institute. Laura is also CEO and managing director of Professional Tax Masters Inc., PTM, a year-round tax business providing tax planning consulting, preparation, and tax resolution. As an enrolled agent, she is *"admitted to practice"* before the IRS.

PTM offers assistance and guidance to all taxpayers with an emphasis on the small business owner. Laura has chosen to share her experience and knowledge as both a businesswoman and tax professional.

Laura, welcome to *Stepping Stones to Success*.

LAURA LYNN BURKE (BURKE)

David, thank you for a wonderful introduction.

WRIGHT

How would you describe a successful person?

BURKE

There are many ways to be successful. Some of us may be "great" at different times in our lives. For example, we were the best at selling Girl Scout cookies, were in one of the popular "in" groups during high school, graduated summa cum laude, or achieved professional success in a career. Others may be successful stay-at-home moms, or entrepreneurs. Successful people may be Harvard-educated or self-taught.

One of the most financially successful people I've had the chance to work with was a home-builder. He came to the United States from Poland, set out to make his fortune with a sixth grade education. By doing a lot of hard work he succeeded. His annual documented income was more than a million dollars. In my opinion he was a true success story.

WRIGHT

How would you describe success?

BURKE

That's a difficult question. Is success the "ability" to purchase whatever you want, whenever you want? Michael Jackson had that kind of success.

Is it the ability to retire early, live comfortably and enjoy life?

Many of us planned wisely for our future years while some of us have not. Those of us who planned inappropriately or encountered life's road bumps along the way still have the opportunity to be successful. New ventures are becoming commonplace in today's marketplace. It is not uncommon to end one's career and start a new one. Open new doors. You are smarter, stronger, less stressed, and more experienced than you were when you first started. Your focus is sharper.

If you're fortyish you can do a complete 360-degree turn and start over. If you're fiftyish, it's time to reinvent yourself (there's still time to reach for the gold). If you're sixtyish you can do a makeover. You still have time to be wildly successful.

Think about the advantages you will have—the knowledge, the school of hard knocks—you are in control this time.

At fortyish you have the ability to do something so different from what you started out doing; you can make a complete change. Add some additional schooling or classes, start over.

The fiftyish group can re-invent themselves. I think reinventing is better at this age than starting over from scratch. You should already have built a network—a core group of associates, colleagues and trusted friends. You may even have a following or a database full of past and present clients. Now is the time to capitalize on your good fortune of having a marketing data base of trusted clients and a sound structure of past associates to network with. You've built this throughout your life. This is why I say, "Reinvent yourself." Choose to do something that is a crossover, cross-sale, or similar in some way. This gives you a marketing and advertising advantage. Your clients know you and trust you. You don't need to invest as many new dollars into an advertising budget as when you start from scratch. Use your connections to help you grow and reinvent you!

When in your sixties, you may not want to reinvent the total you, but a new makeover will work. I'm not speaking about a physical makeover but professionally—career-oriented changes. Many Americans are planning to work well into their sixties; some are even keeping positions during their seventies. We experience paradigm shifts in the nineties, relating to living and working longer. We now have new career paths as we age.

I believe each person is successful in many ways and in their own unique ways. Some may take note of their success more than others.

WRIGHT

Do you believe it's possible to be successful after a previous failure?

BURKE

I have found many successful people I know or have had contact with who have had a past of non-successes on their way up. It's the inner strength created in us by these non-successes, or steps backward, that develops our character, shapes, and guides us to true success.

You must possess the ability to fall down and get back up again. Sometimes you may fall down over and over, like learning to ride a bike. You need time to learn to balance, peddle, and steer, but with the bike, you were taught to just keep getting back on, peddle faster, peddle stronger—just peddle. It's the same theory for success. You have to keep going; sometimes it may be harder to get up when you fall, but we must keep getting up, peddling, and reaching for our goal.

WRIGHT

How has networking influenced your life?

BURKE

I have always had a passion for networking. As a speaker I have presented numerous topics on networking. Awhile back, I presented a program, *Knotworking—beyond Networking* for the Professional Speakers of Illinois speaker's school. A woman who also spoke about networking attended my program with her assistant. I knew who she was, I knew she was a competitor who spoke on the same topics I did, and I welcomed her to my program. It never crossed my mind to be concerned that she might be unethical and use some of my material. I did my presentation and all was well.

Months later I attended an event where she was a speaker presenting her topic on networking. I thought I would sit in on her presentation and see her present. I was asked to leave for fear that I might "steal" her material! I was flabbergasted to say the least. She had attended my presentation a few months back, and why would she even think I would change my material to reflect hers? It left a huge question in my mind as to what was she presenting that she didn't want me to hear?" I left without saying anything; I didn't cause a scene. I simply left.

In my opinion, this is an example of a poor networking. Networking is about building relationships and bonds. If you are going to present to an audience, I believe you need to "walk your talk."

From one extreme to another—Dr. Ivan Misner, the "father of networking," asked me to contribute an article to a book he was writing, *Masters of Networking: Building Relationships for your Pocketbook and Soul.* Misner chose to ask others who were successful with their own networking skills and ideas to share them with him and his readers. He wasn't concerned about being overshadowed or copied.

You wrote your own book, *Networkology™, a Method of Combining Traditional Networking Skills with Technology to Create Award-Winning Relationships.* How does this book relate to your past relationships and success?

BURKE

During my life I have had the ability to meet people in many different settings, through predetermined networking and accidental meetings, chance run-ins, and coincidental discussions. God gave me a gift to bond instantly with others. I have always had this gift; people feel comfortable with me. They open up and discuss personal business, stories, and dreams. I have tried to make it my goal in life to stay connected with as many people as possible. By staying connected I have encountered strange and awesome success stories.

I started to tell this story earlier. Quite a few years ago, Dr. Ivan Misner, founder of BNI (Business Networking International), was writing a book about networking, titled *Masters of Networking: Building Relationships for your Pocketbook and Soul.* I was asked to participate and write a contributing article. During this time my dad was very sick. I tried to offer as much help to my mom as possible. I spent a lot of extra time with my dad. I just kept putting off writing the article. One day I called Dr. Misner and asked him how the project was going. He said it went well; his book was currently on the *New York Times* best-sellers list.

What had I done? I had missed a huge opportunity to be a part of something so great—to be on the best-sellers list. I felt like the world's biggest idiot. However, I went on to congratulated him on his success and explained why I hadn't sent in my article. I told Dr. Misner my dad had passed away and I just didn't do it. He was very cordial and said he understood. He said it was okay and that I should write my own book and he would contribute to mine. I thanked him, and hung up.

I cried and cried. How could I have let such a wonderful opportunity pass me by? I could have contributed to a book that is on the best-sellers list and I didn't do it. I called my best friend Emily and cried even more. She said, "Stop it. It's your turn. He is right—you need to write your own. What are you crying for? You have another chance, another opportunity. He said he would contribute to your book." I stopped to hear what she was saying, she repeated herself, saying, "He said he would contribute to yours!"

I perked up, dried my tears, and called Dr. Misner back. I said, "Okay, I'm going to do it." He offered his support, sent me an e-mail with multiple articles attached, and said, "Use whatever ones you want." That was how I started writing my book, Networkology.

I thought, who else could I ask to share a story about networking? I asked Nick Carter of Nightingale-Conant Corporation. He said, "Sure," and mailed me an audio tape of his stories, and told me to use whatever I wanted. Many others voluntarily contributed their stories and I sought out a few others.

Now I have my own book, *Networkology*. Let's see if I, too, can make it to the best-sellers list.

I was fortunate to be asked to be a part of this book project, *Stepping Stones to Success,* as well. Life has a way of finding you when you least expect it. I have found in business and in life that my best friends have come from networking.

Networking knows no boundaries. You can network with just about anyone. Distance, sex, age, race, religion, or education—none of it matters. What matters most is what you share; that is your common bond. A bond is what is important. Without a bond you are acquaintances. Build a bond and you are networking with friends, business associates, maybe even partners.

Never think you are too good to befriend someone. There will be a time in your life when you will need someone to befriend you. Someone will appear and be there for you! Whether it's a new career, a divorce, a family tragedy, or the start-up of a new business, you will need someone you are not currently networking with. That someone will be there when you need him or her. The question is, "Will you be there when someone else needs you?"

WRIGHT

So how do your relationships relate to others' success?

BURKE

I think that many of the people I've connected with over the years have been very successful. I believe in surrounding yourself with successful people from all walks of life. I think I have helped others to be successful and to accomplish their goals or dreams and to mainly believe in themselves. I feel that staying connected to both past and present relationships is very important.

I believe the more people you help, the more success will come back to you. I have done my best to stay connected to past clients, colleagues, business partners, associates, and friends. It is a connection of time—past, present, and future events—that help build and strengthen our relationships.

My relationships with others have created a strong synergy often used to develop new ideas, expand on current issues, and develop new relationships. It is through these relationships that a new beginning is formed, building trust and creating bonds. This trust can then be built upon as new ventures stem from past relationships. It is the synergy of the union that catapults us forward to experience new endeavors.

WRIGHT

What do you feel are key attributes to building relationships?

BURKE

Being yourself is really important as well as not having a, "what's in it for me" attitude. By building a relationship and rapport with people, being interested in what they are doing and not what they can do for you is really the first step in starting any kind of a bond. I have always thought that my attendance (showing up) and being a friend/ co-worker is more important than what business others are going to give to me.

I have found that connecting to the other person is also important. Whether you connect through mutual friends, activities or, business desires, you need to have a common bond.

Loyalty is also on my top list. If others feel you are loyal, they will most often return your loyalty. If not, then maybe you would choose to build a relationship with someone else. Not everyone walks his or her talk. Learn to choose those you include in your "circle of life." Build a team that is interrelated so you can cross-reference anyone on "your team" or "circle of life" to enhance meetings and future projects. Not everyone on your team will be involved in the same project; some will be involved in more projects than others. Always know who is in your circle.

I have a core inner circle with my most trusted confidants and respected business associates. Then I have an intermediate circle for those I'm not as connected to as my inner core group. I have a very comfortable level of trust with them so that even when we don't see one another or speak as frequently, all that is needed is a phone call, e-mail, or luncheon to pick up our relationship exactly where it was. You should also have a larger circle you are cultivating and working on building to add to the intermediate or inner core group.

WRIGHT

Is there a famous person who influenced your thoughts or behavior?

BURKE

I have a few of them:

Tony Robbins is one. He rose above many adversities in his life. He was thrown out of his home on Christmas Eve at the young age of seventeen. He was a janitor, and twelve years later he was wildly successful as a self-taught millionaire. He lost his wealth not once but twice, and he rose above it. Tony is an *extraordinary* person, who exemplifies that you can change and by changing become very successful. I did the fire walk with Tony here in Chicago, on the rooftop of the Hilton. I will always remember the incredible experience of being able to walk across twelve-hundred-degree, red hot stoked coals in my bare feet for about fifteen feet! I did it, and I often remember the phrase I used to put my mind "in state" to change my physiology to allow me to walk on hot coals and not get burned.

I built relationships with others from all over the world that night. There were about fifteen hundred of us who participated in the fire walk, and maybe ten people received minor burns. Most often the burns were from small pieces of hot coal sticking between your toes. We were hosed off immediately upon the completion of our walk.

Christopher Reeve was the real Superman. He fought until the very end of his life to overcome adversity. His wife, Dana, stood beside him when it would have been so easy to leave. She had courage and staying power. They both were models of success.

Helen Keller had all the reasons in the world to give up, do nothing, and be complacent. She chose success; she chose to be outstanding in what she could do. She was the first deaf and blind person to earn a Bachelor of Arts degree.

During her later years she continued to strive for excellence. In 1964, Helen was awarded the Presidential Medal of Freedom, the nation's highest civilian award, bestowed upon her by President Lyndon Johnson. A year later, she was elected to the Women's Hall of Fame.

I also include Eleanor Roosevelt, because she ran a country from behind the scenes to assist her ailing husband during a time when women weren't considered equal. They weren't allowed to vote, and definitely not allowed to run a country. I think she was a strong-minded, strong-willed woman. She stood by her husband when he needed her.

I love the underdogs—those who grit their teeth and just keep on going to win.

WRIGHT

Who do you believe deserves the accolade as being successful, the person who trains, mentors, and encourages one to be great, or the person who actually achieves success?

BURKE

This question reminds me of the old adage, "is the glass half full or half empty?" I feel that the answer depends on how you see the whole picture. I think that the person who believes in someone else, makes many personal sacrifices, and gives up his or her personal fulfillment to help another person achieve his or her goal is a key component to the success of the other person. It is often "because of the other person's" constant belief and encouragement that success has been obtained. I believe the "encourager" is equally as successful as the actual person achieving the accomplishment.

WRIGHT

What are your favorite stories, thoughts, or paraphrases relating to success?

BURKE

One of my favorite paraphrases is, "Thank God for unanswered prayers." I once heard a woman speak at a convention. She told her story of unanswered prayers. It was a sad and difficult story to listen to. I can't remember her name, but I can remember her story. As a child, she was locked in a closet for long periods of time without food. She would always pray to get out and be rescued. Later in her life, she reflected on being locked in the closet. She now speaks about how it helped shape her and mold her into the person she is today. If someone like that can truly be thankful for God's unanswered prayers, we all can. I think there are many stories of unanswered prayers that we have—cars that have broken down on the way to important meetings, meetings we missed because of wrong turns, illnesses, a missed bus, or maybe we weren't there at Ground Zero on 9/11, but those are all stories of God's unanswered prayers.

How often do I think I know what I need or want in a particular situation, only to learn it may not be what I really wanted or needed as I continue down my pathway? I love the thought of God's unanswered prayers; sometimes I think, "It just isn't going right for me, maybe I should give up," and then my mind reminds me that maybe this is just one of God's unanswered prayers for me, and I will be thankful for this later on down the road.

Think about it for a moment. I am sure that you can think of an unanswered prayer that you are grateful for. As you can tell, I am the eternal optimist—I see good in most people and in almost any situation. I don't know why, but I have always believed that things will work out right.

Someone once told me that you never know where your silver lining lies. What if you were only steps away from achieving success and you stop or you quit without ever knowing that, had you taken those last five steps, you would have turned the corner and success would have been there! This is why I believe that you should always keep going; every cloud has a silver lining.

WRIGHT

How has success influenced your life?

BURKE

I'd like to share a story with you. This is a story about a program I started ten years ago for homeless people. It was called, "Open Your Hearts America." I wanted homeless people to have somewhere to spend the holidays. For two days out of the year—Thanksgiving Day and/or Christmas Day—I wanted them to be able to have somewhere to go. I wanted them to be with a family, have a dinner, and not be alone. This program worked for one year and then the litigious side of our country came forward. The threat of a potential lawsuit from allowing a stranger into homes became the axe. Even churches were concerned with the issue.

We had one year and we had Charlie. Charlie wasn't really homeless—he lived at the YMCA. He had a brother, I believe, but he did not live nearby. I was so excited to be doing something of value and something good. It was Christmas. My dad was suffering from stomach cancer and was very uncomfortable. He was pretty miserable at times. But it was Christmas, and Dad was really upset with me for allowing a stranger to join us during our family's Christmas celebration. He didn't want anyone to see him the way he had become—thin and frail. Dad said, "He wouldn't come if I had a stranger in my home on Christmas day."

I thought about it, I cried a little bit, and I called his bluff. I told him, "If he couldn't share food and friendship on Christmas Day because of his selfishness, then maybe he shouldn't come," because that's wasn't what he had taught me Christmas was about. Dad had taught me to share good fortune with others. My dad was an usher at church, he helped many of our neighbors; whenever they had a car problem, Dad would fix it. This wasn't what my dad did for a living—he was just kind. He had forgotten the things he had taught us. I decided I was having a guest, Charlie, and that was it.

So we had Charlie. He was probably in his late twenties or early thirties. Charlie was excited to be coming to our house for the holidays. He had never met any of us; he had spoken to me on the phone for a few minutes and that was it. My daughter, Jennie, and her friend drove out to pick him up at the YMCA. When they arrived, Charlie asked if she could stop at a store so he could pick up something to bring. He couldn't come empty-handed to our home for Christmas. He used a food voucher to purchase a few bags of chips so that he could contribute to the holiday party.

We all talked with Charlie. We played a traditional dice game that we play every year. Everyone sits is a large circle and throws five dice; if you get a double, you pick a prize. Everyone contributes to the prizes and you can win multiple gifts. You can bring old silly gifts you don't want or you can purchase new items. You can even wrap up money! Everyone goes around the circle choosing gifts when a double is thrown. When the last gift is chosen from the center, a last round is called. Everyone gets to throw the dice one last time. If a double is thrown, you get to steal a gift from someone—you can choose any gift. All gifts are still wrapped. Charlie won a few prizes. He had a lot of fun sharing in our family's tradition.

We also purchased Charlie a set of gloves and a scarf. Charlie cried. He was so joyous to be a part of our family's celebration and traditions. He blended in nicely. Dad showed up as planned, he liked Charlie, and all was well.

Charlie stayed in contact for a year or so afterward. He entered into a college program and he progressed with his life. My children can still remember the Christmas that we had with Charlie, the songs we sang at the piano with our special visitor. Was this a success or a failure? You choose. I could no longer carry on the "Open Your Hearts America" Program, it was too risky, but we had Charlie in our hearts forever.

WRIGHT

Would you tell our readers how your networking has created success in your life?

BURKE

Sure. I have an uncanny knack, as I said earlier, to blend and to meet people. I have strong networking capabilities that have shaped my life. I believe that people are put in places at certain times in our lives because they're meant to be there at that moment. Either they need to touch your life or you need to touch theirs. I've been fortunate because I have a long list of people I've met through networking—both planned and what I call "Free Fall" networking—who have continued to touch my life. I like to turn as many casual networking contacts I encounter into business associates, colleagues, or friends (relationships).

Planned networking is something we all do. We plan to go to particular events to network.

What is "Free Fall Networking"? No, you're not networking without a net, but you really aren't there for business and you didn't plan or position yourself to be there. It's an event that leads you to unexpected networking opportunities. You bond almost instantaneously with someone and before you know it, you're doing business together. This is Free Fall Networking.

It has been through networking that I have met almost all of my business colleagues, business associates, and friends. It has been my core belief to treat others as you would want them to treat you. My list of contacts through networking could be a book.

WRIGHT

Would you tell our readers about some people you consider as successful role models for success?

BURKE

Some successful people I have connected with who have had a memorable influence in my life are:

Chuck Wagner, who was a great teacher and influence when I started a direct marketing venture. He walked his talk and spent numerous hours discussing and training me when he had nothing to gain from it.

Wagner was not in any of my uplines or downlines or in any way remotely near them. He spent hours and hours explaining the process to me. He would encourage me to keep trying. He taught me the language—what keywords to learn. One of the most important things he taught me was how to listen and how to make other people feel good about themselves.

I asked him one day why he was willing to spend so much time coaching me. He said there was an old quote, "When the student is ready, the teacher will appear." He appeared.

I will always hold Chuck in the highest regard because he truly was a great networking partner and business associate who cared first about the other person. He cared most about creating a relationship that would last through time. The only thing he ever asked of me was if I ever met someone who needed a teacher, coach, or mentor to reciprocate and be the teacher. I agreed.

James Greene has been supportive as an instructor and mentor in my becoming an enrolled agent. Through his encouragement and belief in me, I stayed focused to achieve my "Enrolled Agents" designation.

There were many times it was extremely difficult to stay focused and positive while working a full-time job and having a family life. My family life became more involved after my daughter's house was destroyed by a fire. Her family lost everything material they owned. The positive note was that no one was injured, with the exception of her cat, "S'mores;" he didn't make it. We have had the experience of having my daughter, my son-in-law, and my granddaughter, who was ten months old at the time, move in with us while they rebuilt their home.

It has been a lot of fun and yet difficult at times for all of us. We are all used to our own space. Nevertheless, I studied at night—often very late at night into the wee hours of the morning. My hard work paid off—I passed all three of the Special Enrollment Exams, and then passed the IRS background check as well.

James continued to believe in my abilities, as he hired me immediately to teach at the Tax Training Institute. Every time I came up with an idea, a new client, a new tax issue, he was there. He never grew weary of my never-ending questions, ideas, plans, and excitement. It is his belief in me and his continuous support and encouragement that inspires me to pass the tax court exam as a U.S. Tax Court Practitioner.

He has entrusted me as an "enrolled agent" to be a member of his team of tax attorneys with his law firm, James P. Greene and Associates. He has strengthened my knowledge in tax court proceedings as well as challenged me to continuously grow and increase my depth of knowledge.

My mother, Rosemarie, has always given me her unwavering support and belief in all that I do. Without mom I wouldn't have achieved all that I have been able to accomplish. She would send me notes telling me to keep on going; she never once stopped believing in me. She is a loving mother, grandmother, and great-grandmother, Busia.

Then there's Emily Ferguson or "Em," as I like to call her. We met while networking many years ago and have managed to stay colleagues and friends through job changes, a divorce, a couple of break-ups, children with growing pains, parents with health issues, and parents passing. I guess you can say we have been through it all, thick and thin. Thank God for Emily. She coined the term, "Who's on your team?" Em, I'm glad you're on my team.

Phillip Hendle is one of the best networkers I know. I met Phil through Emily. We worked on a direct marketing project together, Prepaid Legal Services. He is very successful. He, too, like Chuck Wagner, was willing to share his expertise with me. I chose Phil to be a part of a national team for Realtors that I was chosen to head up for the Midwest states. He later became my editor and confidante when I started writing *Networkology*. He would read and re-read, edit, and re-edit my manuscript, never complaining. He always made the time to fit it in, even if it meant taking it with him. Years passed and I didn't complete my book project. Phil was still there when I needed him; all it took was one phone call and he took the revised manuscript on the plane with him.

He edited it again, met with me, gave me his viewpoints, and strongly suggested some changes. I believed in him, so I made the changes. Our give-and-take, trust, and friendship relationship through the years allowed us to be candid with one another.

Dr. Keith Laggos believed in me when there wasn't a reason to. He saw in me the person I could be and allowed me to grow into that person—the person he has chosen to recommend time and time again for projects he believes I am an expert in. I have always tried to live up to his expectations of me.

For all the people I've mentioned and others, I hope I have also influenced your life in a positive way, been your guiding light—the person who pushed or nudged you to be more. We are only as successful as we choose to be.

Choose your team members wisely. Your team members should vary in intellect, background, age, and skills. They should be diversified. The one common element they should have is that they should mirror your ethics and push you to be the best you that you can be.

I would be remiss if I didn't mention my husband, Joe. He doesn't say much, but sometimes the unspoken words are the ones we are grateful for. He never complained that I was working too much, studying too late (with the light on while he slept), added additional classes to take, started teaching at night, and added writing two more books. He would just ask me how my day went or did I have to work tonight on a project. He started cooking more, shopping more, and taking care of the things I would have been doing. He seemed oblivious to the added mess and clutter I had in our room and the office. It would be hard to miss, so I am sure he saw it but chose to not mention it. Thank you, Joe, for your quiet support. I love you.

I have a long list of people who have added to my success. I have found that, in networking, people often emerge from nowhere to contribute to your success. One idea or project leads to another and another and a new person and before you know it, you have this huge referral tree.

There is always that one go-to person we all have in our lives—the special person who believes in you no matter what. When you are at your absolute lowest, when you're hurting and not sure which way to turn, this person is your beacon, your light in the dark, your cheerleader when no one else believes in you. When things are good, they believe they can be better. When things are really good, this person is there to share in your glory. My special person is Jaci, my daughter. Jaci is always there, no matter what.

I am sure you all have a special go-to person. The question I ask is, are you a special "go-to" person for someone?

WRIGHT

Success is a journey, one that is different for each one of us. Will you tell us your thoughts about the journey to success?

BURKE

In order to be successful, you have to know how to rebound, rebuild, keep inner strength, and just keep on moving. I think success comes in all shapes and sizes in both monetary and professional ways.

WRIGHT

What have you told your children or what would you like to tell them about success?

BURKE

I would tell them:

1. To never give up and that I believe in them. Sometimes we have to give something up to get where we want to be. A caterpillar has to give up its old way of life to become a butterfly. We must give up what is not working. If it's not bringing us success, try tweaking what you are doing and if that doesn't work, reinvent yourself, your ideas, or your marketing plan.
2. Never let someone else burst your bubble, tell you that you can't do it, or that it's a bad idea. If it's your dream—your goal—make it happen. It's only wise to listen to constructive criticism with a grain of salt. Stay steadfast in your beliefs, keep your inner strength and continue to go forward. You will find success. Only you can make it happen. Success is hard work. If you are fortunate to achieve success, you will more than likely have stumbled upon some roadblocks. Without them you

would have been cheated. Nothing feels as good as the success that comes after struggling and pushing to make it happen.

3. I believe in you! I truly am blessed to have successful children. Jennifer (Jennie), my oldest, is a successful Realtor and mother of two, Owen and Elenore. Even while pregnant, Jen managed to be a top producer in her Remax One office. She has a will of iron, the stubbornness of Archie Bunker, and a heart the size of Texas. Her strength and courage amaze me every day. She is a remarkable person. Jacquelyn (Jaci), is a graduate of Bradley University, and one of the youngest store managers with David's Bridal. She is an aggressive and insightful sales leader. Her management style shows her personality to be the best in all she does. She is an awesome mom to Abbey, her daughter. Dale, my baby, has his own company, Lunsford Flooring, a house, and a son, Devlin all at the age of twenty-two. Dale is a very serious twenty-two year old who accepts hard work and continues to grow because of his will to reach for the "gold". He is an excellent networker, has been since age five. You can read about him in my book Networkology.

I am very proud of all three of my children and their success in life.

WRIGHT

What would you recommend to people who may feel that it's not happening for them—they're stuck at a stalemate and haven't found the success they were looking for yet?

BURKE

I would tell them similar words as to what I would tell my children—make a change. Think about where you want to be, set goals, and make a plan to institute some changes. If you keep doing what you're doing, it probably won't happen for you. Maybe you need to go back and look at something that you've done in the past and do it again, just differently. Perhaps you need to reinvent yourself and do something totally different that will be successful for you.

WRIGHT

Will you tell our readers how success has influenced your life?

BURKE

Success has affected my life in so many ways. I have had many failures and negatives in my life. I also have so many successes in my life that I feel the successes always outweigh the failures. One of the things I feel was a success is writing this chapter and my other books, *Networkology* and *The Home-Based Business Guide: planning a business, choosing an entity and IRS approved tax deductions.*

Changing careers at fifty, taking classes, and studying to pass the enrolled agents exam was a difficult task as well. Starting a new business is exciting and scary, especially in today's market.

I have set my sights high and continue to strive for more. I plan to take the U.S. Tax Court Practitioner exam, which is a test that Congress passed in the mid 1940s. The passing of the USTC test is equivalent to passing the bar. Only a handful of students pass the exam. Statistically six to eight out of sixty will pass every two years. Only 272 have passed the exam since the mid 1940s. Once you have passed, you have earned the right to practice tax law in any federal tax court, the same as an attorney. You are granted equal footing. I am planning to take the exam this November.

James Greene and I have started a not for profit organization, The National Tax Academy II. We will provide tax representation to low to moderate income tax payers. Our belief is in "Equal representation for all". We also offer scholarships for specific individuals to take our "Enrolled Agents Courses". Along with our plan to franchise Professional Tax Masters, Inc., designed to focus on the small business owner. The plan is to offer small business owners unique tax guidance, preparation, and planning. Look out, H&R Block, Liberty Tax, and Jackson Hewitt—Professional Tax Masters has arrived!

WRIGHT

Well, I wish you luck, and I would bet on you.

BURKE

Thank you.

WRIGHT

What an interesting conversation, I have really learned a lot here today and even learned a new word, "Networklogy." I really appreciate the time you've taken to talk to me today, it certainly was a pleasure talking with you and I wish you the best. I've learned a lot and I'm sure our readers will.

BURKE

I have enjoyed sharing my thoughts with you. Thank you for choosing me to be a part of *Stepping Stones to Success*. I hope that I've touched someone's life and given encouragement for success.

WRIGHT

Today we've been talking with Laura Lynn Burke, President of Footprints International, a training company designed with you in mind. Burke is also CEO of Professional Tax Masters, Inc.

Laura, thank you so much for being with us today on *Stepping Stones to Success*.

BURKE

Thank you for allowing me to be here.

ABOUT THE AUTHOR

LAURA BURKE, EA, exemplifies the ideals tax professionals strive to achieve for their clients. She is tenacious, inquisitive, analytical, and has a continual drive to be the best in her craft.

Ms. Burke has moved from mortgage broker to enrolled agent in a seamless transition. She has incorporated tax and mortgage training as part of her client representation. She has authored tax articles and has written a tax book, *The Home-Based Business Guide: planning a business, choosing an entity, and IRS approved tax deductions*, which can be used by small and midsized businesses in minimizing their tax burdens.

In addition, Laura has leadership qualities that are discernable to anyone holding a conversation with her. She is a public speaker on tax matters and new tax laws. Laura also speaks frequently on matters relating to Savvy Internet Marketing, Sales, Presentation Skills, and most notably, The Double "P" principle—Partnering and Power Networking—excerpted from a chapter in her soon to be released book, *Networkology*[TM].

Burke is also an instructor for the Illinois Tax Training Institute in downtown Chicago, where she teaches tax ethics and individual taxes for people pursuing an enrolled agent designation. Ms. Burke is the type of professional who will always bring her best to a professional environment. Laura has a strong desire to help others achieve their goals while she consistently adds new ones to her own.

Laura is the founder of two new LinkedIn groups, Enrolled Agents of America and Networkology. Please join her on LinkedIn. She has also written numerous articles for various print media including industry journals. To read other work by her, visit www.LauraLynnBurke.com.

Burke also incessantly looks for ways to reach out to the tax community. She recently joined work forces with The Center for Economic Progress in Chicago. The Center provides tax preparation for low to moderate income families. During the 2009 tax season, the Center put $52 million back into the pockets of more than 33,000 Illinois families. She has also served as both an instructor and a site manager for this not-for-profit organization.

LAURA LYNN BURKE
Mokena, IL 60448
708-692-6199
LLynn145@aol.com
www.SteppingStonestoSuccess.name
www.LauraLynnBurke.com
www.Footprintsinternational.net
www.professionaltaxmasters.com

CHAPTER NINE

Brain Drain, Brain Gain:
Emotional Intelligence Tools for Top Performance
An Interview with . . . **Dr. Relly Nadler**

DAVID WRIGHT (WRIGHT)

Today we're talking with Dr. Relly Nadler. Dr. Nadler is a licensed psychologist and Master Certified Coach with the International Coaching Federation, corporate trainer, and author. He is President and CEO of True North Leadership Inc., an executive and organizational development firm. He brings his expertise and Emotional Intelligence (EI) to all his keynotes, consulting, coaching, and leadership trainings. He has designed and delivered many multi-day executive boot camps for high achievers in Fortune 500 companies. He has been working for more than thirty years with top executives and their teams to help them become star performers.

In his work, Dr. Nadler answers the question, "What do I do to raise my emotional intelligence and become a top performer?" He has coached presidents and their teams, designed corporate university learning curriculums, and developed cutting edge E.I. tools that people use all over the world.

Dr. Nadler has found that most leaders have underestimated their influence on others, thus they and their teams have underperformed. He helps executives find the few actions that can significantly improve their performance. Co-host of *Leadership Development News*, a top Internet radio show on *VoiceAmerica Talk Radio Network*, Dr. Nadler and his co-host, Dr. Cathy Greenberg, bring advancements to listeners weekly. He will share his Emotional Intelligence secrets with us today from his new book *Leading with Emotional Intelligence*.

Dr. Nadler, welcome to *Stepping Stones to Success*.

RELLY NADLER (NADLER)

Thank you David; it's great to be here today and talk with you.

WRIGHT

So why do you say most leaders and organizations are experiencing a "brain drain," operating in a dumbed down manner and not maximizing their influence?

NADLER

Well, part of this, David, is that the brain drain happens from the stresses that go on in organizations today. My hypothesis here is with all these stresses that people are operating with ten or fifteen less IQ points, so that's where the dumbed down part comes from.

You may ask why executives are operating with less IQ points. Well, it comes from three reasons:

1. The daily chaos of complexity, new people, new systems, global interfaces, different languages, different generations—there are all kinds of complexity, so that's one key factor.
2. There is the sense of urgency—everything is due now, everything is due yesterday.
3. Each individual on the team or the organization is thinking about what can he or she do individually, and people sometimes miss the bigger picture of what the system is doing and what the team is doing because they're focusing on themselves.

So those three things, complexity, urgency, and this individual focus lead to someone experiencing chaos and being overwhelmed.

The way we feel chaos or when we feel overwhelmed resides in a part of the brain called the amygdala. When our blood and oxygen go to the amygdale, it creates the fight or flight or response. When the blood and oxygen go there, less blood and oxygen go to the prefrontal cortex, which is where executive functioning resides. As a consequence, people don't make good critical decisions and they have less IQ available to them because the brain drain is like a brain freeze, which is why they can't think as well.

WRIGHT

So how is brain neuroscience research influencing leadership today?

NADLER

In the last five years, we have learned so much more about the brain. The brain is like a "black box;" we all have brains but we know very little of what's going on in the black box. So with the help of functional MRIs, it is possible to see maps of the brain showing where blood and oxygen are. The red, yellow, and the orange colors on the scan show what parts of the brain are getting energized or activated. Spec Scans are also used to depict what is happening in the brain. Today we're able to see what is going on in the brain—not only in the individual, but also how other people are being influenced by us. This Social Intelligence is now being called a "two-person psychology" by author, psychologist, and science journalist, Daniel Goleman. When you and I speak, neuroscientists are able to see what parts of our brains are activated. Brain neuroscience is really bringing a lot of this information back to leadership and to folks working with Emotional Intelligence and Social Intelligence. There is a brand new field called "Neuroleadership" coined by David Rock, which integrates brain neuroscience into applied leadership knowledge and actions.

WRIGHT

So what does Emotional Intelligence have to do with self-control and top performance?

NADLER

Self-control is one of many competencies in Emotional Intelligence. Emotional Intelligence got its start from a long research study. During the course of about thirty-five years, the researchers studied the difference between someone who is an average performer and a star performer. As a result of this research, about eighteen or twenty key competencies emerged. In addition to the competencies, it was determined what behaviors an outstanding or star performer does regularly that average performers don't. What we've found is the concept of emotional intelligence (EI). EI is simply understanding and managing yourself, and then understanding and managing others. These skills are the key skills that allow someone to excel in his or her organization.

Self-control is probably one of the critical key aspects of emotional intelligence—how you put your own personal braking system on out-of-control emotions. Now we know from brain neuroscience there is a certain part of the brain that has to deal with controlling impulses. Given all the stress we've talked about, it's imperative for an outstanding leader to manage and put the brakes on some of their impulses and their daily stresses. Then, they can deal with people around them appropriately and make sound, calm decisions.

WRIGHT

So how would you define Emotional Intelligence?

NADLER

Emotional Intelligence is made up of a personal side and a social side. The personal side has to deal with a series of competencies about understanding yourself—like accurate self-assessment of emotional self-awareness and confidence. Then there is a side about managing yourself. Emotional self-control, initiative, achievement orientation, trustworthiness, and adaptability are some of the main competencies also on the personal side.

Now on the social side, to which the new brain neuroscience is adding, you have competencies such as understanding others, empathy, and knowing what is going on in someone else's mind. Social awareness includes how you get along in an organization, knowing whom to befriend, and how to get things done. Then relationship management is also on the social side, and includes how you manage these relationships. Those are some of our typical leadership issues—influence, team work and collaboration, developing others, and managing change. So emotional intelligence looks at the four key areas: understanding yourself, managing yourself, understanding others, and managing others.

WRIGHT

What are the characteristics of the top 10 percent performer, and why is it important for corporations?

NADLER

I think that it's very important in corporations because we spend time training and coaching, and we need to know exactly what competencies to encourage with our training and coaching. The goal would be to get somebody who is a solid B player to be a solid A player. So a lot of our focus is getting leaders into the top 10 percent. The top 10 percent, David, is really a tipping point. This means that when you get someone into the top 10 percent he or she adds twice as much revenue to the organization as managers in the eleventh through the eighty-ninth percentile. When people become A players, they are able to be outstanding performers.

So, of the competencies that I mentioned—initiative, self-control, confidence, influence, inspirational leadership, developing others, change catalyst, to just name a few—the goal would be to get a leader to be good in three or four or maybe five of these areas. Depending on the leader's job, that will propel him or her into the top 10 percent. Depending on leaders' positions, they will choose which areas they think are the best to excel in and then get more coaching or more training to excel in those areas.

WRIGHT

So why is training and emotional-social intelligence and brain neuroscience so important today?

NADLER

The good news is that we can learn some of these emotional intelligence skills. You can't change your basic intelligence quotient (IQ). You can't cram and then all of a sudden increase your IQ. In organizations today, what's been shown in the research is that it's the emotional quotient (sometimes called EQ) that is the critical factor for someone to move up in an organization. So it is more EQ than IQ. The other reason why it's important to train in emotional and social intelligence today is that many of the Baby Boomers are going to be retiring and there is going to be a gap of about ten million jobs lost, probably in the next five years as the Baby Boomers retire.

The other really interesting point is that the Baby Boomers and the Traditionals have higher emotional intelligence. The younger folks— Generation X and Generation Y—have less emotional intelligence. One of the areas in which they have less EI is self-management. They may act on their impulses more than someone who is older and wiser. Often, emotional intelligence is just maturity—older people understand themselves more and know how to manage themselves. So training the younger generation in emotional intelligence—how to deal with others, how to motivate folks, how to give very clear feedback, and how to manage themselves—is going to be critical for the future of an organization to grow.

WRIGHT

So the next question, given all that you've said up until, now is how do you raise emotional intelligence?

NADLER

As I mentioned, there are eighteen to twenty competencies and each of these competencies have certain behaviors and certain tools. In my new book, *Leading with Emotional Intelligence,* a lot of these tools are examined in more depth, but typically, what you'd want to do is start off assessing people on some of these emotional intelligence competencies—where are they and where do they need to go?

Many organizations use 360 assessments. People are evaluated on these specific competencies by their boss, their peers, the people who report to them, and then sometimes by others in the organization. These evaluations determine if they are good or average. Their jobs are also evaluated to determine the most important competencies necessary to perform the job well. Then you want to look at what are they already doing well. People are going to excel and be motivated by continuing to do what they do well and what they're excited about. So you first want to look at what you are already doing well, what your strengths are, and if there are some places where you can improve. Often this is identifying how you build and broaden your strengths, which would be the next step.

Then you're going to look at the areas in which, with a little bit of work, they could improve. These are in key needed areas. So first look at strengths, and then look at some of the needed areas in which, with just a little bit of work, they can improve.

I like to talk about micro-initiatives, these are small initiatives. Sometimes they could be activities that would take five minutes, a half hour, or hour that can have a macro effect or a major effect on the person's performance. Then you design a development plan focusing on the small activities. Ideally this is to pick two or three things to focus on, start working on it, start practicing it, and then get feedback from a coach on how well they're doing in those areas so that they can continue and sustain that progress.

WRIGHT

You have said that a derailer can trump good emotional intelligence competencies. Why is that and will you give some examples of derailers?

NADLER

Yes, so a derailer comes from the root of the idea that something derails someone who is on the track or the rail to success. Often these are things that can trump all the good things from emotional intelligence. Examples are the "smartest person" in the room "driving others too hard" and "pushing for perfection." One of the biggest derailers that we see in our media all the time now is "lack of impulse control."

Two unfortunate examples recently include that of John Edwards fathering a child and lying about it and Tiger Woods' sex scandal. These show lack of impulse control. Another is Serena Williams shouting in front of millions of people at a referee because of a line fault. These are all critical outbursts and sometimes they're called the "amygdala hijack." The person's amygdala is hijacked so quickly by overwhelming impulses that it overpowers a person's executive functioning. Of all the derailers, the one that probably acts on people the fastest and that can also derail someone significantly is lack of impulse control.

WRIGHT

One Emotional intelligence competency is change leadership. Would you tell our readers why organization change is so hard?

NADLER

I think one of the things about change is that from brain neuroscience we know that people see something as either a reward or a threat. In simple terms, the brain sees those two things and makes a quick assessment: is this a reward or is this a threat? I think people see any kind of change in an organization, then, as a threat—a threat to their status, their comfort level, or their security. The change can be a threat to what they're doing as far as autonomy, they may be put in a different position, and it can be a threat to relationships they have—some of their good friends may leave.

What happens, going back to what we said of the brain, is that the emotional part of the brain gets aroused and when that happens, the executive function of the brain doesn't work as well. A critical piece for leaders, because they're the ones who are promoting change almost on a daily basis, is knowing how to motivate people, knowing about the strengths and weaknesses of your people, and how you can change your approach to help people move along with the change. Simply stated, people need to be involved in the change; they need to have some ownership of the change. Leaders need to talk about the why of the change, connect the dots, what's going to be important about the change, how people's jobs are going to improve, what kind of training they are going to get in regards to the change, and then asking their people what they think about the change, and how best to implement it. One of the rules of change management is involvement equals commitment. So the more involved the organization is, the more committed they are going to be to the change.

WRIGHT

For a newly promoted leader to be in the top 10 percent, what are a few EI tips that you would give them?

NADLER

These are things that I typically would talk about with leaders in executive coaching and in training. Here are some of the key things your readers can do:

1. *Agree on the top five responsibilities:* Go to the supervisor and say, "Let's talk about my top five responsibilities." Agree on what the top five responsibilities are. Typically, of the five there are usually only one and a half that are the same. So an employee may be working on something thinking that it's the right thing, and the supervisor would rather have the employee working on something else.
2. *Clarifying expectations:* The leader should give a clear target of what the employee should be doing or not doing. Expectations are very important and the clearer a leader can be, the less they're going to create what's called an "error message" in the brain. This causes the employee to think, "Well, I don't know why we're doing that," or "Oh, that's not what I thought was going to happen." When the leader creates an error message, the employee will not operate with as much efficiency.
3. *Know your people:* A leader can get to know their people well enough to learn their strengths and see if the job can provide more opportunities for the employees to do tasks that maximize their strengths.
4. *Build a team.* If there are new members on the team, sometimes there is fear of the new member. It is important to quickly build a team, build camaraderie, and talk about how to operate together. Building a team to move forward is important.
5. *Be aware of trying to add too much value.* Sometimes a leader and new leaders want to be the answer person. They try to add value to every idea that comes up, which can zap some of the involvement and some of the engagement of employees. So try not to add too much value.

6. *Hold individual meetings:* Make sure you're having one-on-one meetings for individual coaching. This is where most leaders underestimate their influence. These meetings can help leaders to understand their employees, their motivations, their strengths, and how they want to be recognized or rewarded.

7. *Be aware of your own triggers:* Determine what your hot buttons are and how you can manage yourself so these buttons don't get triggered and that you don't experience amygdala hijacks.

WRIGHT

Well, what an interesting subject, and goodness knows you know more about it than anybody I've known. I really do enjoy talking with you. I appreciate all this time you've taken with me today to answer these questions. I have learned a lot and I can just imagine how much our readers are going to learn.

NADLER

Well, thank you, David; this has been enjoyable for me also.

WRIGHT

Today we've been talking with Dr. Relly Nadler. Dr. Nadler has coached CEOs, presidents, and their staffs, and he has developed and delivered innovative leadership programs for such organizations as Anheuser-Busch, BMW, EDS, and MCI. He has created and facilitated team trainings for DreamWorks Animation, Comerica Bank, American Honda, and General Motors Defense. He is recognized around the world for his expertise in linking emotional intelligence tools to business objectives.

Dr. Nadler, thank you so much for being with us today on *Stepping Stones to Success.*

NADLER

Thank you, David.

ABOUT THE AUTHOR

DR. RELLY NADLER is a licensed psychologist, Master Certified Coach (MCC) with the International Coaching Federation (ICF), corporate trainer, and author. He is President and CEO of True North Leadership Inc., an executive and organizational development firm. He brings his expertise in Emotional Intelligence to all his keynotes and to his consulting, coaching, and leadership trainings. He has designed and delivered many multi-day executive boot camps for high achievers in Fortune 500 companies. Dr. Nadler has been working for more than thirty years with top executives and their teams to become star performers.

He is the author of five best-selling leadership and team performance books, and is a sought-after speaker and consultant on leadership development, Emotional Intelligence (EI), team-building, executive coaching, and change leadership. His latest books are *Leading with Emotional Intelligence, Leader's Playbook, Leadership Keys Field Guide* (also in audio), and *Leadership Keys*. They are the first in a series of EI curriculum and tool kits for leaders and their direct reports to move into the top 10 percent of performance. Dr. Nadler also has a CD program called *EI Experts Speak,* which has interviews and specific tools for many of the EI competencies.

Dr. Nadler is also the co-host of *Leadership Development News* with Dr. Cathy Greenberg, a top Internet radio show on *VoiceAmerica Talk Radio Network* that brings advancements to leaders weekly.

RELLY NADLER, PSYD, MCC
True North Leadership, Inc
1170 Camino Meleno
Santa Barbara, CA 93111
805.683.1066
Rnadler@truenorthleadership.com
www.truenorthleadership.com

CHAPTER TEN

Discover Your Inner Resource

An Interview with . . . **Dr. Deepak Chopra**

DAVID WRIGHT (WRIGHT)

Today we are talking to Dr. Deepak Chopra, founder of the Chopra Center for Well Being in Carlsbad, California. More than a decade ago, Dr. Chopra became the foremost pioneer in integrated medicine. His insights have redefined our definition of health to embrace body, mind and spirit. His books, which include, *Quantum Healing, Perfect Health, Ageless Body Timeless Mind*, and *The Seven Spiritual Laws of Success,* have become international bestsellers and are established classics.

Dr. Chopra, welcome to *Stepping Stones to Success.*

DR. DEEPAK CHOPRA (CHOPRA)

Thank you. How are you?

WRIGHT

I am doing just fine. It's great weather here in Tennessee.

CHOPRA

Great.

WRIGHT

Dr. Chopra, you stated in your book, *Grow Younger, Live Longer: 10 Steps to Reverse Aging*, that it is possible to reset your biostats up to fifteen years younger than your chronological age. Is that really possible?

CHOPRA

Yes. There are several examples of this. The literature on aging really began to become interesting in the 1980s when people showed that it was possible to reverse the biological marks of aging. This included things like blood pressure, bone density, body temperature, regulation of the metabolic rate, and other things like cardiovascular conditioning, cholesterol levels, muscle mass and strength of muscles, and even things like hearing, vision, sex hormone levels, and immune function.

One of the things that came out of those studies was that psychological age had a great influence on biological age. So you have three kinds of aging: chronological age is when you were born, biological age is what your biomarker shows, and psychological age is what your biostat says.

WRIGHT

You call our prior conditioning a prison. What do you mean?

CHOPRA

We have certain expectations about the aging process. Women expect to become menopausal in their early forties. People think they should retire at the age of sixty-five and then go Florida and spend the rest of their life in so-called retirement. These expectations actually influence the very biology of aging. What we call normal aging is actually the hypnosis of our social conditioning. If you can bypass that social conditioning, then you're free to reset your own biological clock.

WRIGHT

Everyone told me that I was supposed to retire at sixty-five. I'm somewhat older than that and as a matter of fact, today is my birthday.

CHOPRA

Well happy birthday. You know, the fact is that you should be having fun all the time and always feel youthful. You should always feel that you are contributing to society. It's not the retirement, but it's the passion with which you're involved in the well being of your society, your community, or the world at large.

WRIGHT

Great things keep happening to me. I have two daughters; one was born when I was fifty. That has changed my life quite a bit. I feel a lot younger than I am.

CHOPRA

The more you associate with young people, the more you will respond to that biological expression.

WRIGHT

Dr. Chopra, you suggest viewing our bodies from the perspective of quantum physics. That seems somewhat technical. Will you tell us a little bit more about that?

CHOPRA

You see, on one level, your body is made up of flesh and bone. That's the material level but we know today that everything we consider matter is born of energy and information. By starting to think of our bodies as networks of energy information and even intelligence, we begin to shift our perspective. We don't think of our bodies so much as dense matter, but as vibrations of consciousness. Even though it sounds technical, everyone has had an experience with this so-called quantum body. After, for example, you do an intense workout, you feel a sense of energy in your body—a tingling sensation. You're actually experiencing what ancient wisdom traditions call the "vital force." The more you pay attention to this vital force inside your body, the more you will experience it as energy, information, and intelligence, and the more control you will have over its expressions.

WRIGHT

Does DNA have anything to do with that?

CHOPRA

DNA is the source of everything in our body. DNA is like the language that creates the molecules of our bodies. DNA is like a protein-making factory, but DNA doesn't give us the blueprint. When I build a house, I have to go to the factory to find the bricks, but having the bricks is not enough. I need to get an architect, who in his or her consciousness can create that blueprint. And that blueprint exists only in your spirit and consciousness—in your soul.

WRIGHT

I was interested in a statement from your book. You said that perceptions create reality. What perceptions must we change in order to reverse our biological image?

CHOPRA

You have to change three perceptions. First you have to get rid of the perceptions of aging itself. Most people believe that aging means disease and infirmities. You have to change that. You have to regard aging as an opportunity for personal growth and spiritual growth. You also have to regard it as an opportunity to express the wisdom of your experience and an opportunity to help others and lift them from ordinary and mundane experience to the kind of experiences you are capable of because you have much more experience than they do.

The second thing you have to change your perception of is your physical body. You have to start to experience it as information and energy—as a network of information and intelligence.

The third thing you have to change your perception on is the experience of dying. If you are the kind of person who is constantly running out of time, you will continue to run out of time. On the other hand, if you have a lot of time, and if you do everything with gusto and love and passion, then you will lose track of time. When you lose track of time, your body does not metabolize that experience.

WRIGHT

That is interesting. People who teach time management don't really teach the passion.

CHOPRA

No, no. Time management is such a restriction of time. Your biological clock starts to age much more rapidly. I think what you have to really do is live your life with passion so that time doesn't mean anything to you.

WRIGHT

That's a concept I've never heard.

CHOPRA

Well, there you are.

WRIGHT

You spend an entire chapter of your book on deep rest as an important part of the reversal of the aging process. What is "deep rest"?

CHOPRA

One of the most important mechanisms for renewal and survival is sleep. If you deprive an animal of sleep, then it ages very fast and dies prematurely. We live in a culture where most of our population has to resort to sleeping pills and tranquilizers in order to sleep. That doesn't bring natural rejuvenation and renewal. You know that you have had a good night's sleep when you wake up in the morning, feeling renewed, invigorated, and refreshed—like a baby does. So that's one kind of deep rest. That comes from deep sleep and from natural sleep. In the book I talk about how you go about making sure you get that.

The second deep rest comes from the experience of meditation, which is the ability to quiet your mind so you still your internal dialogue. When your internal dialogue is still, then you enter into a stage of deep rest. When your mind is agitated, your body is unable to rest.

WRIGHT

I have always heard of people who had bad eyesight and really didn't realize it until they went to the doctor and were fitted for lenses. I had that same experience some years ago. For several years I had not really enjoyed the deep sleep you're talking about. The doctor diagnosed me with sleep apnea. Now I sleep like a baby, and it makes a tremendous difference.

CHOPRA

Of course it does. You now have energy and the ability to concentrate and do things.

WRIGHT

Dr. Chopra, how much do eating habits have to do with aging? Can we change and reverse our biological age by what we eat?

CHOPRA

Yes, you can. One of the most important things to remember is that certain types of foods actually contain anti-aging compounds. There are many chemicals that are contained in certain foods that have an anti-aging effect. Most of these chemicals are derived from light. There's no way to bottle them—there are no pills you can take that will give you these chemicals. But they're contained in plants that are rich in color and derived from photosynthesis. Anything that is yellow, green, and red or has a lot of color, such as fruits and vegetables, contain a lot of these very powerful anti-aging chemicals.

In addition, you have to be careful not to put food in your body that is dead or has no life energy. So anything that comes in a can or has a label, qualifies for that. You have to expose your body to six tastes: sweet, sour, salt, bitter, pungent, and astringent because those are the codes of intelligence that allow us to access the deep intelligence of nature. Nature and what she gives to us in bounty is actually experienced through the sense of taste. In fact, the light chemicals—the anti-aging substances in food—create the six tastes.

WRIGHT

Some time ago, I was talking to one of the ladies in your office and she sent me an invitation to a symposium that you had in California. I was really interested. The title was *Exploring the Reality of Soul*.

CHOPRA

Well, I conducted the symposium, but we had some of the world's scientists, physicists, and biologists who were doing research in what is called, non-local intelligence—the intelligence of soul or spirit. You could say it is the intelligence that orchestrates the activity of the universe—God, for example. Science and spirituality are now meeting together because by understanding how nature works and how the laws of nature work, we're beginning to get a glimpse of a deeper intelligence that people in spiritual traditions call divine, or God. I think this is a wonderful time to explore spirituality through science.

WRIGHT

She also sent me biographical information of the seven scientists that were with you. I have never read a list of seven more noted people in their industry.

CHOPRA

They are. The director of the Max Planck Institute, in Berlin, Germany, where quantum physics was discovered was there. Dr. Grossam was a professor of physics at the University of Oregon, and he talked about the quantum creativity of death and the survival of conscious after death. It was an extraordinary group of people.

WRIGHT

Dr. Chopra, with our *Stepping Stones to Success* book we're trying to encourage people to be better, live better, and be more fulfilled by listening to the examples of our guest authors. Is there anything or anyone in your life who has made a difference for you and has helped you to become a better person?

CHOPRA

The most important person in my life was my father. Every day he asked himself, "What can I do in thought, word, and deed to nurture every relationship I encounter just for today?" That has lived with me for my entire life.

WRIGHT

What do you think makes up a great mentor? Are there characteristics mentors seem to have in common?

CHOPRA

I think the most important attribute of a great mentor is that he or she teaches by example and not necessarily through words.

WRIGHT

When you consider the choices you've made down through the years, has faith played an important role?

CHOPRA

I think more than faith, curiosity, wonder, a sense of reference, and humility has. Now, if you want to call that faith, then, yes it has.

WRIGHT

In a divine being?

CHOPRA

In a greater intelligence—intelligence that is supreme, infinite, unbounded, and too mysterious for the finite mind to comprehend.

WRIGHT

If you could have a platform and tell our audience something you feel would help them and encourage them, what would you say?

CHOPRA

I would say that there are many techniques that come to us from ancient wisdom and tradition that allow us to tap into our inner resources and allow us to become beings who have intuition, creativity, vision, and a connection to that which is sacred. Finding that within ourselves, we have the means to enhance our well-being. Whether it's physical, emotional, or environmental, we have the means to resolve conflicts and get rid of war. We have the means to be really healthy. We have the means for being economically uplifted. That knowledge is the most important knowledge that exists.

WRIGHT

I have seen you on several primetime television shows down through the years where you have had the time to explain your theories and beliefs. How does someone like me experience this? Do we get it out of books?

CHOPRA

Books are tools that offer you a road map. Sit down every day, close your eyes, put your attention in your heart, and ask yourself two questions: who am I and what do I want? Then maintain a short period of stillness in body and mind as in prayer or meditation, and the door will open.

WRIGHT

So, you think that the intelligence comes from within. Do all of us have that capacity?

CHOPRA

Every child born has that capacity.

WRIGHT

That's fascinating. So, it doesn't take trickery or anything like that?

CHOPRA

No, it says in the Bible in the book of Psalms, "Be still and know that I am God"—Psalm 46:10.

WRIGHT

That's great advice.

I really do appreciate your being with us today. You are fascinating. I wish I could talk with you for the rest of the afternoon. I'm certain I am one of millions who would like to do that!

CHOPRA

Thank you, sir. It was a pleasure to talk with you!

WRIGHT

Today we have been talking with Dr. Deepak Chopra, founder of The Chopra Center. He has become the foremost pioneer in integrated medicine. We have found today that he really knows what he's talking about. After reading his book, *Grow Younger, Live Longer: 10 Steps to Reverse Aging,* I can tell you that I highly recommend it. I certainly hope you'll go out to your favorite book store and buy a copy.

Dr. Chopra, thank you so much for being with us today on *Stepping Stones to Success.*

CHOPRA

Thank you for having me, David.

ABOUT THE AUTHOR

DEEPAK CHOPRA has written more than fifty books, which have been translated into many languages. He is also featured on many audio and videotape series, including five critically acclaimed programs on public television. He has also written novels and edited collections of spiritual poetry from India and Persia. In 1999, *Time* magazine selected Dr. Chopra as one of the Top 100 Icons and Heroes of the Century, describing him and "the poet-prophet of alternative medicine."

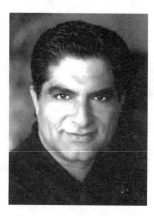

DR. DEEPAK CHOPRA
The Chopra Center
2013 Costa del Mar Rd.
Carlsbad, CA 92009
info@chopra.com
www.chopra.com

CHAPTER ELEVEN

Living Abundantly in the Face of Adversity

An Interview with . . . **Marissa Penrod**

DAVID WRIGHT (WRIGHT)

Today we're talking to Marissa Penrod. In January of 2008, Marissa Penrod's youngest child was diagnosed with Duchenne muscular dystrophy, a degenerative neuromuscular disease with no known cure. Initially devastated and terrified for her son and her family's future, she very quickly made a decision that this disease would not define who her son was and that he would live a full life. Armed with her belief that we can live abundantly in the face of adversity, she has since devoted herself to sharing her message that often happiness is simply a decision. She leads us to an understanding that although we can't control what we are handed, we can indeed choose how we handle it.

Co-Founder of Moving Mountains LLC, and former corporate trainer, speech writer, copywriter, and teacher, she punctuates her story with humor, honesty, and thought-provoking insight, acknowledging that we're all climbing a mountain of some sort. She inspires audiences to believe in the possibility of their future and to move from a life of surviving to one of thriving.

Marissa, welcome to *Stepping Stones to Success*.

MARISSA PENROD (PENROD)

Thank you, David.

WRIGHT

So tell me how you came to embrace and teach this philosophy of living abundantly in the face of adversity.

PENROD

I certainly did not come to this by choice. If I could have avoided the circumstances that led to this I absolutely would have, but it wasn't an option for me. Learning from it, however, was an option.

Two years ago, as you mentioned, my youngest son was diagnosed with Duchenne muscular dystrophy. I thought he was simply delayed in his ability to run, so I asked our pediatrician to take a look. She did a few simple, physical tests, left the room for a minute, and moments later came back in and told me we had an appointment with a neurologist the next day. Now, for any of us, a statement like that would give us reason to pause. When it's about your child, it can be downright terrifying.

So, the next morning, a neurologist who was virtually a stranger to us sat my husband and me down and confirmed our worst fears—our little boy did indeed have Duchenne muscular dystrophy.

He told us that Joseph's disease was degenerative and progressive and there was no cure. Then he said, "I'll give you a few minutes to collect yourself," and left the room. Apparently he didn't understand that after that kind of news it takes the rest of your life to pull yourself together. But when he returned to the room, something had come over me. I was already drying my tears and I just looked at him and said, "What now? What do we do now?" He told us to go home and they would make an appointment for us to see a specialist in eight weeks. When I told him I didn't want to wait eight weeks, he smiled patiently and said that's just the way it works—we would have to wait eight weeks.

I sat back in my chair, crossed my arms, and said, "Well, that's not the way it works anymore. I'm not waiting eight weeks." I dug my heels in and I said that I wasn't leaving his office until he got me an appointment. I said, "You can call the specialist, you can text him, you can e-mail him, you can Facebook him, but I'm not leaving until you get in touch with him." He looked to my husband for some kind of backup but he just shook his head and smiled. So the neurologist agreed to e-mail the specialist and try to squeeze us in. In retrospect, I think he might have been e-mailing security, saying, "Come and get this crazy woman out of my office!"

As we left his office, I explained calmly that if I didn't hear from him by noon the next day, I would drive the hour back to his office and sit there until Joseph had an appointment. He called me at nine o'clock the next morning and told me I had an appointment for the following day.

It was at this moment, when I had to spring into action and start advocating for my son, that I realized my role had changed. We were on a new path and a new journey, and I was about to discover a lot of lessons, including what my purpose was.

WRIGHT

Was there a turning point for you when you decided that you could live a good, full life in light of the burdens you carry?

PENROD

It was probably after allowing myself to wallow for about a day—to be sad and to be fearful and to think about all the things that the doctor had told us, including what our future could look like with this disease. I realized quickly, though, that everything he told us was the history of the disease—all the facts and statistics were a history lesson. They were a reflection of the past. But the future was unwritten. Nobody knows the future, and as much as we want to predict it, as much as we think we have the answers, we don't really know what's coming. I choose to believe that Joseph and all the other boys with this disease represent the future of this disease. All the scientists racing toward a cure or treatment represent the future. And all the volunteers who tirelessly advocate and raise money for research represent the future of this disease—and the future will be bright!

I made a decision very quickly that I didn't like feeling sad, I didn't like feeling hopeless, and I certainly wanted more than that for Joseph, for my other children, and for our family. We didn't choose this, but we certainly had the power to choose how we would handle it. This was not going to define us. That's when I made the decision that we can live abundantly in light of this, and we can be filled with hope and possibility.

It's not always that simple and it's certainly not always easy. Sometimes I have to make that decision every single morning, and that's the way it is for so many people when they're faced with a crisis or even small day-to-day adversities. I call it living consciously—not just reacting to things, but truly stopping and thinking about the way we're thinking and then reflecting on that. It's about really saying this is who I want to be or this is not who I want to be, this is not how I want to approach this. So I just made a decision that I would choose happiness and I would choose to live a really full life for Joseph and for my family.

WRIGHT

You seem to almost embrace adversity; isn't it natural to want to avoid it?

PENROD

Our natural human instinct is to want to avoid adversity, and I think you should avoid it if it's something dangerous or unhealthy. But when you're faced with the kind of adversity that can actually end up being something good for you, something that inspires creativity and thinking beyond your current situation, I think it's beneficial to take a look at it. And here's the bottom line—some adversity, like what my son is facing, is unavoidable. So, the focus should then become a matter of moving forward with what you've been dealt. At some point, we have to accept what we cannot change.

We often try to avoid adversity because it comes along with a healthy dose of fear. But it's helpful to remember that so many good things in life begin with fear. If you think about all the great things, the fun and adventurous things, the most rewarding, fulfilling things you've ever done in your life, most of them begin with some amount of fear. A really simple example is riding a roller coaster—we wait in line, we look up at the roller coaster, we have butterflies in our stomach, we get on, we're afraid, we scream the entire time we're on it, and then, when we get off the roller coaster, we look at our friends and say, "Let's do it again!" It's like that even with big life decisions. I don't know one person who is married who wasn't a little bit afraid to take that step. And I think anyone who is a parent certainly had some trepidation about bringing a new life into the world.

Fear is our natural human radar that tells us something is unfamiliar or could be harmful. It tells us to assess a situation and think twice. Fear can also be a great fuel. It can move us to work through a situation because something better is on the other side. It can inspire us to move faster, try harder, and find strength and courage we didn't know we had. If we looked at our struggles as a chance to do something new and different and to actually improve ourselves, we wouldn't have to avoid them, but we could, in fact, embrace them. Growth and good things only happen outside of our comfort zone.

WRIGHT

Will you help our readers understand what qualities or characteristics are the most helpful for us to have in situations of adversity?

PENROD

I think the most important quality is to think about your thinking—about your own thoughts and how you approach something. We're always faced with decisions, and it's helpful to remember that no matter what situations we're thrown into, we always have choices. We can take back our control, and we have to take responsibility for our success and our happiness.

Another quality that is helpful is what I call "thinking beyond the crisis." Sometimes when we're faced with a challenge or an adversity, we tend to focus on just getting our lives back to normal, back where they were before the challenge entered our lives. Don't just ask for that—don't just ask to return to the status quo. If you lose a job, don't try to get the same job you just lost. If you lose a relationship, don't go out looking for the same relationship you just lost. This is your chance to expand and grow. Think bigger!

In most situations, I don't think we ask for too much, I think we ask for too little and our expectations are too small. With my son's illness, I am faced with the daunting task of helping to facilitate a treatment or a cure. That can be overwhelming at times, but if I want to learn and grow from this adversity, I certainly wouldn't want to simply return to my old life or who I was before this journey began.

In situations of adversity, if we can adopt a desire to evolve, that will ultimately lead to a new kind of success.

Another quality that's helpful in adversity is to dream big, act boldly, and actually make our lives better along the way.

Let's talk for a minute about dreaming big. First, have a huge vision—have a vision so big that it seems unrealistic to smaller thinkers. If somebody tells you your goals are out of reach or your dream is unrealistic, that can be a good sign, as long as you're willing to back it up with action. You can't just be a dreamer and go sit on the couch and think something's going to happen. You have to participate in the results and you have to participate in creating the vision that you've laid out for yourself by acting. Success often comes from actions that are bold.

One of my favorite stories of someone who understood the idea of bold actions is that of world class runner, Glenn Cunningham. When he was just eight years old, Glenn was severely burned in a fire. He lost his brother in the fire and was not expected to survive himself. When he defied those odds, the doctors recommended that his legs be amputated. His mother refused. Within a couple of years, through sheer stubbornness and determination, Glenn was walking again. He went on to compete in two Olympic Games and in 1934, in Madison Square Garden, this brave man who was told he would never walk again when he was eight, ran the mile in four minutes and eight seconds—the world's fastest indoor mile!

One more characteristic that I think is so important for success, especially in times of adversity, is humility. People often think that to be very successful you have to have a huge amount of confidence. That is helpful, of course, but the real advantage comes about if you can be humble enough to acknowledge your weaknesses and gaps in your abilities, and then go out and ask for help. I'm not afraid to say, "I don't know how to do this, will you help me?" When your vision is big enough, your dream is clear enough, and you're willing to take bold actions and ask other people to help you, you've got a formula for huge amounts of success.

WRIGHT

So do you ever feel like giving up?

PENROD

Absolutely! I get tired and sometimes I feel like I need to stop and reevaluate my direction. The bottom line is that feeling like you want to give up is a normal human response. We have a finite number of hours in the day and we have a finite amount of energy. But, no matter where your challenges are— in your business, or your personal life, or with your health or family—if your goals are pure enough and good enough, and if they're what gets you out of bed early and keeps you up late, once in a while you can let yourself feel like giving up. That just might mean that you need a day off or you need an hour to yourself or a good book or a walk on the beach. It's important to recharge our batteries so the urge to quit is fleeting. The key is to acknowledge the feeling, but then be done with it! Fight that feeling with a break and then action.

Something interesting happened to me about a month ago—I ran into someone I hadn't seen in quite some time. He gave me a big hug, and then he held me at arm's length by my shoulders. He looked at me and said, "Wow, Marissa you look . . . tired!" I laughed out loud and I thought, "Who says that to somebody? Who would actually say that?"

Then I thought about it and realized something—I've *earned* being tired! I *should* be tired! We so often talk about how we "spend" our lives, but let's really think about what it means to "spend" ourselves. When I arrive at the end of the road and my time here on Earth is done, I want to be *spent*. I want to have used up everything I've got in pursuit of a huge goal or a great mission. So when I feel like giving up, I acknowledge that. I acknowledge my fatigue and I realize that I'm on the right path because I'm truly spending my time and really spending my life.

WRIGHT

So how do people around you respond to your approach?

PENROD

One of the most rewarding responses I've had is when people tell me that Joseph's story inspires them. To have a child diagnosed with a devastating disease is unexplainable. There is no rhyme or reason and there is nothing about it that makes any sense. But if his story, our story, and our journey can make a difference for someone else, then our burden is that much lighter.

I think sometimes people are surprised at how happy I still am and how I move forward and still have a big vision in spite of the heartache I have. But you know the bottom line, David, is that when we see people who are happy, we have to understand that happiness isn't something that just happens. Happiness does not show up on my doorstep every morning saying, "Here I am! It's going to be a great day!" Happiness is a choice—it's a decision we have to make all of the time.

When we see someone else who is happy, we see the display of their happiness, which is very public—we just see their outside persona. However, the pursuit of that happiness happens in private when no one is watching. It's a personal journey, often filled with reflection and decision-making and hard work. So I always tell people not to make the mistake of seeing me happy and assume it's always easy. It takes focus and persistence and work to be happy and to live abundantly. It takes a conscious effort.

WRIGHT

So how do you apply this to other people—people who maybe aren't experiencing something as dramatic as you are?

PENROD

It would be nice if we lived in a world where there was no adversity for any of us, but everybody has something. Everyone is climbing a mountain of some sort. It may be monumental or it may just be something temporary—something that lasts a day or an hour. Whether you want to go back to school or want a new job or need a better relationship, the bottom line is this—we only get one life and when today is gone, we never get it back. This is it. So I encourage people to think about how they are spending today. Are you taking even one step today, moving forward toward what your definition of success is?

Here's a fun way to look at it, David. If I asked you to name some of the greatest people who have ever lived, who would you choose?

WRIGHT

Einstein would be one. I'd probably pick a great writer to be another, and perhaps someone who's developed something such as the polio vaccine and changed the world, at least medically.

PENROD

Great. So let's think about Einstein or Mother Teresa or Gandhi. We all have something in common with them. Sounds crazy doesn't it? Believe it or not, we do have something in common with those who really had a monumental influence on the world. We all have a common bond with Mother Teresa and we have a common bond with Einstein and Gandhi—every single one of us, no matter who we are, has twenty-four hours in a day. I call it the great equalizer—no matter who you are, what advantages or disadvantages you have, or what crisis you're facing, you get twenty-four hours, just like everyone else.

The critical factor that determines who is going to live a full life filled with abundance, with a focus on success and happiness, is what you choose to do with your twenty-four hours.

WRIGHT

In a time when so many people are searching for answers and looking for that key to happiness, will you tell us a few key tips that will help us on that mission?

PENROD

One thing I would suggest is for people to think about what they really want their lives to look like. Who do you want to be in five years? When you look back—when you're sitting on the porch in your rocking chair, at the end of your years, your sunset years—what do you want to have accomplished; what do you want to be remembered for? Who do you want to be? Be so on purpose about that and don't be afraid to go out and make it happen.

I'm not afraid of anything because my mission and my goals are so focused. I actually feel very liberated. I'm not afraid to ask for help, I'm not afraid to think big.

David, something else that's helpful for people to understand is that no one else can travel your journey for you. At the end of the day, nobody else can be my son's mother. I'm the only one who gets that honor with all its privileges and struggles. And it's the same for every person out there. Wouldn't it be great if you could lie on the couch watching television and eating ice cream, with someone else on the floor doing pushups, but you end up with the great muscle tone? That's just not the way it works. The bottom line is this—nobody can do your pushups for you.

The same goes for success and living abundantly—we have to walk the path for ourselves. No matter how much support we have or how many ways we might try to avoid it, the struggles, the fatigue, and the introspection is all ours. No one else can figure it out for us. The sooner people accept that, the quicker the sense of abundance and happiness appears because you're making progress on your own life. You're not waiting for somebody else to do it for you. You're taking responsibility and you're owning your own journey. That's really what I think leads to success.

One more tip I would suggest is to understand that we're going to have roadblocks along the way to happiness. I believe that roadblocks exist simply to test our resolve and to make us prove how much we really want something. Unfortunately, in the pursuit of the goal, sometimes people see roadblocks as the end of the road. They pull over, they turn off the "engine" and they just quit. It's time to simply question your goals. Do I really want to get to the other side? Do I really want to lose those ten pounds? Do I really want to go to grad school? Do I really want a new job? Do I really want to improve my relationship? Imagine that on the other side of the roadblock are your dreams and your happiness and your success. Instead of slowing down, it'd be a better idea to step on the gas and plow your way through the roadblock. That proves how much you want something. Roadblocks are an opportunity to quit or an opportunity to dig deeper and redesign your life and live large. The decision, the difference, is just a choice that you make.

WRIGHT

So, Marissa, what is the goal on this journey of yours? What would define success for you?

PENROD

A couple of things would define success for me. The number one goal is to be a part of finding a cure for Duchenne muscular dystrophy. That will be the ultimate measure of success. My other mission is to make sure that Joseph's journey is not in vain and that his journey has a higher purpose. I really believe that when we're faced with a big adversity, there is often a bigger purpose for that, there is a reason. Success will mean that I advocate for Joseph in the best way, that I am his voice, and that he changes other people's lives for the better with his journey.

WRIGHT

Well, what great insight you have. I can tell you used a lot of humor along the way. This is a terrible disease and I wish you so much good fortune with your goals. I really appreciate the time you've taken to tell us your story and be with us in this book.

PENROD

Thank you, David, I appreciate being here.

WRIGHT

Today we've been talking with Marissa Penrod whose youngest child was diagnosed with Duchenne muscular dystrophy, a degenerative neuromuscular disease with no known cure. Today, she is Co-Founder of Moving Mountains LLC. She is a former corporate trainer, speech writer, copywriter, and teacher. Marissa punctuates her story with humor, honesty, and thought-provoking insight, as we have found here today.

Marissa, thank you so much for being with us on *Stepping Stones to Success*.

PENROD

My pleasure, David, thank you so much.

ABOUT THE AUTHOR

In January of 2008, Marissa Penrod's youngest child was diagnosed with Duchenne Muscular Dystrophy, a degenerative neuromuscular disease with no known cure. Initially devastated and terrified for her son's and her family's future, Penrod very quickly made a decision that this disease would not define who her son was and that he would live a full life.

Armed with her belief that we can live abundantly in the face of adversity, she has since devoted herself to teaching others that often happiness is simply a decision. She leads us to an understanding that success and fulfillment are attainable in the midst of great struggle, and, although we can't control what we're handed, we can indeed choose how we handle it.

Co-founder of Moving Mountains LLC and former corporate trainer, speech writer, copywriter, and teacher, Penrod punctuates her story with humor, honesty and thought-provoking insight. Acknowledging that we're all climbing a mountain of some sort, she will inspire audiences to believe in the possibility of their future and move from a life of surviving to one of thriving.

MARISSA PENROD
Moving Mountains
3050 Union Lake Road, Suite 8-F
Commerce Township, MI 48382
248-330-0430
marissa.penrod@gmail.com

CHAPTER TWELVE

Believe. Achieve. Succeed.

An Interview with . . . **Merikay Tillman**

DAVID WRIGHT (WRIGHT)

Today we're talking with Merikay H. Tillman MS, owner and CEO of COACH MKay Companies, LLC based in Greensboro, North Carolina. Her mission is to act as a catalyst to help individuals and organizations reach new heights in professional and personal performance. Through her keynotes, coaching strategies, and seminar facilitation, audiences are transformed by her targeted and energetic style. Her personal challenges and triumphs fuel her passion to help people break through barriers to achieve success.

Merikay**,** welcome to *Stepping Stones to Success.*

MERIKAY TILLMAN (TILLMAN)

Thank you.

WRIGHT

So what are the three keys to professional success?

TILLMAN

Embrace Change! In my early twenties while I was working for my father's periodontal practice, I came home one day complaining to a close friend about my job. After listening to me for several minutes, he looked me straight in the eye and said, "Is it the job, Merikay, or are you just unhappy?" I realized at that moment I had to make a critical decision—I had to make some changes. I needed to face what wasn't working and figure out what needed to change in my life in order for me to have more joy and happiness in my work and home life.

One of the first professional development books I ever read was *The Power of Positive Thinking* by Norman Vincent Peale. Reading his techniques and suggestions taught me that what I think about on a daily basis, I bring about. This idea helped motivate me to move forward with the changes I needed to make

Take Risks! Many events in life involve taking risks and facing the unknown. Taking a risk may involve career changes, relationship dynamics, finances, or other life areas. There are several reasons why a person may choose not to take a risk; one of the most common is negative self-talk. Negative self-talk, such as old mental tapes and false beliefs, can prevent us from taking a step forward. Stepping into the unknown takes courage, deciding to take the risk means taking action and that puts everything into motion. Taking a risk allows doors to open and close naturally and opportunities to be presented. Sometimes, we need to feel the fear and do it anyway.

Be on Fire! Find passion and experience true joy in your career. If I can't wake-up each morning and be excited about what's on my agenda for the day, then I need to look at what I'm doing and make some adjustments. I think that is one reason my career has taken so many directions over the years. I started as a restaurant manager and then switched to dentistry and became a dental assistant, then an office manager, and then a dental consultant. With each opportunity, when I wasn't on fire anymore, I set a new goal and embraced a new challenge so I could feel excited about my career.

In 2000, during graduate school, I was introduced to Dale Carnegie Training. Their mission and training style inspired me. After graduation, I went to work for their organization as an instructor and training consultant for more than four years. Today, I continue to teach two of their public programs and participate in developing partnerships with area businesses to customize training and development.

Staying connected with my fellow trainers helps keep my passion for speaking and coaching alive. Working in such a positive and supportive environment gave me the courage to start my own company. It is important to know what inspires you in your career and to find an environment that can be supportive in the journey. Believe in the power of your dreams and goals—it can take you to wonderful places.

WRIGHT

How do you stay enthusiastic about your work?

TILLMAN

For me, it is all about my attitude and maintaining my energy. Some days are more challenging than others to juggle family life and career. It helps to know and accept that some days will go well and some days won't, and it's okay. Enthusiasm is about spirit and energy. Helping people and inspiring them to make positive change helps me to be enthusiastic about my work.

In early December of 2009, I struggled with a project. My mom had died a few days before I was to begin a twenty-day professional development program for unemployed workers in our community. Rescheduling classes would have been a nightmare for the other instructors and disappointing for the participants. At that point, I chose to follow my passion and purpose. I focused on the fact that this group of people needed our help; they were going through their own struggles because of a job loss.

That entire week was challenging. By continuously adjusting my attitude and staying true to the mission of helping people, I was able to be genuine and add value to the program's success.

WRIGHT

Who has had a positive influence on you professionally?

TILLMAN

My grandmother, Freda Hunt, had the most positive influence on me professionally. After she passed away I visited her home in Burton, West Virginia, because I wanted to have something special to remember her by. Among several items I found were two books: *3,500 Good Quotes for Speakers* by Gerald F. Lieberman and the other one was *God Calling*, edited by A. J. Russell, as well as an article about my grandmother. At the time, I was working on ways improve my speaking skills and striving to grow spiritually, so the books offered great inspiration.

In reading the article, I discovered that Grandma went back to school in her sixties to get her teaching degree and played the organ at her church into her nineties. I realized that age is just a number. I decided that if she could go back to school at sixty, then for me to return to school in my mid-thirties to pursue a master's degree in counseling was possible.

When I hear people use excuses about being too old to do something, not having enough money, or doubting their abilities, I encourage them to create a realistic action plan to overcome their obstacles. I tell them the story of Grandma Freda to encourage and show them that anything is possible. If you believe you can achieve. William Arthur Ward said, "If you can imagine it, you can achieve it. If you can dream it, you can become it."

WRIGHT

So what obstacles have you had to overcome throughout your career?

TILLMAN

There have been several obstacles, but it's all about growing and adjusting. One of the first obstacles in my career was going through a job loss. I graduated from the University of North Carolina at Chapel Hill in the winter of 1988 and took a job with a company based in Greenville, South Carolina. This company owned several restaurants throughout the East Coast and I became the youngest assistant manager in their history. I had big plans for the company and myself.

After only eight months, I was let go and I was devastated. I worked more than seventy hours per week and believed I was doing a great job. At the time, I was unclear about how the company operated on the back end. I later found out that the company had a 200 percent manager turnover rate (information they failed to highlight during the interview). In addition, as managers we weren't taught leadership skills, effective communication strategies, how to control stress, or how to build effective teams. Looking back, it was one of the best things that could have happened. It showed me firsthand the importance of effective leadership training and development and what can happen inside an organization when such training is not in place.

Another obstacle I had to overcome was dealing with a divorce. At a young age I became a single mom, but I still had my hopes and dreams about what I wanted for my daughter and myself. I worked two jobs and went to school at night. I realized that hard work, determination, and a belief that I deserved better would be my inspiration to push forward. My former husband ridiculed me about having a college degree and only making ten dollars per hour. He had his own struggles and was negative toward many aspects of my life. What he didn't realize was that I had already spent years living with a tremendously negative mother who was consistently critical. In a way, he was picking up where my mother had left off. In my heart I knew that we were not mature enough emotionally to fix our problems together and it was time to end the brief marriage. The good news is that both of us entered into therapy after our divorce, became friends, and coached our daughter's soccer team together for many seasons.

Dealing with failure is another obstacle. For six years I had pursued a career in dentistry. This was the career path my father had wanted for me for years and I believed I wanted the same. During the six years, I applied to three different dental schools, accumulated more than thirty hours in biology and chemistry classes, and took the Dental Admission Test three times. I applied three years in a row to the UNC-Chapel Hill School of Dentistry and I was denied three years in a row. My heart was broken. The loss of what I thought was my destiny was overwhelming. I worked with friends in my church to deal with the grief and loss. Reflecting on that time continues to reassure me that obstacles, coupled with the right attitude, are building blocks for success.

WRIGHT

We've talked about keys to professional success, what about the keys to personal success?

TILLMAN

BELIEVE IN YOURSELF

If you don't believe in yourself, how can you expect others to believe in you? In my opinion, believing in yourself is about having strong core values, knowing your abilities, and realizing the areas that need improving. Together, these elements create a positive self-concept, along with a sense of peace and joy.

I love anything that has to do with improving oneself and I have participated in many seminars and workshops. I'm inspired by people brave enough to share their journey and their struggles. If I had listened to all the negative and critical people early in my adult life, I would not be the person I am today. I am committed to being a life-long learner and this has given me the confidence to speak and coach others. If I can help others build their confidence and improve their self-belief, then I've achieved personal success.

STAY IN THE PRESENT

In professional coaching situations, many people are too focused about what happened in the past and they worry too much about what's going to happen in the future. This causes them to become paralyzed and not live in the moment. I am a strong believer in "day-tight compartments," a principle I learned from Dale Carnegie's book, *How to Stop Worrying and Start Living*. Participating in the twelve-week Dale Carnegie Course changed my life in many ways. This principle helps individuals focus on today. Short- and long-term goals, as well as learning from the past, are still important. The key concept is to stay mentally focused in the present to maximize productivity.

TAKE CARE OF YOURSELF

There are a lot of stressed-out people in the world. When we're stressed, we don't think clearly and we don't make good choices. This can lead to unwanted consequences. Taking care of yourself comes in many forms—mental, physical and spiritual.

I can remember some dark days when I was recovering from an illness. When I had my third child, I almost died in the delivery room and had another close call later that evening. It was a scary time for both my husband and me. I experienced some depression afterward and realized that I needed to go ahead and take some time to take care of me. I knew that if I didn't use the tools I had learned to focus on myself and my health, I certainly wasn't going to be at the top of my game to help take care of my family or my clients.

WRIGHT

So how do you manage stress and juggle responsibilities on a daily basis?

TILLMAN

Managing stress and doing the juggling act can be a challenge. There are three things that help keep me in check: establishing routines, calendars, and to-do lists. I personally have a morning routine and I have created routines and guidelines for our family.

I begin each day with positive affirmations to enhance attitude, a strong cup of coffee, and ten to fifteen minutes of devotion time. During the day, if I begin to feel overwhelmed and stressed, I take time to pray, talk to a friend, or go for a walk. Exercise has always helped my mood and I try to do something daily for fifteen to thirty minutes that gets my heart pumping. When my back starts to hurt, it's my sign that something isn't quite right. I will then spend some quality time thinking or journaling about what may be bothering me, and then I may schedule a massage. I also make sure to get plenty of rest and eat healthy. If I do both, I have energy and can get a lot accomplished.

Routine for the family includes prepping for each day the night before. Each child has specific, daily household chores to accomplish. Our mornings run much smoother if they have their backpacks ready, clothes laid out, and papers signed and reviewed the night before. On Sunday evenings, I plan the week's menu and make the grocery list. This helps me plan good, nutritional food choices so we can avoid the drive-through temptation and spend quality time enjoying dinner together.

It is important to be in charge of your schedule and not let your schedule run you! Making daily to-do lists help me focus and plan my work. A large, laminated yearly calendar enables me to target revenue opportunities, class schedules, and vacation days. I use a day planner to track business meetings, conference calls, and the instructional days. Each one is color-coded and the block scheduling technique helps me reserve time for sales calls and personal time. I also hire a professional organizer to help coach and review how I manage my administrative chores, ranging from paper flow and file organization to time management. All of us can use someone to review how we are delegating our time. My office (and I) usually need a tune-up every six months to get things back on track.

WRIGHT

So if you could improve and change in any area, what would that be and why would it be important to you?

TILLMAN

I believe life is an ongoing process and we should try to find ways to constantly improve and grow. One area I'm committed to improve is *focus*. I want to reach my personal and professional goals and with increased focus I know I can accomplish them. It is my nature to want to help everyone, but I can't. Staying focused allows me to set and maintain boundaries.

I learned a valuable lesson about my ability to focus more than three years ago when I was working with a healthcare consulting firm. Our new president sent me an e-mail in late January 2005. The first line was one word: FOCUS. Underneath was written, "Merikay, your revenue projection was X, you produced Y—*focus*." However, later in the e-mail he said, "... you have my continued support." This e-mail stung because I realized I hadn't reached my goals and I had let the company and myself down. Letting my emotions take over, I initially packed up all my stuff and left. I had fully intended to quit my job that day.

After reflection and dialoguing with colleagues that day, I was able to reevaluate the situation and apply some of the tools and skills that I had developed. I had to admit to myself that at that time, my priorities and focus were different than what the president of our company wanted. The past month had been personally challenging because my father passed away, a result of amyloidosis, and one of the consultants in our firm died of colon cancer. My focus was not on generating revenue; rather, it was on helping my family and the employees in my father's practice deal with his death. It was also to help the staff in our consulting firm deal with the grief of losing a team member. I decided not to quit my job that day and if I left, it would be for a business reason, not an emotional one. Focusing on doing the right thing is sometimes more difficult than focusing on what your gut feelings are telling you to do. There will be stages in life when focusing is difficult. These times offer a great opportunity to hit the reset button and begin again.

WRIGHT

What is something that happened in your childhood that defines the kind of leader you are today and that describes your leadership style?

TILLMAN

I am a responsible leader and I value people's time. When I was in pre-kindergarten, my mother enrolled me in a half-day program. I was supposed to be picked up each day before lunch; more often than not she was late. I would have to sit to the side and wait while the other kids ate lunch. I would sit there getting more and more hungry from smelling their food. Sometimes the teacher would give me a piece of bread. I would sit underneath the lunch cart and eat the outside of the bread and roll it into a little ball and take little bites. I could make that piece of bread last about twenty minutes. I still remember how I felt every time she was late picking me up.

The message I received as a child was that I was not important. As an adult, the memory of that incident plays a role in my leadership style. I realized that we can send the wrong message when we're continuously late. We can send the message that another person may not be important or that we are tremendously unorganized or unprofessional or uncaring. If I'm ever going to be late for a meeting, I'll always call ahead. This is an area of responsibility and it is one of my greatest leadership traits.

Regarding leadership style, I've been told by people in all areas of my life, throughout the years, that I am dependable, passionate, dedicated, motivated, and committed to helping people. I am energetic and I use my enthusiasm to help encourage and empower others to stretch their comfort zone to achieve their goals.

Faith is a large factor in the foundation of my leadership. Through faith, I gain strength and confidence as a leader and the ability to push through fear. Giving the eulogy at my father's service almost four years ago was tough. Giving the eulogy in December 2009 at my mother's service was challenging. God can give us a tremendous amount of strength as a leader if we will lean on Him.

WRIGHT

You've used the word "faith;" would you describe your faith journey and how faith has affected your life?

TILLMAN

One of the blessings that my parents gave to our family was introducing us to church and volunteering. My faith has given me a foundation to love others, help people, and a tremendous sense of freedom and flexibility. In high school, it taught me how to treat people the right way and faith showed me what happens when you mistreat people. In college I was somewhat lost. I really didn't connect with many people who were on the same journey, but that didn't stop me from keeping my faith even though it was hard. Faith enabled me to be successful and survive college; it also taught me how to be brave in dealing with people. Sometimes people will let you down; often it's not about you, it's about them.

My faith gives me a lot of confidence. During the past five years, I began participating on building mission teams through our church. This was one of the service activities my father enjoyed. After his death, I lost the chance to travel with him. When another chance came around for me to be on a team with people who had traveled with my father, I embraced the opportunity.

My faith has enabled me to reach out to people in other countries and gives me courage to face difficult situations with grace. Every day at noon, the alarm rings on my BlackBerry to remind me to pray. I joke with people and tell them it keeps me from going over the edge and possibly taking someone with me!

Faith enables me to recenter and refocus on what's important, and gain the calmness I need to handle any situation. I keep a prayer list on my desk; the list is always changing and growing. Currently, I have four people on my list; these people are hurting. Some are looking for new jobs, others are suffering from disease and illness, and one of the people on my list died of a brain tumor, so now I have her family on my list.

We have to keep things in perspective. Everyone goes through difficult struggles. It's easy to get trapped in our own stuff and forget that other people need our prayers.

WRIGHT

So what guiding principles keep you heading in the right direction?

TILLMAN

Here is a running list of guiding principles that I feel are important:

- Take time to center daily or have devotion time.
- Pray.
- Don't be afraid to share how you're really feeling.
- Be willing to ask for feedback and listen to it.
- Set goals and keep them in front of you daily.
- Manage your stress so that stress doesn't manage you.
- Be excited and focused on what you do well.
- Don't try to do it all.
- Discover your gifts and talents.
- Be a blessing to others.
- Be willing to change.
- Trust yourself.
- Be generous.
- Let go of past failures.
- Surround yourself with positive people.
- Commit to being a life-long learner.
- Find joy in each day.
- Don't take yourself too seriously. Be willing to laugh at yourself.

WRIGHT

I think that's great advice.

I really appreciate all this time you've taken today to answer these questions. I have learned a great deal and I know that our readers will.

TILLMAN

It's been a pleasure and an honor to share with you and your readers.

WRIGHT

Today we've been talking with Merikay H. Tillman, MS. Merikay's goal is to bring joy and success to the world one person at a time.

Merikay, thank you so much for being with us today on *Stepping Stones to Success*.

ABOUT THE AUTHOR

MERIKAY H. TILLMAN, MS is the owner & CEO of COACH MKay Companies, LLC based in Greensboro, North Carolina.

Her mission is to act as a catalyst to help individuals and organizations create positive change to reach new heights in professional and personal performance. Through her coaching strategies and facilitative seminars, Merikay inspires her clients to create an action plan of success that generates results. The professional development programs are fresh, entertaining, and energetic. Merikay is also the author of *StressBusters: Conquer Stress Before it Conquers You!,* her first audio book.

Ms.Tillman received her undergraduate degree from The University of North Carolina at Chapel Hill and her master's degree from North Carolina A&T State University in Human Resource Counseling. She is a current member of the National Speakers Association, International Speakers Network, National Society of Certified Healthcare Business Consultants, and the Medical Education Speakers Network. Ms.Tillman has more than ten years of experience as a consultant and program facilitator. Ms.Tillman offers keynotes, coaching, and professional development to a variety of organizations. Key clients include: Polo Ralph Lauren, Sealy, Inc., Volvo Business Services, Sara Lee, Banner Pharmacaps, numerous hospitals, as well as medical, and dental practices. Ms. Tillman is a certified Dale Carnegie instructor and customizes all programs to meet the goals of the event.

MERIKAY H. TILLMAN MS
CEO, COACH MKay Companies, LLC
P.O. Box 10115
Greensboro, NC 27404
Phone: 336.255.3273
info@merikaytillman.com
www.merikaytillman.com

CHAPTER THIRTEEN

Executive Whisperer
An Interview with . . . **Eileen Terry**

DAVID WRIGHT (WRIGHT)

Today we're talking with Eileen Terry. Eileen has been a leader in the retail industry for more than twenty-five years. Prior to the launch of her own consulting and coaching business, she most recently served as executive vice president of franchise, emerging brands, Canada and global diversity for Blockbuster Incorporated. She joined Blockbuster in 1999 as a Zone Vice President and successfully progressed through several positions before becoming the only female to reach the top rank of Executive Vice President inside Blockbuster. She was responsible for working with all franchisees across the United States and Puerto Rico, representing one thousand and fifty stores. She also had the company's non-Blockbuster branded retail concepts, and the operation of Blockbuster's four hundred and fifty Canadian stores. In addition, she served as the Global Diversity Officer driving forward Blockbuster's diversity inclusion efforts.

Because she has always promoted the philosophy of equal rights and equal opportunity throughout her career, she has become a widely sought-speaker on a range of topics including Diversity Impact and Inclusion Insights into how to succeed as a female executive, and on a number of business development topics ranging from Emotional EQ (Emotional Intelligence Quotient) and Quality Conflict Resolution to Problem solving via Root Cause Analysis.

Eileen Terry, welcome to *Stepping Stones to Success*.

So let's start with what has brought you to coaching after almost twenty-five years in retail as an executive.

EILEEN TERRY (TERRY)

Well, it's funny—I really believe in the saying that when the student is ready the teacher will appear. I have always been deeply involved in influencing and driving business results by working with and through people. As you mentioned, this has been more than twenty-five years in a variety of leadership roles.

Then suddenly, at the end of 2005, I found myself in a unique situation, at least for me. Due to a necessary restructuring of the Blockbuster business, a significant number of the business units I was in charge of were being sold. That left me with facing the realities of downsizing, and the effect it had on me directly. I took my leave of the business and found that I actually had the opportunity to take some time to revitalize.

When I left BBI at the end of 2005, I decided to take a self-imposed sabbatical. I hadn't had more than ten consecutive days off at any one time in the previous thirty years. So I committed to myself to really step back this time, and do a little reflecting, enjoy some rest and recreation, and perhaps entertain a little academic learning before reentering corporate America.

I reached out to a good friend of mine, Sharon Reedie, who actually provided me with my first experience working with a coach some fifteen years before. Sharon challenged me to take some time off and do a little (to quote Covey) "sharpening of my saw," to add a few more "tools to my tool kit," and to insure I didn't jump right back in, but to enjoy a break and take some time to get reacquainted with my passions and purpose. I hadn't done that since college—really spent time in any kind of dedicated learning place. So I decided to take her advice.

Sharon recommended me to an organization called The Hudson Institute of Santa Barbara. The institute was founded by Fredric Hudson and his wife, Dr. Pam McLean. You may not know this, but Frederic Hudson is one of the founding developers of the adult learning process, and the development of coaching expertise. His book, *The Handbook of Coaching*, is a must read for anyone involved in the coaching field.

As I did a little research on their organization and their program, I thought why not? I would enroll in their program and go back to school. It was an eight-month commitment, but I was intrigued and ready. I didn't intend to take up coaching as a profession, but to simply learn new skills and to pick up some insights on how to be more effective in developing people. So I signed up and attended their program.

It turned out to be quite intellectually challenging. The program requirements seemed equivalent to earning an MBA. It was eight months of really rigorous practicum—reading and research, then more practice, four on-site workshops where we were involved with textbook theory, interactive learning, and additionally, peer-to-peer coaching practice. All of this while under the supervision of a master coach. The peer-to-peer coaching, in particular, was a significant advantage in building one's coaching skill set, as well as self-confidence.

This experience turned into one that became life-altering for me. I began the program to simply sharpen some skills. I left with a new clarity on my life's purpose—to start my own business, in the coaching profession.

I had come to one of those pivotal points in life where you think you're headed in one direction only to look up and find yourself at a fork in the road. I decided then and there that instead of staying with the tried and true—the well traveled road that I was most familiar and comfortable with—to try another approach. I decided to build on the opportunity to influence a large number of companies and their employees and to work on helping these companies deliver great business results through the ongoing development of their people. I wanted to provide this service, however, using an experienced, external point of view, with myself as the external coach. That was quite different from my life so far where I had been employed by a company to deliver business results and develop people.

I'd like to expound on this external view contrast for a moment. There is a certain amount of freedom in being an external coach. Quite honestly, inside an organization, even with a great HR Department, at the end of the day there is still a hiring hierarchy. There are still trust issues when working with internal coaches. Will my boss hear about this? Is confidentiality assured? Can I be heard from an unbiased view point? External coaches represent a firewall. They allow people to be more free in expressing their deepest feelings and thoughts. They help people to readily explore and be open to new opportunities, new styles, new practices, and to be vulnerable or clumsy when trying new skills.

When working one-on-one with the client, the external coach allows a laser point of focus—a "lead from behind" method that prompts each client to learn be in charge of his or her own growth—to learn to ride his or her own bicycle. People can decide their own desires and goals and design a plan that leads them there. They can then use the coach to help guide them as they practice new behaviors.

A great coach is a lot like a set of bicycle training wheels. The coach helps insure clients have a clear path in front of them, with clear milestones along the way. As a coach you ride *with* the clients while they develop conscious competence and confidence in these new behaviors. Once they are in stride, you remove yourself as coach. It is now their journey and your role is now complete. You have helped them to realize their goals, their purpose, and to find their flow.

That's what drew me to the coaching profession. I always had the desire to help people be their best and find fulfillment in what they choose to do. But it was the Hudson experience of seeing how powerful one-on-one coaching and interaction can be, whether it was executive coaching, leadership coaching, or transitional coaching. It is in helping people get purposeful, get intentional, and really drive to a life in flow. I had found my new life's work.

WRIGHT

Would you talk about coaching? It seems to be an emerging profession.

TERRY

Well, it is an emerging profession. Coaching shouldn't be confused with training, mentoring, consulting or therapy. There are distinct differences. Let me explain. In training, the focus is on learning how to do a particular task. It is usually done in a classroom or formal training session. There is a correct way to perform the particular action or task. It is very direct and it is also very repeatable.

A therapist is necessary for people who need to heal when they aren't completely functional in their life and/or their work. It is about healing, working through some pathology, and getting to a place where one can once again move functionally forward in one's life.

Mentors are people you want to emulate because they've demonstrated success in either a particular facet of business or a profession. This person takes on a one-on-one guidance role using their life and skills history to help you develop those same skills. The idea of consulting is slightly different as well.

Consultants are brought in to use their experience and wisdom to review a problem situation, and to make recommendations on specific actions to be taken. It is then up to the client to be persuaded or to agree with the course of action, or not.

Coaching is very different. Coaching is about *the person* identifying what he or she is trying to achieve. It is driven by the client. It is individualized, as no two clients are alike. The two requirements for a successful coaching engagement are 1) clarity on what needs to be achieved or what is desired to be achieved, and 2) is the client able and willing to do that? Those are the two key questions. In any coaching relationship, it's critical to be able to articulate what is it that you're trying to achieve. What does success look like? What would success working with me look like? Of course, it is also being committed to doing different to get different.

Tiger Woods is someone I use as an example of one who understands and uses coaching as an important part of staying at the top of his game. So how does he use it? Well, it starts out on the driving range. Coaching is having somebody stand side-by-side with you, watching you perform, and giving you feedback. Coaching involves asking questions about what happened after you examine results, then modifying the behavior if you didn't achieve the results you intended. That's very different than someone telling Tiger, "Swing the club the way I swing it." That's not at all what coaching him is all about. Coaching Tiger is about what he needs, his intentions, and working with him on ideas to reach them his way. I use Tiger for another reason—I don't think anyone would disagree that he is by far and away the top golfer on the circuit today. Some would say that he one of the top two or three golfers of all time. *And he practices every day with a coach.*

When I talk to people who say, "I don't need a coach. I'm pretty darn good," I ask, "Do you think Tiger Woods is good?" The answer will inevitably come back as a yes. I will then say, "Do you know he has a coach?" Then I add a bit of additional background. Tiger fired his coach for a couple of years and his performance fell off dramatically. Same guy, same intensity, same muscles, but he lost that edge. The edge was having somebody stand side-by-side with him and have him continue to practice to get the results intended, with an observer and guide.

He hired a guy out of Texas, named Hank Haney, to come on board to help him. Hank Haney is a pretty good golfer in his own right, and he also had a reputation as a great coach. Once Tiger started working with Hank, his game swung back to the top.

So when I use Tiger and I talk about the coaching profession and how to go from good to great and stay there, I ask one question, "Do you think Tiger demonstrates the need to stay active, practicing skills and behaviors every day with a coach?" If Tiger can be aware and humble enough to know he needs continued guidance and support for his performance, we all can do that if we're willing to be humble enough to admit we don't have all the answers.

Practice is critical to coaching—you've got to not *just talk* about what you want. You need to *act different* to get different results. You must practice that over a period of time, develop new muscles, and continue to strengthen them. It's about the whole idea of developing habits.

Coaching is becoming a more disciplined approach to assisting people as they work on new goals and behaviors and install them as habits. People are starting to see that it's not enough to have good intentions—you've got to be flexible, you've got to be able to make changes, you've got to be open to learning, and un-learning. Drop what's no longer working. You have to start new practices that are more aligned with achieving your desires. It's so very helpful to have someone who can be there as a presence to monitor and encourage you, to review with you and to practice with you, in a safe and comfortable environment.

With more than twenty years as an active profession, and a multitude of terrific certification programs, coaching is coming into its own.

I think that success is starting to bear out over time. Additionally, there is an emerging protocol and a standard of ethics being established for the coaching profession. The International Coaching Federation is the current certification setter, and aggregator of best practices and leveraged learning tools and services. It is a communication center to support a self-regulated profession that is setting and encouraging all coaches to meet a certain set of standards relative to organization and individual coaching.

There are now some very formidable certification programs in universities and certainly in places like The Hudson Institute that continue to do an extraordinary job upholding coaching standards through their programs.

WRIGHT

Let's talk a bit more about your specialty. So you trademarked the Executive Whisper. What inspired the Executive Whisper process?

TERRY

I think most people are familiar with The Horse Whisperer and The Dog Whisperer. My passion around dogs collided with this, and provided a "Eureka" moment. I learned how to take the situation of bad behavior, and turn it around with quiet and confident certitude. Let me explain.

One day I was talking with a friend about the latest challenges my partner and I faced with the Terry-Walker dogs. Our friend asked me, "Do you live with your dogs, or do your dogs live with you?"

I thought about it, and replied, "To be perfectly honest, we live with our dogs." So we talked some more about that, and what it actually meant. I thought we simply loved our dogs when we were lavishing affection on them and expecting them to behave well. Although we certainly had great intentions and great expectations, we continued to find ourselves in a state of frustration and irritation when they didn't do what we expected them to do.

They certainly were not taking to our approach of training them. We would read all the training books and we would try things suggested, all the while thinking, "Gee whiz, that just doesn't seem like a nice thing to do to for an animal. If they want to sleep on our bed or if they chew our favorite shoes while we are at work, how can we reprimand them when we get home hours later? Maybe they do cost a lot in replacement pillows that were part of an apparent dog pillow fight. Or perhaps we would turn and wonder where we put down our donut, and then notice our mutts licking their chops. Or maybe everyone buys deep cleaning rug machines. And when we do catch them in the act, and when we try to hold firm with them, what do they do? They cry, or whimper. Or simply run away from us." Good grief, Charlie Brown, what to do!

My friend suggested that I try a different approach. Maybe I had been looking at this wrong. She said there was a new program on the Discovery Channel called *The Dog Whisperer,* and if we were to take a look at it, maybe it would be worthwhile.

After watching a couple of episodes, I was hooked. I was watching a master coach. Cesar Millan starts each visit by asking the owners what the problem is and how can he help. He establishes the contract—what is the desired outcome? After listening to the owners and observing them interact with their dog(s), he quickly informs the owners what the real issues are. He explains that he rehabilitates dogs, but he is there to train or retrain the owners. The problem is not with the dogs, but with their behaviors. And their behavior issues are directly related to the lack of leadership behaviors of the owners.

Cesar went to the source. His hypothesis is that owners don't act like real "pack leaders" to their dogs. The dogs weren't getting consistent, calm, assertive, pack leadership from their owners. They would behave differently if they knew what was expected and if they experienced the right cause and effect relationship and if it was done in a calm, repeated, and a well serving way. If this was done, the dog's behavior would improve. It is as simple as that. It never ceased to amaze me (and the owners) on his show each week, how quickly he could adjust and correct behavior. It was all done calmly, with care and the end result was a happy and well-behaved pooch.

So after getting very familiar with his pack leadership model and how he sets up the environment (where both dog and owner can coexist happily and in a healthy loving way), I was ready. His approach brought a wow from me, both in its extraordinary common sense and its practicality.

The even bigger wow was that eureka moment I spoke of a few moments ago—couldn't we adapt his process and use it when looking at performance problems in the workplace? When a problem is identified at work, or at home for that matter, the first thing we normally do is go to the person who has the problem behavior. At work we tell them to fix it, and if it doesn't get corrected quickly, we may even start them on a disciplinary management process. This will document what the person is not doing right, and restate the desired improvement result. We generally operate from the point of view that the employee is the problem. The ah-ha to me is the realization that in most cases, it is indeed the boss's behavior or approach to correcting the employee's behavior that needs to be examined. As that behavior is modified and changed, the employee's behavior changes. Where along the way could the boss have behaved differently so that the employee didn't get into the situation he or she was in?

So it started me thinking about "what if." I was attending The Hudson Institute, working on my coaching certification at the time. I needed to finalize a thesis topic and I thought, "What if I looked up the dog whispering techniques Cesar Milan uses and applied them to bosses? How could they be effective in managing and getting improved performance? What if I went into any organization and was to talk to someone who was having challenges with an employee or multiple employees. What might I coach them to do differently to get a different result?" And so the Executive Whisperer was born. The program is really about how to identify the root cause, the environment needed to work with people to help them understand what's expected, and to ensure that they have that competency to accomplish the end in mind—to focus the efforts on practicing different behavior in a way where people can learn with the emphasis on learning. This can't occur in an emotional state and never in a threatened state. You have to do it in a place and in a fashion where people feel safe and trusted and where they can trust you. Then make sure that the accountability—the why and consequence—are clearly there and understood.

Now, a word on accountability in corporate America. Too often, accountability has meant you get fired if you make a mistake. It carries a negative connotation. Healthy accountability simply is this: here is the consequence—when you do it right, you get rewarded and when you do it right, I give you more responsibility. And here are the consequences and costs if you do it wrong. And I will insure you know how to do something before I put you in position to be held accountable. Wow, that's different!

So I coined the phrase Executive Whisperer, and have developed a process around it. You might wonder if it is really necessary to have one more book, one more idea or process about improving leadership or individual performance. After all, there are walls and walls of books about how to improve performance, whether it's the *Fish!* book, or *Who Moved My Cheese,* or the *One Minute Manager.* And the same holds true for diet books. There are lots of diets for people to choose from to lose weight. The key is, what's critical, is to find one that works for you. They all have some commonalities. For example in diets, eat less and exercise more. But they also offer a special twist, a slightly different approach. Whichever one appeals *to you,* and works *for you* is the right one *for you.* The same holds true in personal and leadership development.

In Covey's *Seven Habits,* he makes the importance of establishing an environment clear so that people can be comfortable as they learn and change. Covey calls it "your emotional bank account." In the "Five Dysfunctions of a Team," what's most critical is to establish the baseline of trust. The same is true in *Speed of Trust.* These themes seem to echo and re-echo.

In reviewing Whispering, as well, I've distilled it to seven key principles I believe are necessary to generate positive behavioral change and improved results. These key steps are:

- Creating a trust/respect relationship (i.e., being consistent in approach and seeking to understand first)
- Setting clear expectation (SMART Goals—specific, measurable, attainable, realistic, and timely)
- Insuring competency through training and validation
- Maintaining a calm, yet assertive pack leader presence

- Training or problem-solving only when the employee is in a thoughtful versus emotional state (demonstrate high EQ—Emotional Intelligence Quotient)
- Focus on the continuous practice of desired behavior
- Insure that accountability is in place and is both reward-oriented and correction-oriented

WRIGHT

So who would benefit from this?

TERRY

Clearly, any business can benefit. Turnover costs, as we know, are extraordinary. It also goes without saying that the higher the level of the position that's turning over, the more significant the costs. So any improvement in retention would show immediate financial benefits to the company. Additionally, the employee benefits because he or she can go from an uncertain and average performance to a more intentional good to great performance. This investment in people starts moving employees from compliant to committed. When you can shift the paradigm from "I have to" to "I want to" (i.e., "I can pass the test at 70"), you've now have people who want to give 100 percent.

When you start to see evidence of that commitment, whether it is in a retail store, a restaurant, or other customer-focused business, when you see that your team delivers excellent services and exceeds expectations, the loyalty factor will jump, the positive word-of-mouth will jump, and business will build. Just think of it. Where are you more likely to spend more of your money, visit more often, and/or recommend a business to others? Will you do so at a place where you had an okay experience or one where you had a great experience?

That's where I see the tangible benefits. You have invested in building a committed group of employees. You've treated them in a way that says, "I find you valuable and your work provides the company and me with great value. Thank you!" If these components are in place, the employee is very likely to say, "This is a great place to work."

For me, the answer to the question of who can benefit and how is almost too simple to explain and almost too simple to present—it is anyone or any company that wants to deliver great behaviors, great results in their lives and business. That said, *this is common sense but not common practice.* The key to the Executive Whisperer is to embed these behaviors throughout your organization and in your daily life and to insure the freshness and quality of the execution through regular practice.

WRIGHT

If you were to pick the key principals to focus on, which ones are most important?

TERRY

I clearly think they all add important value, but there are a few emphasis points.

The first is creating a safe and trusting environment. For example, the real horse whisperer, Monty Roberts (no, not Robert Redford!), has his own whispering program that he calls "Join-Up." His process has a lot of similarities to The Dog Whisperer. He starts by establishing that critical safe environment. Cesar Millan, the Dog Whisperer, calls it "establishing pack leadership." I call it "developing a safe environment based on mutual respect and trust." In all cases, it is *invitational*. Essentially, to really achieve breakthrough performance, you can't demand that people do what you say, but you can invite them to do things because they trust you, see the benefits, and know they can deliver the desired outcomes.

What else can you do to help people feel safe? Create an environment of a trial-and-error phase that is encouraged and supported because that's what learning is, right? Trial and error is different than succeed or fail.

As part of my coaching environment, as a part of our coaching contract, I ask clients provide me with a comprehensive personal profile. I have them finish a series of sentences that are fill-in-the-blank. As I get inside their psyche a little bit, by far and away, the most common fill-in-the-blank answer to "What I fear most is—" is "failure." It's not death or public speaking, by the way, it is failure. We are taught that failure is bad and should be avoided. That discourages people from trying new things. My goal, after establishing trust, is to insure people know that it's okay to try and err. Erring is simply putting a hypothesis out there and testing it. If the results are not exactly right, or what you expected, you evaluate and then you adjust. This is learning. Babies do it all the time. When they are trying to take their first steps, the parents aren't standing there saying, "No, that isn't right." In fact, they typically are cheering, applauding, cooing, and reinforcing the baby even when he or she falls down.

In looking at Tiger Woods, he doesn't say he fails when his shot goes to a place he didn't intend. He does something that I think is very important—he has *a second shot*—a *"recovery shot."* He notes his new situation and corrects it through an adjustment. His goal is to hit the shot he intends—the one he

185

practices. But if he misses, the goal is to get back on track, not find fault or assign blame.

So trial and error not only gives people confidence, it teaches from a learning perspective that if things don't happen the way they originally intended, how to get back on track quickly.

If Tiger Woods hits his ball under a tree, he's got a tough—some would say impossible—next shot. But Tiger manages to get the ball back out and sometimes, I don't know how, onto the green. Luck? No, it's practice.

So establish a great safe environment, and then practice the intention, and a way to recover—the second shot, as it were.

Then insure you are very present and really listen to the person you are working with so that you understand the challenge from his or her perspective. Encourage people to practice, evaluate their effort, and provide "second shot" guidance. To really have the art of listening, you've got to be curious while suspending judgment. In Covey's language, seek to understand. Once you fully understand, then you can choose to agree (continue), disagree (adjust), or formulate a new process (create a third alternative). In the art of whispering, it is get their attention, create a safe learning environment, and help them practice. So set expectations and work on competency.

The next one is building a collaborative relationship. This is where you reinforce with constancy their practicing new, desired behaviors. There is no such thing as a bad person—they just have behaviors that aren't serving them well. Help each person to focus on how to do things better versus finding fault or assigning blame. This is what is called suspending judgment. It means working with each other to develop better, more useful actions, always seeking to improve situations. Stephen Covey calls it "The Win-Win." How can we get to an intended outcome? What does it look like and how will we know when we're there? Keep in mind that your role is to keep the environment calm and to coach from an assertive but caring position. You are there to help them, but insure that they don't feel threatened or judged. You want them to know you're bringing expertise and you're there to guide them along. Focus on win-win. How can they achieve their desired outcome by working with others, not against or in spite of.

Finally, take them through understanding the appropriate consequence of doing things that best serve the intended end. Again, consequence should not be seen as a negative, it should be seen as the conclusion—the outcome, the why it is important, the value it adds, and the problems or costs that can occur if it isn't executed correctly.

So, as in Tiger's golf shot, here is where it lands if we swing the club correctly—when we do things right as practiced. When we're not hitting the ball quite right, this is what could happen. If that does happens, how do we get back on track? You, as the coach, are building their mental muscles around not just delivering it right, but if they err, how to get back on track quickly. And you do this with care and respect.

These are the areas I think are most critical. A final thought: in every situation, approaching each individual with unconditional, positive regard is critical. Focus on people's behavior and give them a break. Assume they have positive intentions.

WRIGHT

So how does this differ from other leadership development processes?

TERRY

I think it differs in a couple of ways. What is observed is not really learned and is soon forgotten.

It's not that the Executive Whisperer has a lock on any secrets. In fact, a lot of commonalities or effective leadership models exist in many different books. The real question is where does the program break down? Why doesn't a particular approach stay with you?

One reason is failure to implement with consistent long-term practice in place. Is it ever really out there being actualized, being reflected upon, improved, and worked out over time? To be successful, to embed something in an organization, the leadership needs to buy in. The best way to secure that commitment is to demonstrate Return On Investment. The investment is of course in time and money. I think part of what happens in too many companies is they think that things like this are warm and fuzzy, they lack the clear financial win—the immediate results. It's not as black and white as a "five-dollar foot-long sub" ad campaign that has a measurable spike in sales or customer count.

So if the tangibility of the value is not as clear—if that's not set up front and clearly understood—it can quickly find itself on the back burner.

Of course, there many ways to determine ROI. Start with the problem statement. Determine effectiveness measures. Then measure them! For example, you can do employee satisfaction surveys, you can evaluate turnover, benchmark succession planning, or contrast a test area performance against the balance of the organization. There are many ways to set up success criteria and measure the outcomes. It does take a thoughtful approach and the dedication and discipline to follow it through. Customize it with each client, based on each contract. There should be documented deliverables.

There are great intentions out there, but delivery with some discipline in measurement and constancy has been missing. When you watch the Dog Whisperer, he doesn't show up, spend an hour, and say good luck and walk away, problem solved. He starts with, "How can I help you? What is it you would like to see happen differently?" He then evaluates where the root cause of the issue is. Is it in the clarity of expectations or competency? Are there other factors getting in the way? Is there clear accountability where the right behavior is rewarded and the errant behavior is calmly readjusted? In his world, he leaves the owners with a path to follow.

Establish a pack leader presence. Trust and lead with calm, assertive behavior. Be diligent about exercise, practice, and predictable consequences.

Cesar Millan returns a month or so later to verify and confirm their learning and practice. The practice and verification of delivery is the area where there's a big gap in many of the programs out there.

WRIGHT

So what are the leading inhibitors to developing leaders and managers?

TERRY

The answer to this question is self-awareness, commitment to investing the time to execute it, verify its effectiveness, and the ability to maintain high EQ when conflicts or challenges/setbacks occur.

First, there can be a profound lack of self-awareness. I think we struggle when we attempt to take an honest look at what we do well and particularly what we don't do well. We tend to blame and shift or move the focus to someone else.

Secondly, conflict management for many is not a strong skill. This is where EQ comes in. EQ measures how aware we are of our own emotions and how well we self-regulate. It is also about how well we can identify emotions in others and act in a way that defuses a situation so that emotions are not negatively affecting the situation or outcome. How this can show up in the Executive Whisperer or viewing the Dog Whisperer is fairly evident. When an owner is yelling at an animal or hitting it, it can get you compliance with your desire, but compliance was accomplished through fear. Fear training will not produce a loving, calm, predictable, healthy animal. It is quicker and less thoughtful, but not as effective in the long run.

So too can emotional behaviors erupt in the workplace. Bosses who command and control, bosses who are toxic, bosses with inconsistent behaviors can all create confusion, fear, avoidance behaviors, and generate a compliant employee or organization that is at best operating in survival mode. That is a different outcome than best in class, highly productive, and a committed organization.

WRIGHT

Is this process restricted to large companies?

TERRY

No, not at all. This process is an individual process. Companies can benefit, however, I don't talk to companies, I talk to people. I don't train companies, I train people, I don't train departments, I train people. So it's how many people you want to influence and where you want to find value.

I have worked with companies that are from as small as three people to companies as large as fifteen thousand employees. But because my program is individually focused and molded to each unique opportunity, the size doesn't matter. It's a matter of commitment from the leadership on what they choose to do and if they have the commitment to stay with it and support the efforts.

I also coach individual clients whose needs range from joining a new company and wanting to transition well to wanting to change jobs or careers to wanting to improve particular skills or develop new behaviors because they feel stuck where they are in life. All are coachable areas.

WRIGHT

So how do our readers get more information on the Executive Whisper process?

TERRY

Well, the easiest thing to do is to go to my Web site, www.etconsult.biz, and visit the "contact us" section. The site will provide a lot of information about the variety of products and seminars I offer, including the Executive Whisperer. That's probably the quickest, easiest way for people to reach out and catch up with me.

WRIGHT

Any final thoughts you would like to leave us with?

TERRY

Well, I'll leave you with this: I know that some people hope we have more than one life. I am certainly one of those who entertains the concept of reincarnation. But I am not sure of that! And I don't want to plan my life thinking I will get a "Do Over!" I know that living in the present and being intentional, purposeful, and in flow is the best bet I know of to get and give the most in this lifetime. I can truly say that I am doing what I should be doing, and it brings me great joy.

My purpose and legacy statement and intention is as follows: "I was both a lifelong student and teacher and I entertained as well along the way. The people I touched were all left better for knowing me." If I achieve this intention, this life purpose, then my life will be one that fills me with pride and satisfaction. If I feel that I've made a difference in how I lived my life and how I have positively influenced others, I will be satisfied. My wish is for everyone to create his or her own purpose and legacy and to end with as much gratitude and appreciation as possible for a life well lived.

WRIGHT

Well, what an interesting conversation, especially your Executive Whisperer program. You've put it in terms that even I can understand.

I appreciate all the time you've spent with me answering these questions, some of which were very difficult.

TERRY

You are very welcome. I look forward to meeting with you sometime in the near future.

WRIGHT

Today we've been talking with Eileen Terry. Eileen is the CEO of her own consulting and coaching business. She has become a widely sought-after speaker on a range of topics including Diversity Impact and Inclusion, Female Executive Success, Insights, and Advancing Careers, and a host of other topics.

Eileen, thank you so much for being with us today on *Stepping Stones to Success*.

TERRY

You are most welcome. And don't forget to keep practicing that whispering!

ABOUT THE AUTHOR

A multi-experienced and dimensional woman, Eileen started an active business career that has spanned the last thirty-five years. Her first business, a Kool-aid stand, fully capitalized with 100 percent ROI (cost of goods and wagon were fully financed by parents). The golfers on the seventh hole of the local golf course were her target market. This first sales and marketing opportunity stimulated Eileen's interest in pursuing a business career.

Eileen graduated with degrees in Philosophy and Sociology (go figure!). After not finding a real market for a "Philosopher-in-Residence," she started her business climb with Procter & Gamble. While employed there, and then at Pillsbury Corporation, she perfected her persuasive selling skills. She moved on to Southland Corporation and then Chevron, taking positions from multi-unit oversight to marketing, merchandizing, and operations management. Eileen's next stop was Blockbuster, where she successfully progressed through several positions before becoming the only female to reach the top rank of Executive Vice President inside Blockbuster! Eileen was responsible for working all franchisees across the United States and Puerto Rico, representing 1,050 stores, the company's non-Blockbuster branded domestic retail concepts, and the operation of Blockbuster's 450 Canadian stores. In addition, she served as the Global Diversity Officer driving forward Blockbuster's global diversity efforts, and she successfully developed a world-class diversity council and program that resulted in several national awards by key ethnic/diversity groups.

Eileen has become a widely sought motivational speaker on a range of topics including Diversity Impact, Female Executive Success Insights in Advancing Careers, and Mentoring. She has always given back to the community by serving on numerous prestigious community and industry boards, the most recent being the Women's Museum Advisory Board, the Susan G. Komen Race for the Cure, the Women's Franchising and Distribution Forum Board, the Muscular Dystrophy Association (MDA), and the Urban League Youth Diversion Board. She was also keynote speaker at the inaugural North Texas Gay/Lesbian Chamber of Commerce as well as the Houston Gay/Lesbian Chamber, and she served for two years as Co-Chair of the Seattle Mayor's Commission on Sexual Minorities.

Eileen belongs to a women's golf association and enjoys spending time with her partner, her friends, and work associates. She loves dogs, playing golf, watching football, viewing movies, participating in a good debate, and being with interesting people (remember those degrees in Sociology and Philosophy?).

EILEEN TERRY
2725 44th Ave. SW.
Seattle, WA 98116
972-740-4531
www.etconsult.biz

CHAPTER FOURTEEN

Coming To America

An Interview with . . . **Siva Tayi**

Today we're talking with Siva Tayi, Founder and CEO of Sai People Solutions Inc., a $30 million company with more than three hundred employees.

What I find most fascinating about your story, Siva, and the incredible success that you have achieved, is that thirty years ago you arrived from Chennai, India, landing at Chicago's O'Hare Airport, in the middle of winter, with just $5 in your pocket and a dream. That's amazing!

SIVA TAYI (TAYI)

I agree! Thank you!

WRIGHT

Your company, Sai People Solutions Inc., has been hailed as *Inc.* magazine's, "Inc. 500" as one of America's fastest-growing private companies and has even claimed as an "Emerging 10" company by the *Houston Business Journal*. Your company has also been recognized several times as a "Houston 100" company having made a significant impact in the city of Houston.

What I want to ask you is what do you know that everyone else doesn't?

TAYI

Well, it is not what I know more than what others do not know. It's really a question of one being able to use the resources they have, adapting to the marketplace at any given time, and using what they know to create what they want. It begins with a vision.

I had the vision about this company from the day I started, and made sure every day I made progress toward that vision. I took meticulous steps day in and day out and things started happening like magic. As the adage goes, the harder I work the luckier I get! I was not more intelligent than anybody else— I just planned my work and then worked my plan.

As employees joined me, I borrowed ideas from them to come up with new road maps and I made sure everybody followed the path. Making everybody participate in the vision of the company was an important factor. To achieve what we implemented, quality management systems were put in place so that all the processes could be managed in bite sizes with everyone working toward the common goal.

WRIGHT

You have to know a little something because Sai People Solutions Inc. is a $30 million company with more than three hundred employees.

TAYI

Well, I also engaged in my own intuitiveness. People can be quite accomplished in their mission and their vision if they also combine some intuitiveness in making decisions. Entrepreneurs are largely more intuitive in nature than executives working in major corporations. So that helps!

Frankly, if I knew all the problems associated with this services business I probably would not have even begun! Well, actually I'm joking, but it has not been an easy road and I think an easy road is what most people expect. They expect a formula of first you do this, and then you do that, and ultimately you, too, can have a company with revenues in the millions of dollars! I'm sorry, that is not the way I learned and neither is it the way anyone who has made a success for themselves would have learned.

Sometimes ignorance is bliss. The only real thing I knew then was to answer these questions: "Does this idea make sense? Is this idea feasible? If so, what do I have to do to be profitable?" Fortunately for me, the answer was "yes" for the first two and I had a game plan for the third, and so I went with it.

WRIGHT

In your book, *Strange Creature in a New Country,* you define the character traits necessary to become a successful entrepreneur. Do you believe intuition is one of those character traits that drives a person toward owning his or her own business?

TAYI

You have to possess an imagination—an intuition—about who you are and what you can do in this world. For entrepreneurs, any opportunity or idea is not old or new. Even old services can be addressed with new business models. The entrepreneur, though, feels deep inside that he or she can alter old ideas with innovation and that is what we need most, right now.

Intuitively one knows—if one makes the effort—to find out what they really want. If people can go within to that place where their vision or desire was created, that sixth sense of intuitiveness will be realized. It's a gift everybody has, but not they may not know how to tap into this resource.

I've always been very intuitive and knew I would one day be an entrepreneur. I was just looking for the right opportunity and for the right time. The window of opportunity presented itself and I grabbed it.

WRIGHT

Exactly. Most people know what to do, but few actually apply what they know.

You have a master's degree, though, so don't you think intellectually you were a little more prepared than the person who is simply has a great idea or a lot of courage?

TAYI

A master's degree has nothing to do with anything. Education is fine, but education is a testing field of how much you can do and how disciplined you are. I've seen great entrepreneurs who have no college education and great entrepreneurs who have a college education, so it's a mixed bag. It is being entrepreneurial and being able to achieve what you want in business.

Also, my master's degree is in chemistry and had no bearing in building Sai People Solutions. However, to address education one needs to look at the fact that certainly they can teach theory on many subjects—chemistry, psychology, finance, law—*but* what makes a difference is when a person applies what he or she knows. What's the difference between a junior attorney and a world-renown criminal defense attorney? One has applied himself or herself, taken ownership, and made the commitment to be the best. The other is still living in that world of theory—"If I do this, then I get that."

WRIGHT

So you land in Chicago with $5 in your pocket, where do you go from there?

TAYI

My sister lived in Chicago so I boarded with her for a while and then started looking at the opportunities I had. I did some small-time jobs here and there and then I moved to Washington, D.C. I educated myself in computer programming and landed my first decent job and built my career from there on.

The challenge was adjusting to the cold after coming from a tropical country such as India. The most difficult part was adjusting to the American English accent and understanding the mindset of Americans. I wish there had been a job lined up, but 1978 was not the best of times. So to answer your question, I had no job, no prospect, and no clue what was going on. This is normally the state of an immigrant that so many fail to appreciate. They, just like I did, come over with shear, raw courage.

WRIGHT

So looking back, what was your greatest challenge at that time and how did you push through?

TAYI

My greatest challenge was to find a job so that I could be independent. I did not want to become a chemist, the job for which I was trained, which put me in a predicament about what I really wanted to do. The options were limited and my family demands were growing disproportionately.

The only way I pushed through the problem was to move to Washington, D.C., along with my sister. This proved to be the first break I had to land a professional job. My knowledge of chemistry came in handy, for the job I landed was with Environmental Protection Agency. That was a cool job with low pay and low responsibility, which was just fine at the time.

WRIGHT

So you ultimately established your citizenship. Will you describe that day?

TAYI

Yes it was a great day. The citizenship application is rigorous, but once completed I felt very deserving of that extraordinary moment. There were thousands of people and I remember the ceremony vividly. I expressed my gratitude to realize one of my dreams coming true right then and there. That day was very special and very meaningful to me. I left feeling one more hurdle had been removed to attaining my goals.

WRIGHT

Much of your success happened in Houston. How did you come to be in Houston and what took you from being Siva Tayi, the individual, to Siva Tayi, CEO of Sai People Solutions? That was a big leap. How long did that take you?

TAYI

It took six years from the time I started the company in 1984. I came to Houston in 1980 because I was transferred from the consulting company where I used to work. But in 1984 the economy tanked and things looked bleak. I secured local consulting assignments and started building from there. As the economy improved, I began building my company at a more rapid pace.

Before I moved, the consulting firm I worked for gave a farewell party for me. They had a cake that was shaped like a shotgun. I asked what it meant and was told then that Texans in West Texas carried shotguns in their trucks and would shoot at anything that looked odd. Being from India, I would be a good target. I was concerned, but still I drove to Houston from San Francisco during the summer of 1980. The drive was a memorable one, especially the passage between El Paso and Houston.

As a kid, I had watched a lot of westerns where John Wayne used to swagger about the saloons picking off his victims with his Colt 45. This scene was fresh in my mind as I went through El Paso and started crossing the desolate West Texas terrain.

It was late in the evening when I decided that we should rest for the evening and took the next exit into a small town. I drove down the main street looking for a motel and couldn't find any vacancies. I asked a resident if he could recommend another motel in the area. After peering through the car windows he said, "If I were you, I would take the freeway and keep on driving." I recalled the shotgun story and I took the man's advice. I kept on driving until I reached a larger town in the middle of the night.

WRIGHT

I trust you now find Texans a friendlier lot, though that had to be an intimidating moment for you and your family.

TAYI

Absolutely, yes, I did find friendlier people there! I love Texas!

WRIGHT

Tell me about Sai Public People Solutions. What exactly do you do and who is your typical customer?

TAYI

At Sai People Solutions, we are both a consulting and staffing company. We began as an IT consulting company and staffing company. Most of our clients are Fortune 500 companies, which is how we established ourselves nationwide. We grew rapidly during the early 1990s and won "The Houston 100" award several times, the "Inc. 500" award, and I was voted "Entrepreneur of the Year" in both 1995 and 1996.

We are still a consulting company and now offer additional service lines. We work extensively with engineering companies and do a lot of engineering staffing placements. We also do healthcare and scientific and accounting placements. We have also started outsourcing companies in India to Houston and across the country.

WRIGHT

In your book, *Strange Creature in a New Country,* you talk about your fascination with America. Were you seeking to capture your slice of the American dream?

TAYI

My fascination was to become an entrepreneur and the only place I knew I could achieve this far beyond any other place was America.

To be honest with you, I didn't come with an idea to make a lot of money, not at all. I was never greedy and never had any ambition to become rich. I wanted to do things differently and see what this country had to offer.

When I left India, I had a comparatively good job. I lived in a nice place. I had a motorcycle. I had a wife and a child and supported them fairly well. I remember my mother repeating the Indian proverb, "Why do you want to run and drink milk and stay someplace and drink water?" But I had to tell her that

I just wanted to see what I could do in America. Most of the migrants who come to America are adventurous spirits.

WRIGHT

So what would you tell others who feel they have roadblocks, such as feeling too old to begin or feeling like they don't have the education to validate their dreams?

TAYI

Basically, everything has the meaning you give it. If you feel too old or too young and that means the difference between success and failure, then that's what it will be. People have a hard time guessing my age because I act very differently. I definitely don't act my age—at least that is what my wife tells me!

Right now, a roadblock might be the economy and there's no question about it, people are being laid off as jobs are being eliminated. Times are changing to be sure.

So when you get stuck during changing times, draw from what you truly believe in, what you have learned, and then set forth to offer your services to others who have value to their business. There is sheer joy in discovering one's own niche market, having a sound business plan, and seeing a positive cash flow coming in. If a person is comfortable with that then he or she should not look back and not even think about a back-up plan. As long as you have a back-up plan to fall back on you will not succeed. To have a "safety net" is to know there is a "Plan B." With most successful entrepreneurs I know, they never have a "Plan B." There is only "Plan A"!

To give an analogy, David, when you start building a structure, you have a plan and you start putting on the bricks. The bricks go up every day until one day, the building is built. But if you don't show up or don't daily add bricks to the structure, then you are never going to finish, plain and simple. That's why I recommend having a plan and then working your plan every day. That is when the magic happens and your vision comes to life—you have a vision, you do the plan, and then you execute the plan. Things will then fall into place.

WRIGHT

So what is essential in creating the mindset for success?

TAYI

First and foremost is to silence the mind on a daily basis and begin the practice of meditation, which prepares you to think better and to access your intuition.

I do yoga and meditation first thing in the morning before I come to work. Once you silence the mind, the whole world opens up and you can start looking at things much more differently. Meditation helps to give you perspective and clarity in how you make decisions, how you think, and how you go about planning your life. You can not only realize your personal vision, but you can also realize the ways and means to make that vision—your desire—a reality. By recognizing one's inner chatter and stilling the mind for even just ten minutes a day in a secluded room, you will bring more clarity to any adversity you will face in life or on a day-to-day basis.

WRIGHT

I think a lot of people will try meditation if it helps them create a $30-million business!

TAYI

Meditation has helped me enormously. The blend of Eastern mysticisms and the Western way of living gave me a unique opportunity to express my inner longings. When I talk about my experience to fellow entrepreneurs and tell them what I do on a day-to-day basis and how it benefits me and the people I work with, they hesitate to believe how searching in the inner world can benefit the materialistic world. My answer to this is that having a better understanding of one's own inner world throws a flood of light onto the workings of the outer and the material world.

Let me explain how meditation helps me in my day-to-day affairs running my companies. Every Monday I have several conference calls with management staff. As usual, problems come up. Some seem to be insurmountable and some are regular day-to-day mundane situations. What I observed in me is that there has been a gradual transformation over the years regarding the clarity with which I addressed the problem and came up with workable solution. A situation can be or not be a problem, depending on the state of your mind. In essence, if you improve the clarity of your mind by regular meditation, you can label a situation challenging or not so challenging. So the anxiety of problem-oriented situations vanishes and is replaced by stimulating challenges so that you can address it with clarity and calmness, which normally produces better results.

The experience and clarity you attain by regular meditation is contagious and will spread rapidly among your associates on a daily basis. They observe the changes in you and wonder what it is that brought about the changes. Eventually their curiosity will make them inquire and take up the path of inner inquiry.

WRIGHT

Even with the gift of meditation, do you feel that you would have been able to enjoy this kind of success had you not come to America? What if you had remained in India?

TAYI

If I had remained in India I probably would have been successful in a different manner because I was bent on doing that anyway. I wouldn't have been as financially successful as I am now but it is very difficult to answer a hypothetical question.

WRIGHT

It is apparent that you have a high sense of self-confidence. Did you always have a strong belief in yourself?

TAYI

Yes, I always had very high self-esteem. Self-esteem is something that is developed when you're growing up. If you're lucky enough to build up your own esteem and confidence, you can go a long way; nobody can take you down. I was always a keen observer of successful people, as well as a keen observer of people who were much smarter than I was. I had good self-esteem and was never jealous of them, their success, or their intellect. I appreciated that about them and learned from them.

I had my own rules and I followed them. This developed my personality to be more unique without a whole lot of ego intertwined. For aspiring entrepreneurs, irrespective of who you were in the past, you can help yourself by starting a new day with a new chapter of your life. By tapping the eight unique characteristics I have written about in my book, you can let the professional side of your dreams come true.

WRIGHT

So how does one develop that kind of confidence? For you it comes naturally, but how does one go about obtaining that kind of charisma?

TAYI

Confidence exists in everybody, yet only the degree of confidence is in question from person to person. Say for example you never rode a motorcycle. The first time, you probably were worried whether you were going to stay on it. Once you went around the block, you began to build up your courage and confidence and soon you wanted to take it for a spin on the freeway.

Everything boils down to how you nurture your inner confidence from one level to the next. If you had a certain level of experience in business and you have decided to become an entrepreneur, try with that innate confidence you possessed to get the idea off the ground. To reemphasize, if you decide to become an entrepreneur, obviously you have a degree of confidence.

Now the real work begins. Never try to take a big bite that you cannot swallow. The best way to build your confidence is to accept projects or assignments in a step-by-step manner. Upon completion of each assignment, your confidence will grow exponentially and very soon you might even fall into the trap of over-confidence. If you do, you will start making mistakes.

WRIGHT

Is that what you talk about when you speak to business groups?

TAYI

I do, and I talk about mediation and how to discover and develop your desire, your passion, your ambition, and your vision. My topics vary according to the type of audience I have been invited to address. If I am addressing a group of young adults who have entered the business world, I will talk about zeal and enthusiasm at the workplace. When I address these young professionals, I talk about enthusiasm, sense of ownership, and empowering one's self. I stress the fact that these characteristics should be cultivated diligently on a daily basis. The best part of this practice is that it comes in handy when becoming an entrepreneur.

For the stressed-out business executive, I talk about other things in relation to stress and how to manage that stress. Stress is built up in the mind when one vacillates between past knowledge of the incident and trying to predict the future result while being unnecessarily bogged down with multiple scenarios. When that happens one completely misses the present by not acting with the correct solution.

For an aspiring entrepreneur I would talk about the wide world of opportunities and how one could develop one's own niche and build one's dreams in a practical manner.

For companies that have survived the first few years and are ready to build an infrastructure and a management team to grow exponentially, I talk about my years of experience in building companies from the ground up. I discuss the do's and the don'ts. I also discuss Remote Management and Metrics Management so that leaders can manage the company using quantitative principles.

Lastly, I talk about sales management, motivating sales teams, and training management to manage their teams with byte management techniques.

WRIGHT

Launching your own company, you describe several experiences of handling conflict and maintaining integrity. You say specifically that honesty is the best policy in every aspect of a business. As I look at businesses today, I think others would learn something from your ethic. Is being honest risky?

TAYI

No, being honest is easy and being honest makes you more money because you are giving more value to your customer. They know intrinsically that they are not being taken advantage of. It's a paradigm shift from thinking selfishly, wanting your own gain over your client's benefit. Let me give an example.

I was working with one of the directors of a growing Fortune 100 company. In one of our conversations, the procurement manager said his goal was to make sure I didn't make a dime by the time this deal was done. That got me very curious. When I asked what he meant, he stated that he wanted to get as much out of me as he could, ensure that I did not make any profit, and complete the project. At the end of the contract, he asked me to get involved on the next assignment. But then I said thanks, but no thanks.

That is the wrong way of doing business. My philosophy is give the correct advice, be upfront with customers on expectations and be interested in completing the job because in return, they'll get value. That will get me more business than telling them I'm the best guy and I can do all these wonderful things.

Being honest in business reduces stress and improves your overall integrity, which will enable you to get more repeat business and references.

When you question whether you are doing business ethically, just imagine yourself being on the receiving end of the deal. If you are fine with it, then you are probably doing the right thing.

My spiritual focus is based on Cosmic Law. Cosmic Law has no awareness of religion, color, or nationality. For the Cosmos, man-made boundaries do not exist. The Cosmos has its own logic for what is right or wrong based on the emotional, mental, and physical hurt you cause others. If you do any one of these due to your dishonest behavior, it will be noted in your Karmic diary to which certain actions have to be facilitated by you to clear up the Karma you created in the first place.

Again, this is just how I hold myself to a higher standard in accordance with my beliefs, which so far have not steered me wrong. But this is not a new idea in American culture. Some people put it this way: "you get what you give." Another such phrase is "what goes around comes around." Basically, this is karma.

WRIGHT

So what you're doing is obviously working for you. You've won award after award especially in the early years of establishing your company. You even called one of your acceptance speeches your "academy award" speech. What did it feel like as a "strange creature" to win these prestigious awards?

TAYI

Winning awards is an addiction. It's a good addiction, though! It tells me I am doing something right and that feels great.

During the early part of my career, we used to win awards every year. One of the prestigious awards was winning the Inc 500. When I first started the company, it was a good thing to create a lot of buzz as a way of drawing attention to my products and services that improved my sales.

As I won each award over the years, I figured that the ultimate award was to win the Earnest & Young Entrepreneur of the Year award. We had to work hard for this, since Earnest & Young was not giving awards on sheer sales volume, but on financial viability, the potential for growth, as well as quality management systems that assured sustained growth. It took us more than three years to participate. We were nominated twice and won the second time.

It was a thrill to win this prestigious award. And I remember it was a spectacular evening with more than a thousand people in attendance in the ballroom of the Hyatt Regency. The decorations were festive and people were in high spirits. Many companies brought their families and employees with the overriding anticipation of winning, similar to Hollywood's Academy Awards, I would imagine.

The celebration started with different categories. There were several large screens around the ballroom and announcements were continuously explaining the different classifications of the entrants, their accomplishments, and at last, the winner in each of those categories. My company was representing the high-tech telecommunications classification.

Our segment was on, the expectations were rising, and there was anxiety in the air at our table. The music was blaring, the video was running, and the tone of the announcer was becoming animated. At last my name was called! That particular moment was the glorious moment I had been waiting for. My whole life flashed in front of my eyes, from my boyhood days of desperation, to the expectations of adulthood, and finally, in that very moment, I felt that the main movie of my life had come to a great climax.

I highly recommend this experience because for me it was not the end, but the beginning of building even greater things. It was like a launching pad for me. This was a superior milestone for me, my family, and my employees. I kissed my wife, hugged my colleagues, and raced to the podium to deliver my five-minute "Academy Award" speech. I was not shy or intimidated. I had worked too hard. I said everything I wanted to say, and in an animated way the audience generously roared with laughter when they heard how I squandered $20 in the transit lounge in Frankfurt drinking German beer.

People enjoy a "rags-to-riches" story, and I was indeed that "Strange Creature" who ventured to lands unknown to achieve success.

WRIGHT

Siva, you have an inspiring story of success. Please tell us you have a formula whereby many can follow your lead, practically applying what you know.

TAYI

Yes, I've developed eight principles: Resourcefulness, Investigative, Persistence, Discipline, Diffusing Objections, Can-Do Attitude, Enthusiasm, and creating a Sense of Urgency.

Briefly, I'll explain, but you'll want to get my book so you can work the strategies for yourself.

Resourcefulness means capitalizing on who and what you know. Investigative means to discover what you do not know to create your own opportunities. Persistence is self-explanatory—you must keep going on. Discipline is a frame of mind, really. I could not have done what I have done without strict discipline. Diffusing Objections is to not allow roadblocks. Some people are looking for them and even create them. Maybe they are afraid of success. But to diffuse an objection is to eliminate these blocks in your path toward success. Another "must have" frame of mind is a "Can-Do" Attitude. If you don't believe you can, then you won't. You have to have that spirit of success already in mind and then raise the bar. Enthusiasm is important because people want to work with those who are excited about what they do. And lastly, Sense of Urgency is important because you have to act long before your competition even knows what to do next.

WRIGHT

So which of those do you feel is the most important?

TAYI

Every one of the characteristics is required. A good dish can be prepared only when all the ingredients are mixed in the right proportion. However, clarity of your mind is essential to everything and very important to becoming successful.

WRIGHT

So your eight principles are: resourcefulness, investigative, persistence, discipline, defusing objections, can-do attitude, enthusiasm, and creating a sense of urgency, is that right?

TAYI

That's right.

WRIGHT

So why did you write your book? What do you want people to know about you, your life, and your success, and how will the book help them?

TAYI

Good question. All these years and during my travels conducting seminars and conferences, young people entering in the services business ask me how I did it. I have repeated the abridged version of my story several times to many people and it always evoked the same awe-inspiring feeling from my listeners.

This compelled me to write my story and after meeting my publisher, Donna Wick, it materialized.

WRIGHT

So what do you have to believe about yourself, Siva, to coach others?

TAYI

Most of the time, the fear of failure stops people dead in their tracks and they don't even wish to take the first step. I know my book will help them to get over that type of fear.

To tell a crowded auditorium the "how, why, and when" is what people are looking for. I want to impart the strong beliefs behind my core values necessary for a person to become a successful entrepreneur. No matter if you feel you have "been there, done that" or if there is a crowded auditorium of people who wish to just begin, I ask you, who is better to teach them?

Who am I to do this? And why should I do this? It is an intrinsic nature of all humans to share what they have learned with others, sometimes for profit and sometime just for the love of it. In my case it is both. I love teaching others and yet, I have to make a living, especially since my retirement vanished in the March 2009 downturn. I have to start from scratch and work for another ten years to bring it back to the stage where it was. Thus the game to be successful and to strive towards one's success is never really over. Life is full of twists and turns and surprises!

Businesses and great ideas are built from the bottom, up. Even an inconceivable idea can be built with a workable business model. Ten years ago, microlending was unheard of. Now, all the major banks are getting into this segment of the marketplace. Microlending was started by an American of Indian origin, Mr. Vikram Akula, who founded SKS Micro Finance. He had this idea, traveled to India, and made this venture a successful business model.

In the current economic times when unemployment is not improving, start thinking about your strengths and assets. See how you can bring the value of service to others and how you can bring that value to a profitable revenue stream. This is the time to sell services! Any kind of services to large companies will be a good idea. When these companies are reducing staff in all areas, the pent-up demand from their user community rises. This is a great environment for an entrepreneur to be creative and fill the void.

I want to make sure that when I talk in business forums and public venues, I impart my wisdom and lend my inspiration so people can reevaluate themselves, their worth and value, their capabilities and their talents to venture out on their own. I wish everyone could have their "moment on the stage" of the entrepreneurial theatre, delivering their own acceptance speech of a job well done.

Success is essential, no matter if your achievement is announced on a nationally recognized platform or in the living room in front of your family and friends. Everyone has something to give. Everyone has value. I look forward to being a part of that person's success!

WRIGHT

Well, Siva, I really appreciate all this time you've taken with me to answer these questions. This is really going to be a great entry as a chapter in our book and I am so glad that you're in it. You've given me a lot to think about today and I'm sure our readers are really going to really appreciate this chapter.

TAYI

Thank you very much.

WRIGHT

Today we've been speaking with Siva Tayi. CEO of Sai People Solutions Inc., a $30-million company with more than three hundred employees.

Siva, thank you so much for being with us today on *Stepping Stones to Success*.

TAYI

Thank you very much. I enjoyed the interview.

ABOUT THE AUTHOR

SIVA TAYI is the founder of Sai People Solutions, Inc. An outstanding IT professional, Siva has more than twenty years of data processing experience, which includes many years as a programmer/analyst and project leader. He is directly responsible for the dramatic growth and continuing success of the company. With a high level of management skill, Siva continues to insist that the company maintain its thrust toward excellence. His integrity and competence have been solely responsible for the high degree of success of the company, and he demands nothing less from his staff. Siva holds a Master's of Science degree in Chemistry.

SIVA TAYI
2313 Timber Shadows Drive, Suite 200
Kingwood, TX 77339
800-929-1858
281-358-1858
Fax: 281-358-8952
sivatayi@saipeople.com
www.saipeople.com

CHAPTER FIFTEEN

Your Glass is Full:

Living in Optimism & Wellness

An Interview with . . . **Jane Drucker and Catharine Randazzo**

DAVID WRIGHT (WRIGHT)

Today we are talking with Jane Drucker and Catharine Randazzo.

Jane L. Drucker, PhD, PCC, is the founding explorer behind "Inner Journeys Coaching." Dr. Drucker brings more than thirty years of professional experience to developing wellness in the caretaking community.

Catharine E. Randazzo, PhD, PCC, is the creator of Coach2Rewards. She is a huge fan of the power of optimism to enhance one's innate creativity. Dr. Randazzo has been coaching and creating positive change for more than twenty years.

Dr. Drucker and Dr. Randazzo, welcome to *Stepping Stones to Success*.

Isn't "coaching" just another word for therapy?

CATHARINE RANDAZZO (RANDAZZO)

When I tell people I am a coach, I am often asked, "What sport?" If only folks knew how funny it would be for me to coach a sports team. But "coach" is quite a versatile word. Definitions from various sources will say that a coach: guides a team, is a pricey purse that uses itself as a billboard, is a wagon that was once pulled by horses to transport people before the gas guzzler was invented, or is a less expensive way to travel—you know, for those of us in the back of the plane. I am none of those. I am a Life Coach who helps people guide themselves.

Life Coaching finds its roots in Positive Psychology and big business mentoring. Coaching was developed by a group of self-defined gurus and is based in the fundamental belief that clients can and will prosper. The coach helps clients to reach beyond the midline of being okay and toward the state of being great. This, in a nutshell, is where coaching departs from what we know as psychotherapy.

Traditional psychotherapy focuses on illness and on ways to alleviate it. It assumes that patients require assistance in order to live healthy lives. In college and graduate school, I was the annoying young woman raising my hand and asking "But when do we help people be happy?" In our healthcare system, therapists of all sorts are allowed to treat patients only to alleviate an illness. Thus, as a psychologist, once I have helped guide you out of depression, I am supposed to set you free. Once your phobia is under control we are to part ways. Once you are no longer beating your spouse I am to call you "cured." But what about being better? Not just better than ill, but better than that place that is the thin line between ill and well.

Positive psychology and its offshoot, coaching, are important vehicles for helping us to reach higher and happier states of being. These fields provide important ways to find satisfaction in our lives and to be the sort of "well" that I believe we were created to be. That sort of wellness finds us singing, creating, offering help to others, succeeding in ways we choose, and living in balance and optimism.

Finding balance is an important component of being "well." Let's take, for example, the many competing negative, positive, or neutral messages we hear about ourselves daily. Some are aimed at us personally like a boss's criticism or a friend's compliments. Some might be directed at us because we are part of a group. Think of the happy people eating chips in the store display ad. Maybe you get messages as part of a subculture such as "blondes have more fun."

Looking and listening in just one day, I was bombarded with the following messages: I saw on my computer that I'm too short and need a tan. I heard from a therapy patient that I was mean. I was told by a coaching client that I was great and the reason for her success. The television news implied that air travel isn't safe and that I should rethink my travel plans. I was called "young lady," "doctor," "aunt," "a good friend," "business partner," "our new tenant," "the coach," "brilliant," "a great writer," and "funny." I received all these messages, and it was not even lunchtime yet! So many opinions. So many labels. So much information!

Positive psychology/coaching is an effective way to help us decipher terms, make choices about meanings, discard what doesn't fit, and keep what is useful information to apply to our lives in meaningful and optimistic ways. It challenges me to be mindful of what I say to myself when I hear the cacophony of messages. Does my private voice defend me or betray me? Am I indeed too pale and too short? Do I optimistically decide I am just fine and don't need new shoes to give me height or a tanning product to make me golden? Do I pessimistically buy the product and cower because I believe the messages? Do I believe I am truly brilliant, or can I just accept the compliment happily, knowing it was enthusiastic and sincere, even if I believe it to be just a tad exaggerated?

While traditional psychotherapy steers patients toward a statistically defined norm, coaching is designed to optimize personal success, however clients define it.

For our Readers: What messages did you hear today?

WRIGHT

What is wellness?

JANE DRUCKER (DRUCKER)

You are here for a purpose. You may not know your purpose, but you wouldn't be here if you didn't have one. Wellness is a state of being in full and profound alignment with your purpose. As you move toward greater faithfulness to your life's purpose, you also begin to become most authentically who you are. You become most real and most well. Wellness is not a simple matter of enjoying physical health. Achieving true wellness requires that you dig down to the roots of your self—to your soul.

I have been asked if wellness can be taught. That's a little like asking if musical talent can be taught. Music theory, musical technique, and music composition can be taught, but musical talent is innate. Wellness itself is not a skill that is created by instruction. It is an innate quality of all living beings. In that sense, no, it cannot be taught. It must be uncovered and developed. What can be taught are tools for uncovering the potential that exists in each of us to be "well." Much as Dorothy learned from her adventures in Oz, wellness generally resides right in our own backyards.

Unless it is taught out of them, young children have a remarkable connection to the truth. They exist in a state of curiosity, optimism, and honesty about the world around them. When asked what they want to be in that world, they offer up the most imaginative ideas that touch deep to the heart of what matters to them. They want to be ballerinas, firefighters, baseball players, princesses, and trash collectors. But what they are really saying is that they want to be graceful, courageous, skillful, desired, and helpful.

As we grow up, we tend to loosen our connection to our core values. That's not to say that we lose our values, rather that we spend more of our conscious time and energy focused elsewhere. As we travel into adulthood, we move further from our natural state of wellness.

Jody sat slumped down in my client chair and sighed deeply that she simply did not know what she wanted to do with her life. She was single, in her mid-thirties, and had recently been laid off from the most recent of a string of low-paying clerical jobs. She had a college degree in nineteenth century American literature. She also held a high school teaching credential, but she did not want to teach. As a matter of fact, she reeled off a long list of jobs she did not want to do.

I let her vent her frustration for a few minutes before asking her how she thought I could help. Again, she knew what she did not want from me. She did not want me to tell her what job she should do. That worked out just fine, as I am not in the business of telling people what they should do with their lives. So I reflected back that I heard her saying she did not want job advice, and she sighed again, and nodded. Then I asked her what she had wanted to grow up to be when she was a child.

"A mermaid!" The answer came without hesitation. "But that's not a job in the real world."

Well, I couldn't argue that there are not a lot of mermaid jobs in the real world, although some do exist in theme parks and theatres. However, she didn't really want to be a mermaid *per se*. Further probing revealed that what Jody had really wanted was to be surrounded by the ocean and its mysteries. In her core, she wished more than anything else that she could be part of exploring, discovering, and sharing hidden knowledge. Rather than dismissing her childhood fantasy of becoming a mermaid, Jody began to reconnect to the real dream, the dream of uncovering treasures, and in that moment, she embarked on a journey to wellness.

For our Readers: What do you dream of being?

WRIGHT

What is "Wellness Coaching"?

DRUCKER

Have you ever felt that something in your life is just not clicking? No matter what you do, where you turn, how you try to reboot, the zing that once animated your days has fizzled. You feel as if the rug has been yanked right out from under your feet. Your energy level is hovering around empty, and you just don't recharge as readily as you used to. Time slips by, and with its passage you begin to wonder how you are ever going to get a handle on everything you need to fix or want to accomplish.

We all go through periods during which our rhythm is out of whack, when life seems to be fighting us, and when the path ahead that once seemed so clear has blurred. Wellness Coaching helps people find their way back to a life of renewed optimism, vigor, and *joie de vivre*. Through Wellness Coaching, they are able to reconnect with their essence and to live from a place of honest engagement with whatever life presents.

The role of a Wellness Coach is at once simplistic and multi-layered. On the simplistic side, a Wellness Coach is someone who knows that you have all the resources you need to create the life you desire. He or she uses that simple knowledge to help you to explore your options for making the changes you want to make. On the multi-layered side, a Wellness Coach employs a toolbox of experience, techniques, and insights to support you on your journey.

Mary, a forty-seven-year-old musician, came to me one day and talked about feeling overwrought and confused. She was accomplished in her profession, happily married, and involved in many community activities that used to interest her. Despite everything looking bright and wonderful "on paper," she felt strongly that something was missing. The performance work she once loved felt tedious. She and her husband rarely talked about anything other than the mundane details of running a home and getting through the week's tasks and errands. Her many committee meetings drained her. She was clear that nothing was wrong in her life, but she also knew that life was not fulfilling in the way that it once had been. She desperately wanted to turn the blahness around.

Starting from the knowledge that Mary was a whole, healthy, and resourceful woman, I challenged her to explore ways to reinvent herself. One of the first ah-hah moments that Mary had was when she began to keep a running list of a typical day's activities. Nearly every entry on her inventory started with the word "go." She was gobbling up huge amounts of time and energy going from one place to another without any real down time. Twenty years earlier, this was a rhythm that had suited her, but it was no longer a match for the woman Mary had become.

Mary made a commitment to herself to carve out half an hour twice a week for "Mary Time." During that "Mary Time" she could read a book, take a walk, paint her toenails, or write in her journal. She could not "go" anywhere for any purpose other than to reconnect with her inner spirit.

Eventually Mary began to create "Mary Time" every day, and she used it to implement a personal spiritual practice that helped her to feel a deepened connection to the creative drive that had drawn her into music so many years ago.

She dropped some of her committee work and used the found time and energy to teach singing at a nearby senior center. By giving her soul the attention that it had been lacking, Mary created a match between her inner life and her life in the outer world. Her renewed passion inspired her husband to follow a similar plan, and the two of them reconnected as life partners.

For our Readers: What would you be doing if you took the time to listen to your soul?

WRIGHT

What role does optimism play in the coaching process?

RANDAZZO

"Some say the glass is half empty; some say the glass is half full. I say, 'Are you going to drink that?'" Offered by writer Lisa Claymen in jest, this is a poignant reminder that there is risk in simply seeing the world through rose-colored glasses and merely maintaining a "half-full" outlook. Half full means very little if we aren't going to drink up and make the most of the potential in whatever our glass holds!

In coaching, half-full, rose-colored glasses, pie-in-the-sky fantasies are out. True wellness and optimism are about personal awakening. Coaching helps us to make better sense of feedback, to view ourselves realistically, and to be more fully aware of our worlds. Mike's story is a simple example.

Mike had a severe weight problem and mounting health issues associated with his weight. He was placed on a routine of diet and exercise, and he swallowed a number of drugs to regulate his high blood pressure and diabetes. His health concerns continued to escalate, and he felt excluded from family meals. Still, his weight was increasing and additional medications at higher doses were being added to his regimen with every visit to his physician. Mike was discouraged. The doctor suggested coaching to help him stick to his diet and exercise program.

Mike came to coaching very reluctant about the process. He doubted that hearing "more of the same" would be useful. He was right—"more of the same" was unlikely to be of any help. It would probably frustrate Mike and bore the coach. Coaching thrives on discovery. So, my place as his coach was to help Mike discover what he needed and to uncover what he wanted. Mike was a mentally healthy man with the best knowledge of himself, even if that knowledge was well hidden.

What came to light was that Mike felt he was depriving himself when he dieted. He lacked creativity and so took an all-or-none approach to life. This proved self-defeating and dangerous, as it led to overeating and too many "just this once" episodes. Despite feeling deprived, Mike saw his weight moving in the wrong direction, and he was further punished by reprimands from his concerned physician. It was time for Mike to get serious!

Serious in Mike's case meant time to get creative. To his delight, we were able to brainstorm several ways to cut calories and not feel cheated. Weight started falling off him. As the weight dropped, he became motivated to exercise. Within three months of beginning his coaching, Mike was off most of his medications and was more than thirty pounds lighter.

Mike had been hit with the truth of his health with each visit to his physician, with each pill he swallowed, with each injection he administered to himself, and every time he set foot on his scale. Nothing was rosy there, but when Mike brought his concerns to coaching, he was awakened. He learned to recognize his role in creating his problems and what options he had. Mike became aware of his actions, his feelings, and his goals. He focused on how he treated himself. He lived in the here and now, he learned to put old habits behind him, and he found his creativity. As a result, he found his health. The elements of Mike's life that were not working were reframed as hurdles to be overcome. Mike moved on to apply this learning to other issues with further coaching.

What positive psychology and coaching know is the same thing that every successful video game developer knows. Modern society tries to teach us to forget this bit of knowledge and even insists that it is something from which we must be protected. What is the dirty little secret? Adversity is useful! What no one told Mike was that the adversity of his poor health and impending early death was a challenge and an opportunity for him to remake his life.

Think of that video game you or maybe your teenager can't get enough of. There is sufficient challenge to get you involved in the game by testing your skills. You can see a goal, the next level, and it can be attained. So you try and try until eventually you reach your goal. When you miss the goal, you blow out the exasperation in a quick puff and optimistically try again. That is what Mike found through his coaching program. His big life change had many small steps, the first of which was approaching his "problems" with an optimistic understanding they were simply challenges to be met.

Wouldn't it be great if our diets, exercise regimes, office organization, household clean up, job searches, and all daunting tasks worked this way? Well, they do. All that is missing is the funky music or the haunting sound effects of the video game. In life we fill in our own sound effects that tell you that you are succeeding or that you are off the path. "If you realized how powerful your thoughts are, you would never think a negative thought," says Peace Pilgrim. (www.peacepilgrim.com/)

Long ago an old comedian joked that there are two types of people in the world. The first wakes up and thinks, "Good God, morning!" The second wakes up and thinks, "Good morning, God!" The coaching process helps to refocus us on life's potential for wonder.

For our Readers: What adversity can you reframe as a challenge?

WRIGHT

How does coaching help clients who are stuck?

RANDAZZO

People who look through keyholes are apt to get the idea that most things are keyhole shaped. Facing a problem that has been close to you for a long while is often like looking through a keyhole. You see the issue from just one angle. You see just one small part of the whole. You come to see the issue as keyhole shaped. Such a limited view doesn't allow for much movement, so you become stuck.

In life, keyholes come in many forms. Exhaustion is one. Exhaustion comes from competing forces taking up the energy you require to fight the good fight on an issue. With a lack of energy your lingering concern never moves sufficiently high on your priority list to get it tackled.

Being overwhelmed is another keyhole. Through that keyhole, a dilemma can look big, especially if it is very close. Something big can be scary, like a monster hiding under your bed. But if you weren't looking at it through a keyhole—if you opened the door and took a good look—you would see that the monster is a fly that landed on the keyhole. Sometimes, when a problem is very close, it can seem huge and can overwhelm you.

So what can coaching do? Isn't that just cheerleading? No. Coaching is not a matter of simply cheering on the efforts of another. In fact, as a coach, I often recommend that my clients find the cheerleaders in their lives and ask for their help too. As a coach I can't use our precious time simply to cheer.

Let's look at weight as a coaching issue again. If cheering were all it took to achieve a healthy weight, America would not be suffering an obesity epidemic, nor would our icons be anorexic. We cheer ourselves and each other a lot of the time, but we don't always acknowledge the difference between applauding real accomplishment and giving polite but unwarranted flattery.

When you live in a keyhole shaped world, you find yourself frantic in the search for answers. "How do I conquer the monster? How do I get through that keyhole and into the room?" By giving in to the frenzy, you are exhausting your time and energy, but beneath the worry, you are full of valuable resources you can use constructively to accomplish your goal.

Stephanie was a young mother, a wife, and a career woman working on an advanced degree and struggling to make it all work—or so she said. Stephanie told me she wanted it all, but she turned all her issues into keyhole monsters. She complained that her mother and father compared her to her brother who made more money, to her "perfect" stay-at-home sister who was a terrific mom, and to her very smart sister-in-law. Her husband was staging a silent war by being difficult at home. Stephanie stated that her primary issue was being overweight.

For years she remained stuck in a cycle in which her weight went up and down with a gradual increase overall. Stephanie said, "I want to focus on my weight," but I also heard that she was getting sabotaging negative messages from her "support system" about her overall life choices and abilities. Weight seemed primary to her because it was the only goal on which her husband, mother, brother, sister, and sister-in-law agreed. Those people are not Stephanie. No wonder she was stuck. Stephanie was sent to find her real cheerleaders. Then we got to work.

With her cheering friends in her pocket, Stephanie learned to ask, "What do I want?" Up to this point she had been stuck asking, "What do I deserve?" She deserved plenty, but deserving plenty implied it would come to her. She deserved a good life, a loving family, a supportive mom and dad, and a helpful husband. Deserving all of that just didn't change reality.

Coaching did change her reality. Stephanie switched her focus from expecting to be valued by her family to learning to value herself. She became mindful of how she was getting lost in the negativity she was hearing from others. With this awareness and her newly found value of herself, she was able to move forward again.

Stephanie worked out some issues at home with her husband. He became more responsible as she developed the skills to create the working partnership she wanted with him. This effort helped to move him into her corner as they focused on moving into their mutual future. He became one of her cheerleaders and helped to make school easier for her by taking on more responsibility at home than she had even asked for him to own.

Success with this early step and her rediscovered optimism led Stephanie to realize that her other family issues might not be quite what she perceived them to be. We worked together so that she could decide what feedback to hear from her family, how to use the information constructively, and how to ask that useless comparisons stop. She learned to restate the criticisms for herself, and later for her family. Since hearing the negativity that Stephanie perceived, her family members' voices have changed. They no longer speak the same words and they know that Stephanie has been listening.

The result was that Stephanie learned to believe in herself. Her problems took on forms she could conquer. She kept her eye on the real goal and made substantial changes to get the life she wanted. Along the way, her stress was reduced, and so was her nervous eating. Without weight loss even being a coaching goal, without changes in diet or exercise, Stephanie lost twenty pounds.

For our Readers: Where are you stuck?

WRIGHT

What is coaching's most profound effect?

DRUCKER

Change comes hard to most of us. We want to change. We intend to change. We promise to change. But change comes hard to most of us. Think back to every New Year's Day for the past, oh, forever. If you are one of the millions of people who have ever made a list of New Year's resolutions, you know that this is true. Every year the same basic goals appear on your new list. You are going to get in shape, sleep more, spend more time with the family, clean the garage, and balance the checkbook every time a statement comes in. Yet somehow the list remains pretty much the same year after year. Why? Because change comes hard to most of us.

At the point that we realize this very simple truth, we can begin to change.

Although many clients come to coaching thinking they are on the verge of a great transformation, most are only beginning to test the waters. They have spotted the diving board and perhaps announced that they intend to use it. But they still have to climb the ladder, create a clear mental image of their dive, and embark on the run to the end of the board. Only then does the actual dive into change begin.

For Orin, a fifty-two-year-old family physician, encouraging healthy lifestyle habits in his patients had become important to him. He was reluctantly realistic about the likelihood that many of them wouldn't follow his recommendations. Frustrated that he couldn't seem to convince them to make wise decisions for themselves, he began to think about his own life. He worked long hours, took few breaks during the work day, often skipped lunch to make phone calls, and ate a lot of rich or fast food. He frequently read medical journals at home without giving much time to his family. He realized that he was asking his patients to do as he said, not as he did.

Then he hit on an idea that he wanted to implement in his group practice. What was the grand idea? He wanted to start a "wellness" program for himself and his colleagues. It was a terrific concept, but he didn't have a plan, and more importantly, his colleagues weren't interested.

When he first approached me about coaching, he was frustrated and confused. He thought he was ready to jump right in and get the whole office running on the path to wellness. However, he had neglected the first step—taking the first step.

Orin realized that the best way to motivate his colleagues (not to mention his patients) was to make some changes himself so that his own journey could become an example to the men and women he hoped to influence.

Orin laid out a plan for changing his own habits. Over the next several months, he enlisted the support of his wife and best friend to help him watch what food went into his mouth and how much time he spent holed up in his man-cave reading. He began a practice of daily meditation.

Not much changed at work, but a lot changed inside Orin. He felt healthier and was more content with his personal life. His patients noted his deeper attention to their care. They did not necessarily follow his medical recommendations any better, but Orin was able to feel more fully appreciated as a physician because he knew that he was providing care from a place in his soul that sincerely respected his patients' journeys. His colleagues did not get on board with him, but to Orin, the importance of his transformation was that he had learned to be true to himself. He became content to follow his personal truth without feeling frustrated that others were not ready to make the change with him.

As Orin's story illustrates, the most significant progress is not necessarily the superficial alteration of your behavior. It is often the shift of awareness that allows you to become "well."

For our Readers: What is keeping you from making the changes that you say you want to make?

WRIGHT

What does it take to create balance in one's life?

DRUCKER

I have yet to meet anyone whose life is in perfect harmony and equilibrium. We live in a culture that makes outrageous and often contradictory demands on us. We are told we can "have it all," but we are warned about burning out too soon. We say that we value leisure time, yet we work more hours in a week than any other Western workforce. We always seem to be in the middle of some fitness or diet craze, yet we are surrounded by the world's most varied and plentiful array of unhealthy food and laborsaving devices.

How exactly does anyone find the happy medium needed to be our best selves? First of all, it is crucial to understand that there is no such thing as permanent life balance because life is fluid. Creating a working sense of life balance is best looked at as the pursuit of constant realignment, and it has to start from wherever an individual is.

Dana was a single mom who knew she needed to make some changes before she burned out. Her days were chock full of things she needed to do so that everyone else in her family was taken care of. She also held down a responsible job.

She got out of bed long before her two sons, who were nine and twelve when I first met Dana. She would put in a load of laundry, lay out clothes for the boys, and wake them each up just before she cooked a nutritious breakfast and made their lunches. While the kids dressed, Dana would make their beds, and as they ate their meal, she would take fifteen minutes to shower and dress for work. As she drove them to school, she would look over her work schedule for the day. During her lunch hour, Dana made sure her bills got paid, exchanged dirty clothes for clean at the dry cleaners, or ran similar homemaker errands. After work, she shuttled the boys to their sports or music activities and usually shopped for the evening meal, which she cooked while she finished the laundry started in the morning. Her weekends were spent cleaning and running more errands.

By the time Dana put her head on the pillow at night, she was exhausted.

Dana had bought into the whole story that a "good" mother does everything for her family always. What she forgot in the process is that you can't burn the candle at both ends. Who was taking care of Dana? No one. She expected little of her boys, and Dana was running on empty.

Guided visualization showed Dana that there was plenty of wiggle room to simplify some of her chores, and the boys were old enough to pitch in around the house and still have time for schoolwork and extracurricular activities. For Dana, the first step to creating balance in the life of her family meant asking more of her sons and less of herself. Often, doing less for others allows them to do more for themselves—or for you. By saying "yes" to doing all the drudgework for her family, Dana was saying "no" to living a balanced life with her children.

For our Readers: What would add balance to your life?

WRIGHT

Why do successful people hire a coach?

RANDAZZO

Top performers win because they know that no matter how talented and dedicated they are, they can always do better with a helping hand. The more a person has accomplished in life, the more keenly aware he or she is of the power of teamwork. Many high achieving people find that adding a coach to their team leads to increased success.

In sports, the coach is the person in charge of strategy and decision-making. A Life Coach plays a very different role from a sports coach or a business mentor. The job of a Life Coach is to be a supportive team member and to take direction from the client.

Successful people rarely need someone else to create a winning strategy or to make decisions for them. What they need is someone to provide supportive feedback, to ask thought-provoking questions, and to speak honestly to them. Life coaching is different for everyone, but the essence of effective coaching is that your coach becomes a team member who helps you to rekindle the sense of mind/body/spirit wholeness that is at the core of your being.

Many successful people find that they have money, fancy belongings, famous acquaintances, and expensive rooms in which to live. Still, they lack for wellness. They are not ill in that they do not sneeze or cough and are not bleeding. They carry out their daily responsibilities quite effectively, but they fail to be well. Once people have reached a significant level of financial or creative success, they find themselves living behind a façade that they believe they must maintain in front of others. They feel alone and unable to confide openly in anyone about their personal doubts and unfulfilled dreams. They come to believe that they can remedy this disquiet by acquiring more "stuff."

For all of his professional achievements, Brian was not a success. He decided he needed to work at building a personal life that was as fulfilling to him as his professional life was. He also knew that he had the judgment to assemble a good support team for this project and enlisted me as his coach.

Brian's pursuit of success began with a "treasure map." In devising his map, Brian realized there were many promising paths ahead of him. He needed to think about which way to point himself. Brian selected a path toward getting more "stuff." Committed to following my client's wisdom, I helped him on his way. Brian was surprised to find that he did not like that path. Although he found baubles along the way, none was a treasure. Nothing he gained increased his joy.

After that epiphany, we went back to the map, and Brian made what I thought was a more promising choice. Brian sought the treasure of friendship. We planned his path, we prepared for the trip, we decided his traveling speed, and I set him on his way. As Brian's coach, I was the person at his checkpoints. Each week I made sure that his course was set and that Brian was on track. We re-evaluated his speed and we tracked his triumphs.

It wasn't long before Brian found treasure! He uncovered an old jewel where he least expected it, but he was finally prepared to recognize its value. He now saw that his brother was a great friend if he let him be. So we searched for a key to unlock that treasure. Brian soon had concrete plans with his brother. That led to plans with people he met while with his brother. Through these new social connections, Brian began to value himself as a person whose thoughts and dreams mattered. He awakened to the truth that his famous acquaintances were people he served and idolized but not people who added any value to his life. He also came to realize that he, in many cases, set that pattern of interaction. Once Brian had stable friendships that satisfied him, he planned to remake the relationships with the people he had not treated as friends but as idols. Brian came to believe he had something to gain from personal relationships.

As a psychologist I teach the difference between mental illness and mental health. I direct change. As a coach, I collaborate with my clients as they direct their own growth. Brian did not know he was not well. Why then, did he come to me? Brian came in search of "more." Often, successful people like Brian come seeking more money, a bigger title, or a route to more "stuff" with less effort. These are all valid goals, and they are results I help people to attain. But on the way, one must acquire wellness because without wellness, you are unlikely ever to have enough.

For our Readers: What is your key to unlocking your authentic happiness?

WRIGHT

What difference does coaching really make?

DRUCKER & RANDAZZO

When all is said and done, when the coaching calls are ended, when clients' goals are met, I have the chance to look back at the whole process. Coaching offers a method for pursuing change, but as a coach I do not change you, the client. You learn to change yourself. My role as coach has been to partner with my clients on their journeys of awakening, to help highlight revelations, and to help my clients stay on their chosen paths.

The words of Galileo ring true for the coaching process, "You cannot teach a man anything. You can only help him to find it within himself."

The rewards of coaching come in the form of discoveries and awakenings. Wellness is the big reward. As a collaborator in the change process, I aim to help you recognize your inner spirit and learn how to be true to it. It is only then when you can achieve authenticity, and authenticity is the most fundamental element that you need to create optimism and wellness in your life. Where do optimism and wellness come from? They come from you, and developing them is like going on a treasure hunt. I help you to find the map, the treasure chest, and the key, but only you can open the lock.

ABOUT THE AUTHORS

JANE L. DRUCKER, PhD, PCC, is the founding explorer behind "Inner Journeys Coaching." Dr. Drucker brings more than thirty years of professional experience to developing wellness in the caretaking community. Additionally, Jane is a seminar leader and author.

Dr. Drucker's background is in counseling psychology and special education. She is a Professional Certified Coach member of the International Coach Federation.

Jane serves on the Board of Trustees of the Colony Theatre in Burbank, California, and volunteers widely in her community.

Dr. Drucker believes we are on Earth to show up as our authentic selves and to be of service to others.

JANE L. DRUCKER, PhD, PCC
3950 Laurel Canyon Boulevard, #1152
Studio City, CA 91614
ijcoaching@aol.com
www.InnerJourneysCoaching.com
(818) 754-2622

CATHARINE E. RANDAZZO, PhD, FACFEI, PCC, creator of Coach2Rewards, is a believer in the power of optimism for positive change. Catharine has been coaching, leading seminars, and speaking professionally for more than twenty years. She has helped people in many walks of life, from across North and South America, Asia, and Australia to acquire and use optimism to discover the rewards of their unique lives.

A Professional Certified Coach with the International Coach Federation, Dr. Randazzo is also a clinical-, forensic-, and neuro-psychologist. She practices in the beautiful horse country of New Jersey where she also rides.

Happiness is a choice that requires effort at times™. Catharine invites you to make that choice.

CATHARINE E. RANDAZZO
PhD, FACFEI, PCC
Coach2Rewards
PO Box 5226
Clinton, NJ 08809
coachCER@aol.com
www.Coach2Rewards.com
(908) 410-0952

CHAPTER SIXTEEN

Develop a Disciplined Life

An Interview with . . . **Dr. Denis Waitley**

DAVID WRIGHT (WRIGHT)

Today we are talking with Dr. Denis Waitley. Denis is one of America's most respected authors, keynote lecturers, and productivity consultants on high performance human achievement. He has inspired, informed, challenged, and entertained audiences for more than twenty-five years from the boardrooms of multi-national corporations to the control rooms of NASA's space program and from the locker rooms of world-class athletes to the meeting rooms of thousands of conventioneers throughout the world.

With more than ten million audio programs sold in fourteen languages, Denis Waitley is the most listened-to voice on personal and career success. He is the author of twelve non-fiction books, including several international bestsellers. His audio album, "The Psychology of Winning," is the all-time best-selling program on self-mastery. Dr. Waitley is a founding director of the National Council on Self-Esteem and the President's Council on Vocational Education. He recently received the "Youth Flame Award" from the National Council on Youth Leadership for his outstanding contribution to high school youth leadership.

A graduate of the U.S. Naval Academy Annapolis, and former Navy pilot, he holds a doctorate degree in human behavior.

Denis, it is my sincere pleasure to welcome you to *Stepping Stones to Success!* Thank you for being with us today.

DR. DENIS WAITLEY (WAITLEY)

David, it's great to be with you again. It's been too long. I always get excited when I know you're going to call. Maybe we can make some good things happen for those who are really interested in getting ahead and moving forward with their own careers in their lives.

WRIGHT

I know our readers would enjoy hearing you talk about your formative years. Will you tell us a little about your life growing up in the context of what you've achieved and what shaped you into the person you are today? Do you remember one or two pivotal experiences that propelled you on the path you eventually chose?

WAITLEY

I believe many of us are redwood trees in a flowerpot. We've become root-bound by our earlier environment and it's up to each of us to realize that and break out of our flower pot if we're going to grow to our full potential.

I remember my father left our home when I was a little boy. He said goodnight and goodbye and suddenly I became the man of the family at age nine. My little brother was only two, so I had to carry him around as my little shadow for the ensuing years. To this day my kid brother has always looked at me as his dad, even though there is only seven years' difference between us. He'll phone me and ask what he should do and I'll tell him, "I'm your brother, not your father!"

Our dad was a great guy but he drank too much and had some habits that took a firm hold on him. He never abused me and always expected more from me than he did from himself. I had a push-pull—on the one hand, I felt inadequate and guilty when I would go to succeed but on the other hand, Dad kept feeding me the idea that he missed his ship and I'd catch mine. The only thing I could do to get out of that roller coaster impact was to ride my bicycle twenty miles every Saturday over to my grandmother's house. She was my escape. I would mow her lawn and she would give me such great feedback and reinforcement. She told me to plant the seeds of greatness as she and I planted our "victory garden" during World War II. She told me that weeds would come unannounced and uninvited—I didn't need to worry about weeds coming into my life, they didn't even need to be watered.

I said, "Wow! You don't have to water weeds?"

"No," she replied, "they'll show up in your life and what you need to do, my grandson, is model your life after people who've been consistent and real in their contribution as role models and mentors."

She also told me that a library card would eventually be much more valuable than a Master Card. Because of my grandmother reading biographies of people who'd overcome so much more than I was going through, I thought, "Wow! I don't have any problems compared to some of these great people in history who really came from behind to get ahead." I think that was my start in life.

I went to the Naval Academy because the Korean War was in force and you had to serve your country, so the best way was to run and hide in an academy. If you earned enough good grades you were put through without a scholarship or without money from your parents. Since my parents didn't have any money, it was a great way to get a college education.

I became a Navy pilot after that and learned that if you simulate and rehearse properly you'll probably learn to fly that machine. But much of it has to do with the amount of practice you put into ground school and into going through the paces. As I gained experience being a Navy pilot, I eventually decided to go on and get my advanced degree in psychology because I wanted to develop people rather than stay in the military. I pursued a program where I could take my military and more disciplined background and put it into human development. That's basically the story.

I earned my doctorate, I met Jonas Salk, and Dr. Salk introduced me to some pioneers in the behavioral field. Then along came Earl Nightingale who heard just a simple taped evening speech of mine and decided that maybe my voice was good enough, even though I was a "new kid on the block," to maybe do an album on personal development, which I did in 1978. It surprised me the most, and everyone else also, that it became one of the bestsellers of all time.

WRIGHT

Being a graduate of Annapolis and having been a Navy pilot, to what degree did your experience in the Navy shape your life and your ideas about productivity and performance?

WAITLEY

David, I think those experiences shaped my life and ideas a great deal. I was an original surfer boy from California and when I entered the Naval Academy I found that surfer boys had their heads shaved and were told to go stand in line—everyone's successful so you're nothing special. I found myself on a team that was very competitive but at the same time had good camaraderie.

I realized that I didn't have the kind of discipline structure in my life that I needed. I also discovered that all these other guys were as talented, or more talented, than I was. What that shaped for me was realizing that the effort required to become successful is habit-forming. I think I learned healthy habits at the Academy and as a Navy pilot just to stay alive. To perform these kinds of functions I really had to have a more disciplined life. That set me on my stage for working more on a daily basis at habit formation than just being a positive thinker only.

WRIGHT

In our book, *Stepping Stones to Success,* we're exploring a variety of issues related to human nature and the quest to succeed. In your best-selling program, *The Psychology of Winning*, you focus on building self-esteem, motivation, and self-discipline. Why are these so crucial to winning and success?

WAITLEY

They're so crucial they're misunderstood. I think especially the term "self-esteem" is misunderstood. We've spent a fortune and we had a California committee on it—we formed the National Council on Self-Esteem. What has happened, in my opinion, is that self-esteem has been misused and misjudged as being self-indulgence, self-gratification—a celebrity kind of mentality. We've put too much emphasis on the wrong idea about self-esteem.

Self-esteem is actually the deep down, inside the skin feeling of your own worth regardless of your age, ethnicity, gender, or level of current performance. It's really a belief that you're good enough to invest in education and effort and you believe some kind of dream when that's all you have to hang onto.

What's happened, unfortunately, is that we've paid so much attention to self-esteem it's become a celebrity and an arena mentality kind of concept. Most people are "struttin' their stuff" and they're celebrating after every good play on the athletic field, whereas, if you're a *real* professional, that's what you do anyway. A real professional is humble, gracious, and understands fans. I think that what we've done is put too much emphasis on asserting one's self and believing that you're the greatest and then talking about it too much or showing off too much in order to make that self-esteem public.

The real self-esteem has two aspects: 1) Believing that you deserve as much as anyone else and that you're worthy. Someone may look at you and tell you they see real potential in you. If you can feel that you have potential and you're worth the effort, that's the first step. 2) The second step is to start doing things to give you confidence so that when you do something and learn something it works out and you'll get the self-confidence that comes from reinforcing small successes. That combination of expectation and reinforcement is fundamental to anyone who wants to be a high achiever. That's what self-esteem is really all about—deserving on the one hand and reinforcing success in small ways to get your motor running and feel the confidence that you can do better than you have been.

Fears crop up and get in the way of our motivation. In my case I was afraid of success. Nobody had ever succeeded in our family and because they hadn't, I felt inadequate to be able to succeed. Whenever it would show up around the corner I would think, "Well, this is too good to be true for me—I don't deserve that." So I would feel a little bit doubtful of my abilities. When I would succeed, there would be an attendant, "Yelp!" I would feel because I would not believe I deserved what I had achieved.

I think fear is the thing that gets in the way of our motivation because we're all motivated by inhibitions and compulsions. You should be motivated more by the result you want rather than the penalty. That's why I've always said that winners are motivated by reward of success rather than inhibited or compelled by the penalty of failure. If you get this conviction that you're as good as the best but no better than the rest—I'm worth the effort, I'm not Mr. Wonderful, I'm not the center of the universe but I can do some things that I haven't done yet—and then apply this motivation to desire rather than fear, that is when self-discipline comes into play.

I'd have to say, David, I could spend the entire interview on self-discipline because I missed it as one of the most important ingredients in success. I've always been a belief guy, an optimism guy, a faith guy, and all the self-esteem things but I think, as time went on, I forgot the amount of discipline it takes for anyone who is a champion in any endeavor. I think I'm back on that track now.

WRIGHT

I can really appreciate the Flame Award you won from the National Council on Youth Leadership for helping high school leaders. I've got a daughter in college and I know how difficult and important it is. But in some circles, self-esteem has gotten a bad reputation. For example, in many schools, teachers won't reward high achievers for fear of hurting the self-esteem of others in the classroom. Many people feel this is not helpful to these children.

In your opinion, where is the balance between building healthy self-esteem and preparing kids and adults to cope and succeed in a competitive world?

WAITLEY

I think that there has to first of all be some kind of performance standard. A good example is the Olympic Games. The idea of the Olympic Games is to set a standard that you've tried to live up to in your own way as a world-class person, realizing that there can only be so many Olympians and so many gold medalists and so on. I think, on the one hand, it's really important to have standards because if you have a standard, then you have something tangible to shoot for or to measure against.

I think there's a problem, however, in that only so many people can be medalists and win medals at the Olympics. One of the reasons that the high jump bar, for example, is set so that everyone can jump over it the first time, is to experience the feeling of success that first jump produces. The feeling of success is working in the competitor before the bar is raised to world record height and to much higher standards than even the normal Olympian.

I'm one who believes in testing. It's difficult when you have a "No Child Left Behind" concept because many times today we're going pass/fail. We're moving people up through the grades regardless of their performance simply because we don't want them left behind and therefore feeling that they're not able to function simply because they can't compete with some students who've been given many more opportunities to succeed than others.

Having said that, I'd say that healthy self-esteem is gained by giving specific stair-step, incremental, bite-sized pieces; perhaps there needs to be several different standards set. Usually the grading system does that and the point system does that where you have someone who has a four point three grade average because of all the extra credits they're taking. Then you have those with a three point eight and then those who are just barely passing. Unfortunately then, what that does is enable only a few people to get into universities and the others have to go to community colleges.

What I will have to say, however, is that we in the United States have to be very careful that we don't dumb down or lower our standards for excellence in our schools. Traveling as much as I do, I have discovered information about this. For example, there are 300 universities in Beijing alone—just in one city in China. The way it goes internationally is that the public schools in Japan, for example, are much more competitive than the private schools. If you're in Japan going to a public school, you have to really perform up to the highest standards in order to ever think of qualifying for any kind of university. You'd have to go into a vocational school if you didn't compete in higher standards in public schools in Japan. The same thing is true in Singapore, China, and in the developing nations.

We have a situation brewing here where we've got global developing countries with really high standards in English, mathematics, engineering, and science. And we have educators in the United States who are more concerned about making sure that the self-esteem of an individual doesn't get damaged by this competitive standard. I think we have to maintain standards of excellence.

I wish we had kept dress codes in schools. I have found schools that have marching bands. A certain amount of uniformity not only encourages greater athletic performance but higher academic standards as well. The same is true globally. There's an argument that if you put kids in uniforms, you're going to limit their creative thinking. The truth is, if you can standardize the way people appear in their style, then you can focus more on substance—their experience, imagination, contribution, and their study. The core of an individual rather than the surface of an individual can be developed much better. It would be great if we could combine the more disciplined aspects of the developing countries with the more entrepreneurial, creative, free-thinking aspects of our society, which means we're critical thinkers (i.e., you throw us a problem and we'll try everything we can possibly think of to solve it). In the developing countries they'll use a textbook or an older person's experience rather than using critical thinking.

We're very entrepreneurial here in America, but I'm very much concerned that our standards are being lowered too much. If we're not careful, we're going to take our place in the future as a second-rate educational country and therefore forfeit the idea of being a technological and market leader.

WRIGHT

I also hear grumbling about motivation. I'm sure you've seen business people roll their eyes a bit at the mention of listening to "motivational" tapes or

CDs. Some tire of getting all hyped up about change or sales goals, for example, only to lose their excitement and fail to reach their goals. Are they missing something critical about the nature or application of motivation?

WAITLEY

I really believe they are, David. I think they're missing the idea that what you *want* in life turns you on much more than what you *need* in life. Too often business managers even today focus on the hard skills because they say that the other skills are "soft skills." Well, there's no such thing as a hard or soft skill because you can't separate your personal from your professional life anymore. You get fired more for personal reasons—for being late, for your habits, for you hygiene, your behavior, your anger. This idea that technical training as opposed to motivation is the way to go is misguided.

I have found that employees are excited and are full of desire and energy because management listens to them, reinforces them, is interested in their personal goals, and is interested in keeping them inspired. That inspiration is what we remember. So, when we go to a meeting we remember how we felt about the meeting, not the specifics of the meeting.

I think this emotional component—keeping people's energy and desires foremost and doing a desire analysis of employees rather than just a needs analysis—is very, very important. I often think this is lost in the idea that we're giving a pep talk, or a quick fix, or a Band-Aid when, as Zig Ziglar has mentioned so many times, "Motivation is like taking a bath. You take a bath every day and you might say why take a bath—you're going to get dirty anyway." But the very nature of doing it, and doing it on a habitual basis, makes this positive energy continue to flow and motivation becomes habit-forming. I think you need a lot of it to keep these habits of excellence or else you'll just be running scared—you'll be afraid not to do well because you'll lose your job.

Believe it or not, we have a lot of employees in America who are working harder than they ever have before so they won't be fired. That's not really the way to go after a goal—constantly looking through the rear view mirror trying to cover your behind.

WRIGHT

If you don't mind, I'd like to change the focus a little to the topic of self-discipline. People seem to know what they should do and how they should change, but they just can't discipline themselves to take the necessary steps to do so. What is the secret to becoming a disciplined person?

WAITLEY

I think the secret is to get a team, a support group, a mastermind group because not only is there safety in numbers but there's accountability in numbers. When we are accountable to one another to maintain a certain standard of discipline, it's much easier to work out if someone else is getting up at six-thirty in the morning with you. It's much easier to have a support group if you're interested in maintaining a healthier diet, for example, because the temptations are irresistible to procrastinate and to fall off the wagon. That's why I believe you need a team effort.

It also has to be understood in an immediate gratification society that there is no "success pill" that you can swallow. There is no quick way to get rich and get to the top. There is this steady ratcheting to the top and that's why I think leaders need to say it's going to take us about a year to get any permanent change going. So, I think we should all understand there may be a little dip in productivity as we start this new program of ours—a little dip at first and a little uncertainty—but over time, over about a year, we're going to become like an astronaut or an Olympian. We need to engrain these ideas so they become reflexive. It takes about a year for an idea or a habit to become a reflex. This idea of being able to do it in twenty-one days is misguided. I don't think it takes twenty-one days to learn a skill. It may take twenty-one days to learn to type, it may take twenty-one days to begin to learn a skill, but it takes a year for it to get into the subconscious and take hold.

I think we have to learn that discipline is practicing on a daily basis for about a year so that it will become a habit—a pattern—that will override the old inner software program.

WRIGHT

I'm a big believer in the greater potential of the individual. I remember a fellow—Paul Myer—who helped me a lot when I was a young guy. He was in Waco, Texas, with a company called Success Motivation Institute. You may know him.

WAITLEY

I know him very well. Actually, he's one of the icons and pioneers in this entire field. He and Earl Nightingale were the first ones to ever have a recorded speaking message other than music. Earl and Paul were pioneers in audio recording and I have still a great respect for Paul. I spoke for his organization some time ago.

WRIGHT

He personally helped me a lot when I was younger and I just really appreciated him. In your book and program, *Seeds of Greatness*, you outline a system for nurturing greatness. Will you give us a brief overview of this program?

WAITLEY

It's taken me thirty years to get this thing to where I want it. I wrote the book twenty years ago titled, *Seeds of Greatness*, and sure, it became a bestseller but so did *One Minute Manager, In Search of Excellence, Iacocca,* and every other book at that time. I have trouble keeping that thing pumped up.

Over the years I've found that *Seeds of Greatness,* for me, has been a system. What I've had to do is go back through all the mistakes I've made as a family leader. I knew I was a father and not a mother *and* father so I had to find a mother who was also a good clinical psychologist and who had worked with every form of behavioral problem. We put our efforts together so that we had a man and a woman as family leaders with clinical and other experience who could give parents or leaders of the day a certain track to run on where they could coach their small children and adolescents on a daily basis.

I provided a perpetual calendar that gives coaching tips of the day—what I call "sign on the day" and "sign off the day"—for parents to use to communicate with their kids. Then I had to put nineteen CDs together—audio tracks—that covered these "roots and wings," which I would call the "core values" and the more motivational or, if you will, ways to set your kids free.

The idea of parenthood should be to lay the groundwork, make it safe to fail an experiment, and then send them off on their own as independent, not codependent, young adults so they can reach their own destiny. I divided it into "roots of core values" and "wings of self-motivation and self-direction" and tried to balance the two so that whether you're from a blended family, or a single parent family, and whether you're structurally religious or whether you're spiritually religious, it would work, regardless of your personal core belief system.

I'm very happy that we've finally put together a self-study program that can be taught by the authors or by people who are licensed facilitators. It's something that a family leadership group could take and work on their own at their own speed by watching, listening, interacting with their kids, and using a combination of a written book, the audios, the DVDs, and this coaching calendar to maybe put it all together so that over a period of six months to a year they might be able to effect some changes in the way they interact with their kids.

Sounds great! Before our time runs out, would you share a story or two about your real life coaching and consulting experiences? I know you've coached astronauts and Super Bowl champions as well, haven't you?

Well, I have. I've been lucky to work within the Apollo program in the simulation area. I found that simulation prevents failure of the first attempt. In other words, if you're going to go to the moon and they're going to shoot you up a quarter of a million miles up and back in a government vehicle, you had better have your rehearsal down and really pat. The astronauts teach you that the dress rehearsal is life or death. The Olympians teach you that at the moment you go to perform, you need to clear your mind so you can remember everything you learned without trying—you develop muscle memory and reflex.

Twenty-one years ago when Mary Lou Retton was doing the vault, she needed a nine point nine five to tie the Romanian for the gold medal in women's all around gymnastics. I asked her what she was thinking about when she went to vault and she said, "Oh gosh, I guess what everyone thinks about—speed, power, explode, extend, rotate, plant your feet at the end. When the pressure is on I get better just like drill. 'Come on, Mary Lou, this is your moment in history!'"

I thought, "Wow! That's not what everyone thinks. What everyone thinks is, 'Thank God it's Friday,' 'Why me?' 'Don't work too hard,' 'Countin' down to Friday,' 'Looking to five P.M.,' 'Romanians are better trained, probably on steroids,'" So I get these stories of Olympians who have internalized this wonderful running the race in advance and simulating as well.

I guess the one story that I'll share is about a ten-year-old boy. In about 1980 this boy came to a goal-setting seminar. He told me that none of the people who had paid their money were really working on their goals. They were really thinking about what they were going to eat and golf. I gave him a work book and told him to go back and do what they were supposed to do and write down his abilities and liabilities, what he was going to do this year and next year and five years from now and twenty years from now. He got all excited because he thought it was this wonderful game that you can play called, Write the Future, or Describe the Future.

So he ran back and worked on the project and forty-five minutes later he astounded the adults in the audience by saying he was earning money mowing lawns and shoveling snow so he could go to Hawaii on the fourteenth of July to snorkel on the big island of Hawaii's Kona Coast. Then he said next year he'd be eleven going into the fifth grade and he was going to build models of what was going to be a space shuttle and he was going to begin to learn more about numbers and math. In five years he'd be fifteen and as a tenth-grader. He said he would study math and science because he wanted to go to the Air Force academy—he was all excited about that. I asked him what he was going to be doing in twenty years and he said he'd be an astronaut delivering UPS packages in space.

I forgot all about him and twenty years later, sure enough, I saw him on the *Today Show* as they showed a picture of an astronaut on a tether line pulling the satellite into the bay of the space shuttle. I thought, "My gosh! This kid did what I only talk about in the seminars." He was a living, breathing example of someone who was focused on this. I said to my family, "Look at what he did!" And they said, "What have *you* been doing for the last twenty years?" I said I was a goal tender. They told me I should be a goal achiever too.

WRIGHT

What a great conversation. I always enjoy talking with you. It's not just uplifting—I always learn a lot when I talk with you.

WAITLEY

Well, David, I do with you as well. You've got a great program and you do a lot of good for people who read and watch and listen. I think you give them insights that otherwise they would never get. I'm just grateful to be one of the contributors and one of the members of your global team.

WRIGHT

It has been my sincere pleasure today to visit with a truly great American, Dr. Denis Waitley.

Denis, thank you for taking so much of your time to share your insights and inspirations for us here on *Stepping Stones to Success*.

WAITLEY

Thank you very much, David.

ABOUT THE AUTHOR

DENIS WAITLEY is one of America's most respected authors, keynote lecturers and productivity consultants on high performance human achievement. He has inspired, informed, challenged, and entertained audiences for over twenty-five years from the board rooms of multi-national corporations to the control rooms of NASA's space program and from the locker rooms of world-class athletes to the meeting rooms of thousands of conventioneers throughout the world. He was voted business speaker of the year by the Sales and Marketing Executives Association and by Toastmasters International and inducted into the International Speakers Hall of Fame. With over ten million audio programs sold in fourteen languages, Denis Waitley is the most listened-to voice on personal and career success. He is the author of twelve non-fiction books, including several international bestsellers, *Seeds of Greatness, Being the Best, The Winner's Edge, The Joy of Working*, and *Empires of the Mind*. His audio album, "The Psychology of Winning," is the all-time best-selling program on self-mastery.

DR. DENIS WAITLEY

The Waitley Institute
P.O. Box 197
Rancho Santa Fe, CA 92067
www.deniswaitley.com

CHAPTER SEVENTEEN

Steps to Living a WEALTH STRONG® Life

An Interview with . . . **Evonne Ryan**

DAVID WRIGHT (WRIGHT)

Today we're talking with Evonne Ryan. Evonne is founder of the Certified Financial Coach™ program. We are talking with her about steppingstones to living and building a wealth-strong life and learning how money serves a person's wealth versus the person being a servant to his or her money. Building on her background as a teacher, lobbyist, author, speaker, Emmy[1] award-winning television producer, and financial radio commentator, Evonne Ryan dedicated five years of her life (from 2003 to 2009) creating tools, programs, and systems to empower individuals in their financial life. She is so committed to helping people live an empowered life that in 2007 she founded the company WEALTH STRONG® International to spread the word. Then in 2009, she co-founded Fin LAB (Financial Literacy and Beyond) to move financial literacy training to a new level.

A wealth-strong life—it may not be what you think. Evonne believes the work of Certified Financial Coaches and the use of financial literacy tools are critical for people to build wealth in the future and to be prepared for the future. She tells us of her concern about what she calls the "Retirement Shortfall Tsunami," which is projected to happen in the next twenty years. She

---

[1]EMMY Award, St. Louis Chapter, National Academy of Television Arts and Sciences 1988.

tells us that more than seventy-seven million Baby Boomers will be faced with retirement during that period, but there is research showing a window of opportunity for individuals to make informed financial decisions.

How do we all prepare for possible events in the future that may dwarf the economic crises of 2008–2009? Evonne tells us there are answers. The answers lie in changing a person's relationship with money and through finding financial clarity. She discusses an exciting new concept to help people become clear about where they are— the Unbiased Resource Sustainability Longevity Age (URSLA™). URSLA is *one number* that tells people, with a 90 percent probability, how long their financial resources will last given what they are doing and planning today. Evonne states that the URSLA number is to a person's retirement what the FICO is to a person's credit. As she states, "The URSLA gives clarity to what has been a mystery for too long. Once people know this one number, they may make more rational decisions to correct direction and build on the wealth they already have in their life."

"You can put your relationship or your focus in any area of your life on hold for a while and you probably will be okay. But if you have a terrible relationship with money, *money will eventually own you*. You need money to survive. So you need to have the right relationship with money so it can serve your life instead of becoming your master."

All of this information seemed overwhelming at first, so I started my interview with Evonne beginning with step one.

Evonne, what is the first step to building a wealth-strong life? I know you are excited about URSLA, but it is only one step in building what you call a "wealth-strong life." Let's start at the beginning.

EVONNE RYAN (RYAN)

STEP ONE: *Understanding or developing a positive relationship with money.*

The fact is that when it comes to money, people feel shaky. In fact, many people feel shaken to their core. We all know the statistics—stress is the number one cause of sickness in the United States and money is the number one cause of stress. The first step to building a wealth-strong life is to give yourself permission to stop suffering when it comes to subject of money.

To do that, you need to take yourself out of your stories about why everything has happened. The truth is, things that have happened in the past have happened and there is little you can do about it now. When we make the reality into a story about us, we are making life much harder than it needs to be. This first realization is one of the reasons I founded the Certified Financial Coach program. Some of my former clients were so much into their story about what had happened in the past that they couldn't move to make a difference in their future. They also were afraid to face financial reality.

WRIGHT

What is a relationship with money? How would someone like me define what my relationship is with money?

RYAN

A person's relationship with money can be defined in different ways. People may use money unconsciously, ignoring their relationship with it. They can see money as the full definition of wealth (making what it can buy the focus of their life) or they can see money as a utility (this is where it serves their wealth). Defining money as a utility is the best way to start on the road to a healthy and powerful relationship with money.

The problem we have at this time in our society is twofold. Many people don't define money in the "utility" role *and* even if they do, they may not have a relationship with money that allows them to focus on the true wealth in their life.

I talk to people about Eleven Areas of Wealth and Human Strength (EAWAHS). These are areas of life that contribute or bring full life satisfaction throughout a person's life. A Certified Financial Coach is trained to help people transform their relationship with money and wealth so they can find clarity, ease, and grace in that relationship. These coaches are trained to help people move forward quickly, so they can address the next issue most people have: *fear*. This is a very critical issue that must be resolved for people to have a healthy relationship with money.

WRIGHT

A person's fear? What exactly does that mean? How do you address a person's fear and what would that mean to me if I were a client?

RYAN

Let's face it—the area of finance can be scary. Most people—even those who are financial professionals—fear they are missing something or that they don't know enough. The fear of not knowing stops people from taking steps they may need to take to grow money for their retirement or even protect themselves when something is going wrong.

Research shows there is lack of knowledge about the most basic financial information in large segments of the population in our country. Annamaria Lusardi (Dartmouth College and Harvard Business School) and Olivia S. Mitchell (director of the Pension Research Council of the Wharton School at the University of Pennsylvania) stated in the January 2007 *Journal of the*

National Association for Business Economics, "Our review reveals that many households are unfamiliar with even the most basic economic concepts needed to make saving and investments decisions. Such financial illiteracy is widespread: the young and older people in the United States and other countries appear woefully under-informed about basic financial concepts [like compounded interest and percentages]), with serious implications for savings, retirement planning, mortgages and other decisions . . ."

To take the first step and start living a wealth-strong life, we need to address the fear. To accomplish this we need to get over the fear of not knowing and find ways to educate ourselves. Let's face it—if you are a Baby Boomer or older, you probably didn't learn these things in school. We need to help people take steps to fill in the gaps we all have around financial issues. One of my biggest causes of concern is when a client walks into my office and tells me he or she has this or that investment or the person is using a financial strategy because a financial advisor or trusted friend said, "Don't worry, I will take care of it, I know what is best for you."

When working with clients, financial professionals need to provide educational components for them. This doesn't mean individuals don't need to take personal responsibility for their wealth. We developed Fin LAB, which is a way people gain simplified hands-on experience to help them make sense of both financial literacy concepts and wealth concepts. This is the reason we call it Financial *Literacy* And *Beyond.* It doesn't matter what program a person utilizes, there are plenty out there. The key is to feel okay about admitting there are gaps in our financial education and to become empowered to expand our knowledge. If a financial professional belittles a client for asking questions or ignores clients' need for information to help them become more financially aware, the professional is not working in the best interest of the client.

WRIGHT

So are you advocating that people take care of their finances themselves? Again, if I were in this position and had all this education, wouldn't I be able to take the next steps without help?

RYAN

Well, it is interesting that you ask this question. Let me tell you a story. I had a wonderful client (I will call her Mary) who came into my office and was truly quite brilliant in the area of finance. She was in need of solid financial strategies and was seeking a professional to help her handle her finances. She was in her sixties, had several degrees, and was going back for a master's degree in the area of civil engineering. Needless to say, her life was very busy.

Mary was a great client. We worked diligently developing powerful strategies for her portfolio. Each time we met, she would ask for a compilation of books, articles and Web references regarding what we discussed. While it was fun to meet with Mary, suddenly it seemed something was not quite right. After we met several times and she kept asking me how this or that was accomplished, I stopped and asked her this question, "Mary, are you interested in taking the test to become a Registered Investment Advisor to manage money for clients?"

She looked at me with a surprised look and said, "What do you mean?"

"Mary," I replied, "at the rate we are going, if we keep meeting like this, you can take my position and then work with clients. From what I have calculated, if you have read all the materials I have given you and researched all the Web sites I've referenced, you have put in at least fifty hours of time in research. The reason people hire professionals is because they don't want to have to know every detail of the investment process. My typical client doesn't have the time to do all the work alone. I will partner with you as much as you wish, but I just need to know if this is the best use of your time or energy."

With that, Mary's face lit up and she smiled. "Oh," she said. "I get it. This is what I am hiring you to do for me!" With that we both laughed.

That was a great lesson for Mary and for me. Just as I didn't want to know every detail about how Mary would build a bridge, Mary realized she didn't need to know every detail of how to manage her own money.

WRIGHT

So the difference is in understanding versus doing it all yourself, right?

RYAN

STEP TWO: *Developing an educated gut and empowering yourself through knowledge.*

I say to clients, "I want you to develop an *educated gut*, which means you can identify what you don't know because you have a sense of discomfort about it. When your gut is telling you that you are cloudy in your understanding of a concept or about how something works, this indicates that you need to be empowered with knowledge about it."

In other words, know that you don't know and
be willing to take the step of learning.

I think it is imperative that people work with someone or partner with a friend or family member who will help them from a place of non-judgment. We are all beginners at something. Standing up and saying, "Hey, I am unfamiliar with that, let's review what that means!" or "I am sorry, but until I can get clear answers to a list of questions I will send to you, I can't move forward," is a definite step to a wealth-strong life. If someone makes a crack because you don't know something, just say, "Hey, it is what people who are wealth-strong do—they keep asking questions until they are clear about financial concepts that affect them."

WRIGHT

Makes perfect sense to me—I understand it. So now I essentially know what I don't know and am willing to take the step of learning. Where do I go from here?

RYAN

Okay, now you are ready for a great next step. **STEP THREE:** *Financial Awakening.*

WRIGHT

Wait a minute; isn't that what I just did?

RYAN:

Well, yes and no. You see, you have opened your eyes to the fact that you didn't know certain things that may have been a gap in your financial education. You learned concepts or facts about how something works. Or you may have found out what a certain concept may mean in a case study or a specific segment of your life. Now it is time to take an even more powerful step—learning your own financial reality. That means putting your own numbers and plans together in an integrated way to see how it all relates to your financial picture.

WRIGHT

Wow, that could be scary. Some people might not be ready for that step for a long time.

RYAN

Well, let me explain something very important about the steps in this process. It is important that you don't see these as steps on "elephant rocks."

WRIGHT

Elephant rocks! What are elephant rocks?

RYAN

Oh, I am sorry. I spent twenty years in St. Louis, Missouri, and about eighty miles southwest is a park called "Elephant Rock State Park." The rocks are extremely large (as you can tell by the name). Go on the Internet and look it up. The point is, if you are using elephant rocks as steppingstones, you will definitely have great difficulty.

WRIGHT

I guess I am showing my ignorance about state parks!

RYAN

That shows we are all beginners at something!

But, David, here is something to know: When taking the first steps to living a wealth-strong life, you have to be easy on yourself. Take short steps and feel free to move around a bit. If you just stay in one place, trying to master something completely with a disregard of everything else, you tend to lose balance with the rest of your life. It is like standing in one place for a very long time—you tend to lose an understanding of what is going on in the rest of the world. Sometimes you need to just take little steps and move back and forth. Life is not a chunk—it is to be lived moment by moment. That means you have to experience wealth *while* you are building wealth. (Whoops, I guess my coach training is showing.)

WRIGHT

That is perfectly all right. So people may work on step one—their relationship with money—for a while, then gain some financial knowledge as the next step. Then they would move on to this step, Financial Awakening, right?

EVONNE

Yes. You are seeing that the steps are all interrelated. And that is the key. When we talk about Financial Awakening, we are becoming awake to a bigger picture. But you have to have some basic mastery of the first two steps to feel comfortable with this one. It is like someone who has been focused to go back and forth from one rock in a stream to another and then the person stands up and looks around. He or she sees the big picture and realizes that what he or she has been focused on (or sometimes fixated on) is just one small piece of real estate.

Now, that is not good or bad, but we all need to keep perspective and that means we need to find our bearings once in a while. When we are back to being focused on living our daily life, we also know we are still moving toward our chosen destination. And that is what this step is all about—standing up and seeing how what we have been learning and experiencing relates to where we are in the big picture. It is the process of getting your bearings. When you think about it, it isn't *that* scary, is it?

WRIGHT

Well, when it comes to a seeing the large financial picture, it depends . . .

RYAN

Let me finish that thought for you. I would say it depends on who you are on the journey with, and the instruments (guidance system or tools) you are using to find your bearings. And that is something you get to choose. Choosing the right guide is one decision; choosing great tools to use on your journey is another decision. Here comes another story. Are you game?

WRIGHT

Yes, this is fun. I feel as though I am on an adventure!

RYAN

Let me tell you the story of URSLA. I know it sounds like someone's name, but it is a tool developed to help you find out where you are in your financial life.

As we discussed, I founded the Certified Financial Coach program in 2004. One of the things I stressed to coaches in training was that they needed to help clients work with financial professionals in a planning capacity. I recommended to the coaches that they tell clients to visit with several financial professionals so they could decide with whom to work on the financial planning and investment side.

Something very curious happened. When the clients started visiting with different financial professionals who said they did financial planning, the clients came back confused. They would come back to their coaches and say, "Wait a minute. These three, four, or five different financial professionals all told me different stories about how I was doing and what my danger was about running out of money." One professional might run a scenario and say, "Oh, you're going to be okay" and another professional would say, "Oh, you're in real big trouble." There was no benchmark upon which people could confidentially know where they stood financially.

WRIGHT

In other words, people were having trouble finding real answers that made sense.

RYAN

There is no doubt that the financial area is very complex and, for the majority of people, it is confusing. People have always said that planning is an art, not a science. This can be a real problem for individuals who need to know where they stand.

Our coaches asked for our help because clients started saying they wanted to find a starting point that made sense. By having a base from which to start, they could then visit various financial professionals and gauge how the financial professional might help them.

We were asked to give direction, but I felt uncomfortable recommending specific Web sites or software. The problem we encountered was that each software program we tested measured different things and came up with different results depending on the variables measured and the underlying assumptions in the calculations. Just as our clients found it frustrating to end up with different answers to the question, "how long will my money last?" we felt the same frustration after our testing. Consumer software just didn't give us the confidence about what was being measured and how the answers were derived.

In an effort to fulfill the request for help, we undertook the task of finding at least three consumer software programs our coaches could recommend to their clients. Our criteria for the software was that it had to be easy to use, have relative accuracy, be inexpensive, and be without bias. It seemed an impossible task. In the end, we couldn't come up with a single program to recommend, let alone three.

Because I had been a co-founder of a company that developed a software program using artificial intelligence to manage money (resulting in our firm's CFO receiving national recognition for positive performance), I felt it was necessary to dig deeper to answer the call for something that worked for our coaches. People on the Board of Directors at WEALTH STRONG agreed. We felt it was important to have a program that would help a coach's client find a base number—a place of clarity from which he or she could stand and move forward. This program also had to find the base number quickly and easily.

WRIGHT

Well, that is a pretty tall order.

RYAN

Yes, it is. But think about it—the ability for people to find clarity regarding their finances is a global need. There needs to be a benchmark that is unbiased, easy to understand, and that holds the most common financial variables affecting the general population (many of which were missing from other measurements.) Also, it needs to be inexpensive and something all people can easily use.

With that, the concept for URSLA (the Unbiased Retirement Sustainability Longevity Age) was born and we funded the continued development of a tool to measure it. URSLA is the concept that we created by setting up a not-for-profit organization whose goal is also to determine and hold the standards that define the URSLA benchmark. We then pushed to make sure the software tool (WHEN-Score) that WEALTH STRONG was developing measured the exact URSLA criteria and exceeded the standards we developed in an *unbiased* way.

The WHEN-Score tool was developed over a three-year period to measure URSLA. The financial cost was high and additional staff hours (paid and unpaid) were involved in the design, programming, and initial release of the software. Each input data cell and underlying data set was questioned, researched, and scrutinized. In refining the WHEN-Score tool we continually asked, "How does this or that variable relate to the majority of Americans approaching retirement?" and "What variables can the client control on his or her own?"

WRIGHT

So, that's why URSLA was developed and why WEALTH STRONG built the WHEN-Score?

RYAN

Yes. We undertook this effort because we saw the need for an unbiased tool to fill a critical gap. The URSLA and WHEN-Score software were created for our coaches *and* to help the millions of people needing to find their financial grounding and needing clarity. Later, we realized the URSLA was similar in nature to Fair Isaac Corporation (FICO). We see that URSLA is to the financial industry what the FICO is to the credit industry. The FICO measures credit worthiness, the URSLA (the number being a person's age) measures financial sustainability and longevity.

WRIGHT

Okay, I have another question: what happens once a person knows this number?

RYAN

Well, statistics show the biggest fear people have is that they will run out of money when they can't do anything about it. So once you know your number, you're on higher ground. You can look around and say, "Ah, if my URSLA is ninety-two, do I feel comfortable with the idea that I may run out of money at the age of ninety-two?" Regardless of the answer, by having this valuable information, a person is now empowered and can begin making informed financial decisions.

You see, being wealth-strong isn't about money, it is all about wealth. It is also about recognizing the wealth you already have in your life and then determining what wealth you want enhanced, and what really doesn't serve you as you continue on your life journey. So knowing your URSLA is terrific tool that enables you to know where you are *now*. Then you look at the money you are spending and determine if it is bringing value to your life, specifically what dollars are and are not bringing value. You can also go to financial professionals and ask them, "How can you help me extend my URSLA?" In other words, you work with them to not only help your financial resources grow, but also to find ways to have your financial resources last longer.

WRIGHT

So let me see if I can put this in context: I am on this journey or adventure called life, and on this journey, once in a while I need to get my bearings. URSLA helps me to do that, right?

RYAN

Exactly! You see, you can't get a sense of where you are going by watching only your feet or by standing inside a canyon. Going back to our journey metaphor, you can't see or plan to get to your destination if you're so focused on today's details that you don't take a few minutes to get the big picture. You need to figure out the landscape, get your bearings, and then see if you have enough provisions to make the full journey and not run out of the essentials before you arrive.

So, how do you get your bearings? That is how URSLA helps; it is a tool that gives you a clear picture of what you are doing today (what you are spending today, planning today, and your total financial picture today) and how long (to what age) your financial resources will last. Once you have your bearings, you can begin making immediate adjustments.

So here is an example: By taking the time to get my bearings now, I might find I have a 90 percent probability that my resources will last until the age of ninety-two. What if I believe I may be one of the increasing demographics of people living to one hundred? I want to feel confident that my resources will last an additional eight years so that I can continue to enjoy my life. Now that I have my URSLA, I can begin making sound decisions. I can lighten my load by taking on less debt, possibly determining to downsize my home or lifestyle, or reevaluating how my money is serving me. Also, I can pick up more provisions (work a little longer to ensure I will have additional income later in life). Additionally, I may take fewer risks with the provisions that I have, knowing that retirement planning is more about risk management than asset management, or I may decide to change some plans along the way. I'll at least evaluate what I truly want in life.

I don't want to be surprised at the age of ninety-two years that I'm out of money and have to go live with my children or try to rely on government assistance.

URSLA is the beginning. I get my bearings and figure out the landscape, so that I can plan now to get where I want to be. Maybe that is only two steps over from where I am now or it might be somewhere far away.

Wherever you go, you want to be sure that when you get there, and along the way, you are living a wealth-filled life.

WRIGHT

Okay, so I am on this adventure called a wealth-strong life and I know I want it to continue. I may want to be living in another country or maybe I just love my home town or somewhere else. Evonne, I guess I need clarification here. When you say "destination," what exactly do you mean?

RYAN

The question is not for me to answer. You see, you know the answers yourself. You know how you feel when you are in that place where you are at peace and life is really good. It is inside you—the physical location of your wealth-filled life is something you, of course, choose. It probably has something to do with money, but when you really think about it, it is more about other factors—things revolving around EAWAHS (those Eleven Areas of Wealth And Human Strength I previously mentioned) and "ways of being" that bring true wealth to your life.

But we are getting a bit off track; we are talking about why, instead of how to actually accomplish the step of Financial Awakening. That is done by first finding your URSLA and then taking on the simple task of accepting your current situation from a state of non-judgment, without guilt, blame, or shame. When you run your URSLA, you are like a scientist—an observer—just looking at the facts and how they fit together. If you can do that without making the results a judgment about yourself and what you have done—right or wrong—you are able to move forward and make a real difference in life. Now, David, do you think, under the right circumstance that is possible?

WRIGHT

Well, Evonne, you said it before and I think it makes sense that you need to have the right guide. So is that where the Certified Financial Coach comes in?

RYAN

Exactly. And there are other professionals who are trained in helping with the URSLA tool. They are being trained to stay in a place of non-judgment and from the heart of an educator. There are some terrific guides out there.

WRIGHT

What is the next step? Having the right outlook, learning enough to take responsibility, and awakening to your own financial reality are great first steps, but that is not enough to make sure a person avoids the Retirement Shortfall Tsunami you talk about.

RYAN

You are so right, David. It isn't enough. And this is where we start having fun. We look at the wealth we already have and we look at the possibilities.

STEP FOUR: *A time for decision making and taking action.*

I already mentioned EAWAHS and it is important for people to realize and build on the wealth and strength they already have in their life. It is great when you see how much wealth you already have and how much you have already accomplished in your life. Nothing breeds success like the success you already know you have.

Now you start to understand your own power. With that you know, you are capable and ready to take total responsibility for moving forward. You decide the most important pieces of how you define true wealth in your life and determine what is most important and what you want to build on. Then you begin developing scenarios around the things in your life that you want to enhance.

WRIGHT

Are you having any fun along the way?

RYAN

Fun is the name of the game—fun, peace, joy—if you don't have those, how can you really have true wealth? And part of the fun is putting money on the hot seat.

WRIGHT

Okay, now *that* I have to see.

RYAN

We help people create what is called a *Money Flow Effectiveness Index* and also a *Life Satisfaction Index*. Using this, you see how money is serving you! It is an enlightening experience to put money under the microscope. Is it doing its job? If not, we need to whip it into shape in order for it to serve us!

WRIGHT

Interesting . . .

RYAN

Yes, Step Four is where it really gets interesting. It is about building the quality of your life, which includes determining what positive actions to take to maximize the wealth you currently have in your life, enrolling others in making it happen, setting up benchmarks, and monitoring feedback systems.

In our Fin LAB we even created a game to help families learn how to do that. It is called *Journey to Life Satisfaction* and it teaches families how to expand their view of money, communicate with each other, and see how they can stand on common ground around money decisions. Now, I think that is truly empowering.

WRIGHT

This sounds really different. You have a goal for people to have a new experience with money.

RYAN

Well, I think it is time for people to stop being in such a weird place about money. We as a society have been too focused on it as something that runs our life or we try to ignore it because it is too painful to think about. We don't discuss it as a family in a way that empowers us or builds our ability to experience wealth together.

So let's be in a different space and put it in the place where it is meant to be; it is truly there to serve our purpose. It needs to be seen as a utility throughout our life and as being our trusted servant.

WRIGHT

That surely is a different way to look at it.

RYAN

David, that also means we need to take care of it. If it is to serve us, we need to make sure we don't do things that ignore it, abuse it, or waste it. And if we can truly take the steps we have outlined here we get to Step Five.

WRIGHT

What is that?

RYAN

STEP FIVE: *Setting up reinforcement and celebration systems.*

It is the best part. It includes setting up reinforcement and celebration systems to continue building a wealth-strong life, continuing to build core strengths, and reinforcing the success of others. You feel that you have reached your destination when you are living the *wealth-filled legacy* you continue to create in your life, your community, and in the world.

You never stop moving growing and loving life because you see how amazing the journey has been and now *you* get to be the guide and spend more time helping others.

The key throughout this wealth-strong life of ours is moving forward with a sense of purpose, clarity, and peace. You know, David, you said it—it is not steppingstones on a journey, it is taking steps while on an incredible adventure.

We have been on this incredible adventure all our lives but we haven't been able to reach outside ourselves to see it. Now we can. It all starts with that first steppingstone and the willingness to be at peace with ourselves no matter what happens. So David, what do you think?

WRIGHT

Well, I think this time has been very valuable! I have learned a lot about money and I really appreciate this time you've taken with me answering these questions. You seem to have it all worked out. I certainly wish that I had spoken with you twenty or thirty years ago.

RYAN

I love that you said this because we talk about this Retirement Shortfall Tsunami often. There are so many people who have come in for coaching with us who feel very hopeless saying, "I messed it up; I didn't do certain things at a certain time in life, and now I am not sure if there is anything that can correct it."

In late 2006, Dr. Moshe Milevski at the University of Toronto published "Asset Allocation and the Transition to Income: The Importance of Product Allocation in the Retirement Risk Zone," showing there is a twenty-year period when decisions and strategies that people make are the most important decisions for retirement. That twenty-year period is the ten years prior and the ten years after retirement happens. The strategies that people make during that twenty-year time period make all the difference for financial longevity. So the key is that people don't give up by saying, "Oh, I'm too old to really think about this. I guess whatever happens is going to happen." They need to know that strategies *do* make a difference. It is not only about asset allocation. Of even greater importance is actively employing various timing and strategies (timing of what you do, risk management of your investments, and distribution plans for income) that make all the difference in the world. I encourage people to work with someone in a strategic way and build on the information disclosed in your URSLA.

It is only by realizing that you, yourself, need to choose to have a healthy relationship with money, that you, yourself, choose what your wealth-filled life looks like, and that you, yourself, are in charge of your financial future. Only then, will you see the wealth-filled life you have and be able to continue to live your life in a wealth-filled capacity.

WRIGHT

I must say, this conversation has been very enlightening. I am serious about that, and I'm sure it will be enlightening for our readers as well.

Thank you for being with us today on *Stepping Stones to Success*.

RYAN

Well, thank you, David, for the opportunity to share this exciting information.

WRIGHT

Today we've been talking with Evonne Ryan. She is the founder of the Certified Financial Coach program and recently became an adviser, serving as a benefit specialist for federal employees.

ABOUT THE AUTHOR

EVONNE RYAN has spent the last three decades serving clients, building systems, and creating software to serve people committed to living a wealth-strong life. She founded the Certified Financial Coach™ program, building on her background as a teacher, lobbyist, author, speaker, Emmy award-winning television producer, and financial radio commentator. Evonne dedicated five years of her life to creating tools, programs, and systems to empower individuals in their financial life. She is so committed to helping people to live an empowered life that in 2007 she founded the company WEALTH STRONG® International to spread the word and then in 2009 co-founded FinLAB, Financial Literacy and Beyond, to move financial literacy training to a new level.

She founded these companies building on her commitment to enable people to transform their relationship with money. Her dedication led to the development of unbiased technology tools to clarify people's understanding of their financial situation. For more information on the tools and concepts covered in this interview visit the WEALTH STRONG Web site or contact Evonne directly using the information below.

EVONNE RYAN
5944 S. Kipling, Ste302
Littleton, CO 80127
303-904-3177

CHAPTER EIGHTEEN

Your Life Purpose: Do You Have a Clue?

An Interview with . . . **Helen Paulus**

DAVID WRIGHT (WRIGHT)

Today we're talking with Helen Paulus, known as the "Out of the Box Mentor~for Life." She is co-author of several books with best-selling authors including Deepak Chopra, Dr. Wayne Dyer, Steven E, David Riklan, and Helene B. Leonetti, MD. In addition, Helen is the Founder and Principle of Out of the Box Institute and Out of the Box Financial Services. As the Out of the Box Mentor~for Life, Helen created and facilitates highly successful teleconference programs titled *Zero to Abundance in 77 Days* and *Zero to Out of the Box in 35 Days*. Dr. Helene Leonetti considers Helen's programs and techniques to be "legendary" and added, "Helen has the courage to call you on your dysfunction and gently and lovingly nudge you with laser sharpness to your potential." Both programs assist you in uncovering and living your life purpose and how your purpose relates to life balance, vision, values, and goals. Helen believes that when we know our purpose or our unique talents and gifts, life flows with ease and grace.

As a professional member of the National Speaker's Association she created and facilitated a number of programs including a stress and money program, which she taught at Lehigh University. Other certifications include meditation and yoga acquired through the Chopra Center for Well Being and financial and estate planning. Helen plays and resides with her two beautiful daughters in Allentown, Pennsylvania.

Helen Paulus, welcome to *Stepping Stones to Success*.

HELEN PAULUS (PAULUS)

Hi David, how are you?

WRIGHT

I'm just fine.

So what were your steppingstones to success?

PAULUS

My personal steppingstones to success were presented to me in 1997 through three very loud wake-up calls. I was married and working with a broker/dealer for twenty-three years. In December of 1996 I made the decision to leave my broker/dealer. In January of 1997 my whole being shifted as I came to realize I would no longer work with the family that *was* Lincoln Investment Planning. By June of 1997, I separated from my husband of twenty-three years with a protection from abuse order. In July of the same year I entered a sixteen-day rehab for prescription drug abuse. These steppingstones are a significant part of the journey that motivated me to where I am today.

I left rehabilitation with the daunting awareness that my best thinking led me here and it would be crucial for me to listen to some other ideas from this moment to prepare for a future with purpose. Someone suggested meditation, so I discovered and ordered a Wayne Dyer meditation tape. In my early experience of meditation practice, I often fell asleep. Since that time, my meditation practice has grown as I have continued to grow and it continues to be my ultimate steppingstone to success.

WRIGHT

What is meditation?

PAULUS

Meditation is a vehicle that assists us in relieving stress but is so much more. It is a spiritual journey that allows us to remember who we really are and what we really want.

My personal practice of mediation is being quiet—being still. I'm a certified meditation instructor and I'm also a certified yoga instructor through the Chopra Center for Wellbeing. I was a Type A personality and worked eighteen hours a day, six days a week. I began to realize that I *needed* to be still. This is when I first started meditation and I would fall asleep. For many people, meditation is jogging or walking in the park. For others, meditation is simply sitting in nature. Gardening is meditation for some people. So you can see that meditation takes on many forms and it depends on the person's personality as to what form is going to serve him or her best in the moment.

The form of meditation that serves my higher purpose is stillness. I use a primordial sound—a mantra—as my focal point to release thoughts as they come up and to connect me to the universal field where all things are possible. Being still will serve anyone. There is a biblical quote from Psalm 46:10: "Be still and know that I am God." One could actually use this as a mantra.

WRIGHT

Why meditation?

PAULUS

Meditation helps us to uncover thoughts that are blocking our vision. Negative thoughts are stressors stored in the body. Through stillness they arise to awareness where they are witnessed and released. In my practice, I imagine a cloud passing through and as it passes, I lay the destructive thoughts on top of this willing cloud. In its place, clarity rises to the surface of my awareness and I enjoy the surprise and synchronicity that is my life. *That* is why I meditate—I recognize a synchronistic life that is my birthright. It is everyone's birthright.

In 1978, Robert Keith Wallace completed a ten-year study of meditators. He evaluated their biological age using three indicators: blood pressure, hearing, and near-point vision. He found that the subjects who meditated for five years or less were on average five years younger biologically. The subjects who meditated more than five years were on average twelve years younger biologically (e.g., sixty-year olds had forty-eight-year-old bodies).

Now, I let myself *be*. In the act of *being* we start to experience deeper clarity regarding our life and we wake up to this wonder every day! Looking and feeling younger may be the benefit that starts you on the practice of meditation. In time, however, I believe the magic and wonder is what will keep you practicing.

WRIGHT

Like everyone else, I am so busy. How do you suggest I find the time to meditate?

PAULUS

David, we don't *find* the time, we *make* the time. My personal opinion on that (and if you ask Deepak Chopra, I believe he will tell you the same thing) is you can't afford to *not* take the time to meditate. Meditating twice daily for twenty minutes is the most precious time-enhancing gift I give myself. As I mentioned, I used to work six days a week, eighteen hours a day. Today I work four days a week, seven hours a day, including one evening. Rarely will I work on the weekend, and most of the work I do today is fun and feels more like play than work. Meditation transformed my reality. I find that I get more done and many things get done without my active participation.

As an example, I'll have a thought to ask Liz, my colleague, to call a company with an order and to my amazement, the item shows up that day. There was a time, before meditation, when I would not have recognized this synchronicity. Meditation creates awareness.

Prior to meditation, I believed I had to do *everything!* Now, I embrace the very magical events that happen daily. In the *Zero to Abundance in 77 Days* and *the Zero to Out of the Box in 35 Days* programs, meditation is the single most important process. It leads to living a balanced, abundant, successful life filled with passion and wonder.

My friend has a medical practice that requires her to see twenty-five patients a day and she makes the time to meditate. She recognizes the value of meditating daily, as it allows her to be fully present with each of her patients. If *she* can make the time, all of us can!

WRIGHT

So how do you define success?

PAULUS

Success is being awake, aware, and grateful. I enjoy all the synchronicities that happen on a daily basis. Socrates said, "Wisdom begins in wonder." I discovered having fun and being in the wonder of it all are two life expressions I like to live by.

WRIGHT

What is life purpose and why do you feel everyone has a life purpose?

PAULUS

I believe every soul who comes into this reality comes with a unique talent and special gift to share with the world. The Universe resembles a huge puzzle and we are the puzzle pieces. Once we recognize what our unique talents and gifts are, our puzzle piece fits into place. Presuming we make the choice to act on our discovery, our action creates a ripple effect. This decision to live your life purpose and leaves room for others to do the same—your action acts as permission.

I think the unrest and the chaos in the world could find balance if everyone on the planet recognized that they have a unique piece to contribute here. Once they tap into their talent, that's when the *real* magic begins.

WRIGHT

I have a daughter who is a junior in college right now, and she's so concerned with what she's going to do when she gets out and what kind of a job and all of that. I may be advising her wrong, but in my life I didn't know what my purpose was until I got out and did a few things. Am I advising her incorrectly?

PAULUS

As a parent, I know you only want what is best for your daughter. I believe all of us, including our children, know what they are here to do. Our life journey takes us down many roads and I believe all of them serve us in some way.

When teaching students at Lehigh University, I found most of them were on a journey someone else chose for them. They shared they were at Lehigh, not because of a desire to be there, but because their family members were alumni. Actually, *their* passion was to do something else—a vet, therapist, or a teacher—not an engineer. I instructed them to make a list of all the things they were good at and they also loved to do. That list is the beginning of uncovering their purpose, passion, and unique gifts they came to share with the world. I also suggested that if they share this information with their parents' eyes, they would more than likely support their journey. This was the result for one of my students.

If you wish, I would be happy to walk your daughter through a few exercises. Please invite her to give me a call.

WRIGHT

I can almost hear our readers as they are reading this chapter asking the question, so I'll ask it for them: what if my purpose has nothing to do with what I'm doing now?

PAULUS

Your purpose *always* has something to do with what you are doing now. Utilizing my own life as an example, I participated in a unique meditation designed to connect me with what I came here to do. This guided meditation slowly and purposefully took me back in five-year increments of time. Eventually, I found myself at the approximate age of five. I was a project child, moving from one dilapidated building to the next, often moving on a Sunday to beat the rent.

As the oldest of six children it was often my responsibility to get food on the table. I remember thinking at this tender and impressionable age that I wanted to do something that helps people to not have to live like this. Sure enough, I went into retail for a while and I was in cosmetics. I did all kinds of things, went down a few different paths; all of it was helping people in some way, shape, or form. Then I went into financial planning, which of course is helping people manage their money. Now I'm doing these programs that help people uncover their purpose.

Everything I did from the beginning until the present moment developed the tools necessary for living my purpose. What I did then served me then. What you are doing now is serving you now. When you see your purpose, you see the connection.

WRIGHT

How did you discover or uncover your life purpose?

PAULUS

Well, the meditation journey to my five-year-old heart assisted in the development of the following purpose statement: My purpose is to wake up every day learning and growing and to be around other people who are also learning and growing. I developed a mission statement for my financial planning business without a fully conscious connection to my *life* purpose. I find it interesting that it sounded like this: to assist others in being totally independent without dependency on anyone else. This was a primary and common goal I heard repeatedly from most of my clients in financial planning.

Then more recently, I was moved in the direction of mentoring and coaching people in the area of their purpose, vision, and values and I followed that path. Meditation gave me the courage and clarity to "follow the yellow brick road."

WRIGHT

So what benefits did you receive through the practice of meditation?

PAULUS

My life became synchronistic and I recognized that every day things came to me when I needed them. In the past, I thought I had to make them happen. The reality is that if we are having fun living our purpose, life flows with ease and grace.

By the way, my number one value is to have fun. When considering anything that involves my time and talents, I ask myself, "is this going to be fun?" Meditation brought that to me. Life inspired. Now that's a benefit.

WRIGHT

What does synchronicity mean to you?

PAULUS

Synchronicity means I am awake and aware of all the magic that happens every single day. It is when I think to call a client and the phone rings. Synchronicity means that on some level we are taking care of details without direct involvement. There is an energetic alignment that goes on that we are not always privy to. Synchronicity is knowing you don't have all the cards, just the one you need.

WRIGHT

Don't you ever worry about where the money will come from if you're living in your purpose having fun with the wonder of it all?

PAULUS

If we're doing what we came here to do, the money will follow. There is a book titled, *Do What You Love and the Money Will Follow,* by Susan Jeffers. The book is really wonderful; it is timeless, relevant, and I highly recommend it.

WRIGHT

So tell me a little bit about your life purpose.

PAULUS

The purpose of my life is to inspire others to embrace and express their life purpose—their unique talent and their special gifts—with fun, love, and laughter.

My favorite week in the *Zero to Abundance in 77 Days* teleconference (that's eleven weeks) is the *purpose* week. Everyone develops and writes a purpose statement. There is magic in having a statement that encompasses what you believe you're here to do. And I know when people are writing their purpose statements whether or not it's really resonating with them. We rework it until how it *feels* is how it *sounds*. The purpose of *my* life is to inspire others to embrace and express their life purpose with fun, love, and laughter. And I have the pleasure of playing out my life purpose daily with fun, love, and laughter. Always fun. Always love. Always laughter.

WRIGHT

I could argue that you could use that purpose in almost anything you do that you enjoy and have fun.

PAULUS

That's exactly right—a purpose statement is all-encompassing. That's why I advise people not to limit the expression of their purpose statement. I suggest they try not to be too specific and be very broad about what really inspires them.

WRIGHT

Well, what an interesting conversation. You've given me a lot to think about here today and I really appreciate all the time you've taken with me to answer these questions for our book.

PAULUS

You're welcome. Feel free to have your daughter give me a call.

WRIGHT

I will.

Today we have been talking with Helen Paulus. Helen's programs help her clients uncover and live their life purpose and how their life purpose relates to balance, vision, values, and goals. She believes that when we know our purpose, life flows with ease and grace. It sounds like she knows what she's talking about to me, at least I'm listening to her.

Helen, thank you so much for being with us today on *Stepping Stones to Success.*

PAULUS

You're welcome. Thank you, David.

HELEN PAULUS is known as the "Out of the Box Mentor~for Life." She is co-author of several books with best-selling authors including Deepak Chopra, Dr. Wayne Dyer, Steven E, David Riklan, and Helene B. Leonetti, MD. In addition, Helen is the Founder and Principle of Out of the Box Institute and Out of the Box Financial Services. As the Out of the Box Mentor~for Life, Helen created and facilitates highly successful teleconference programs titled *Zero to Abundance in 77 Days* and *Zero to Out of the Box in 35 Days*. Dr. Helene Leonetti considers Helen's programs and techniques to be "legendary" and added, "Helen has the courage to call you on your dysfunction and gently and lovingly nudge you with laser sharpness to your potential." Both programs assist you in uncovering and living your life purpose and how your purpose relates to life balance, vision, values, and goals. Helen believes that when we know our purpose or our unique talents and gifts, life flows with ease and grace.

As a professional member of the National Speakers Association she created and facilitated a number of programs including a stress and money program, which she taught at Lehigh University. Other certifications include meditation and yoga acquired through the Chopra Center for Well Being and financial and estate planning. Helen plays and resides with her two beautiful daughters in Allentown, Pennsylvania.

HELEN PAULUS
The Out of the Box Mentor~for Life
314 North Marshall Street
Allentown, PA 18104
610-770-9972
helen@outoftheboxinstitute.com
www.outoftheboxinstitute.com

CHAPTER NINETEEN

The Heart of Success: "Perfect Size System"

An Interview with . . . **Gail Fallon McDonald**

DAVID WRIGHT (WRIGHT)

Today we are fortunate to have Gail Fallon McDonald as a contributing author for our discussion about the steppingstones to success. Gail is a personal and business success coach who assists her clients in achieving immediate momentum toward the execution of their goals. Gail is the creator of *The Heart of Success Perfect Size System.*

She has taken her own personal experience with weight loss strategies combined with her experience as a trainer, consultant, and speaker and designed a unique practice that encompasses a pragmatic system for success. The design of the *Heart of Success Perfect Size System* is designed not only to clarify what has prevented you from achieving *and* maintaining your perfect size goals in the past, but to also provide a direct means to attain that.

Gail, welcome to *Stepping Stones to Success.*

GAIL FALLON MCDONALD (MCDONALD)

Thank you David, it is a pleasure to be here today and share the steps that I took to achieve my perfect size. I would like to begin by sharing a powerful story first.

Many years ago, people asked the great Michelangelo how he sculpted the beautiful statue of David. He simply and humbly replied that the statue was already there, he just chipped away the excess stone.

I would like to share with you and our readers how my excess weight was finally successfully chipped away and how that ultimately gave birth to the *Heart of Success Perfect Size System!*

WRIGHT

Yes, that is indeed a powerful illustration. It certainly sounds like you have had a major transformation. Tell us more Gail.

MCDONALD

It was a month after New Year's Day many years ago and, once again, I was miserable—I faced yet another failed New Year's resolution that I had held with so much hope and promise. I was a size twenty-four and considered morbidly obese. I was overweight and unhappy.

My struggle with my weight had been a lifetime challenge. If someone had asked me, I would have told them that it was my core issue—the one that controlled who I was in all areas of my life. My misery had become a constant companion. I had resigned myself to the fact that this was just my painful challenge in my life and that it would be with me forever. Diet pills, counselors, fad diets, support programs, hypnosis—I had tried them all and nothing had worked. I *hoped* that I would become a "not fat" person. I *hoped* that by osmosis I would let go of the weight and become happy. Sure, I had released twenty, thirty, and even more than forty pounds here and there, yet the pounds—the misery—always came back. Each time, I sank even deeper into my own private despair.

Sadly, my story is not unique. I hated the fat, I hated being fat, and I hated being a fat person. Most of all, I hated me.

In order to survive, I overcompensated in taking extra good care of my outward appearance. I would just get dressed and then do everything I could to try to forget about my body for the rest of the day. Now, since my body was with me all day that was not an easy thing to do!

As I talk about this with you now, waves of tremendous compassion for that woman wash over me now. That woman did not know that she was doing the very best she could with who she was or, to be more explicit, who she believed herself to be.

Interestingly enough, I had begun to have a nagging little voice inside of me telling me there was something inside of me that was blocking me. The key point here is it was inside of me. What was it? How could I unlock it? What was I to do? How could I have access? What specifically needed to change?

You know, David, it's said that when the student is ready the teacher appears. The exquisite nature of my longstanding pain, coupled with my growing awareness that both the problem and the solution were simultaneously within me, literally gave way to my breakthrough.

My first teacher appeared in the form of an NLP workshop that was geared to assist people break through their barriers to achieve the success they wanted. I heard the advertisement on the radio. The ad was about how our *limiting* beliefs concerning what we think is possible and how we view ourselves can actually prevent us from achieving our goals. I honestly felt as if it were a personal invitation to me alone! I pulled my car over and immediately called and booked my spot. Something had already shifted within me; I just intuitively knew that this would unlock what was blocking me.

> I have learned that if one advances confidently in the direction of his dreams, and endeavors to live the life he has imagined, he will meet with a success unexpected in common hours.
> — Henry David Thoreau

This workshop ultimately opened the door for me to walk toward my *perfect size* and freedom from the pain, misery, and conflict that had been my regular companion for over forty years!

I left this workshop with new core beliefs about the person I could be and that it was truly achievable. I also understood that I had been trying to create a new reality for myself from the same thinking and beliefs that had blocked me for so many years.

My identity had shifted along with my beliefs. The very foundation of my being was being rebuilt. Indeed, a major transformation was well underway.

The release of over seventy-five pounds and the sustained achievement of that release have birthed the identity of a woman I had only dreamed about.

Not only did my breakthrough allow me to release the seventy-five pounds of excess weight and maintain it, but I also established a powerful new identity. This new identity, coupled with my experience, created *The Heart of Success Perfect Size System*.

WRIGHT

What a powerful story that is Gail. I can sense your freedom and joy, not to mention the additional health benefits you have experienced as a result of your breakthrough!

Tell us about *The Perfect Size System.*

MCDONALD

Thank you, David!

Let's first begin with the presuppositions of the system. The basic definition of a presupposition is to *believe or suppose in advance.*

It's important to note here that it is crucial to move people out of blame and regret and into an understanding of the magnificent beings they are.

The five presuppositions in *The Perfect Size System* that set the stage for that to occur are:

1. **THE PROBLEM IS A SOLUTION.**

    The current problem is a solution to a former problem.

    One of my clients was told as a young child that to love yourself and think you are great was conceited, and it was not okay to stand out. So, as part of a coping mechanism and her solution to this problem, she gained weight to make herself less attractive. The extra weight she carried as an adult was the solution to the problem of a nine-year-old girl!

2. **BODY AND MIND ARE CONNECTED.**

    Chang the mind and change the body. You can eat all the right foods but if the mind is not aligned with the identity associated with the desired result, you will not be able to shift and sustain changes to your body.

3. **YOU CANNOT CREATE A NEW IDENTITY OUT OF RESISTANCE TO THE OLD.**

    Hating the present reality does not change the reality, it actually maintains the reality. Hating being fat does not create an energetic vibrant body. Each of us is a creative being, and creation does not occur in opposition to something else.

    Often we fall into the trap of focusing on what we don't want:

    - I don't want to be fat.
    - I don't want to be broke.
    - I don't want to be alone.
    - I don't want to feel deprived.

None of those thought forms have the power to create what you want. They actually support maintaining the unwanted present state *just as it is!*

 As has been said before—what you resist persists.

4. IF YOU COULD HAVE DONE IT DIFFERENTLY, YOU WOULD HAVE.

So often we berate ourselves for our *perceived* shortcomings and limitations. In hindsight, the right choices seem to have been so clearly marked. But the truth is that each of us made the best choices we could, given what we knew, what we saw, and our level of understanding at that time.

For years I struggled with the misery of self-loathing. All the while, I told myself that I should stop—I should do or be different. Yet, in reality, if I had had the ability to behave differently I would have.

5. THERE IS NOTHING WRONG WITH YOU THAT CANNOT BE CORRECTED BY WHAT IS RIGHT WITH YOU.

Each of us already has the resources we need to achieve what we desire. The key is to be able to access those already existing internal resources.

WRIGHT

It seems as if those presuppositions alone can actually begin to free people up from their own self-defeating patterns of self-judgment.

McDONALD

Yes, David, great point! The design of *The Perfect Size System* is to initially loosen the person's grip on the problem.

WRIGHT

Once that happens, what does *The Perfect Size System* address next?

McDONALD

As I have said, David, this system was created out of my own personal breakthrough and is based on the NLP Logical Levels of Change.

Let me begin by first briefly defining NLP. Neuro-Linguistic Programming (NLP) is a technology for success that uses your conscious and unconscious mind to identify vital factors to transform disempowering beliefs, meanings, values, and decisions, while increasing self-esteem, clarity, and a strong sense of self and purpose. NLP has a profoundly effective set of tools designed to produce the specific results you want.

WRIGHT

Great! Now, will you explain what you refer to as the Logical Levels of Change?

MCDONALD

Noted linguist Gregory Bateson points out that in the processes of learning and change there are natural hierarchies of classification. Our brains also have different levels of processing. When we are working to change our behavior, we need to address these different levels. These are called the Logical Levels of Change.

The five levels from lowest to highest are as follows:

1. ENVIRONMENT ⟶ Your external conditions
2. BEHAVIOR ⟶ Your habits
3. CAPABILITIES ⟶ Your skills and strategies
4. BELIEFS ⟶ What you consciously and unconsciously know to be true
5. IDENTITY ⟶ Who you unconsciously believe yourself to be

Changing something on the lower level sometimes can influence the upper levels, but changing something on the upper levels almost always has a significant impact on things at the levels below.

What I have found is that by making changes at the upper levels of belief and identity, change at the lower levels becomes much easier.

WRIGHT

That's very interesting. I wonder at what level people most commonly operate when attempting to lose weight?

McDONALD

That's a great question, David. Interestingly enough, most people work at the level of behavior or environment. They will try a new diet (behavior) or throw away all unhealthy food (environment). Yet that alone will not make the difference when the issue relates to identity level beliefs.

I want to point out here that *The Perfect Size System* does not tell you what to eat or how to eat.

The Perfect Size System is about uncovering your current identity and creating a new identity that supports your perfect size. This system reveals the beliefs that have kept you in that unwanted state and uses the belief revision process to change and replace those beliefs with supportive ones. The system assists you in developing capabilities and behaviors while managing your environment, all to support the healthy, vibrant, energetic "perfect size" you.

WRIGHT

This surely sounds very different from just another diet and exercise plan!

McDONALD

It absolutely is, yes. What is decidedly different is that this system recognizes that to truly adopt new behaviors and develop new skills you must have an identity and beliefs that support those behaviors.

An individual with an identity of being a fat person cannot develop the resources, capabilities, and behaviors of people who view themselves as energetic and healthy.

WRIGHT

That would make perfect sense. At the same time, I'm sure it's not always easy to recognize that.

McDONALD

Yes, that's very true. I had the identity and beliefs of a fat person, yet desperately wanted to have the behaviors and results of someone with a different identity. I didn't know or understand that I was pushing a rock uphill. Berating myself for my perceived shortcomings wasn't going to change anything.

> Our achievements of today are but the sum total of our thoughts of yesterday. You are today where the thoughts of yesterday have brought you and you will be tomorrow where the thoughts of today take you.
> —Blaise Pascal

I was doing nothing wrong. I was doing the very best I could. I was behaving consistently with my identity, which is to be expected. It was actually a huge relief when I really understood that!

One of the things I tell my clients who have struggled with weight for years is that even though you have an unconscious belief and an identity that has kept you where you don't want to be, the good news is that you don't have to stay there!

When I work with clients, I work with them initially on identity and belief level changes and then we move to the other levels. At each level, we have a Power Question to assist the client in focusing attention on the proper logical level.

1. IDENTITY ⟶ WHO AM I?
2. BELIEFS ⟶ WHAT DO I BELIEVE ABOUT MYSELF?
3. CAPABILITY ⟶ WHAT SKILLS AND STRATEGIES DO I NEED?
4. BEHAVIOR ⟶ WHAT NEW HABITS DO I NEED?
5. ENVIRONMENT ⟶ WHAT CHANGES CAN I MAKE IN MY ENVIRONMENT?

WRIGHT

This is so completely different from most other approaches—almost exactly the opposite. I can imagine that a person's identity is a crucial component in this process. Will you describe a bit more about the identity Logical Level of Change?

McDONALD

Yes, David, you are right on target. Identity is a most powerful steppingstone in the logical levels of change.

POWER QUESTION 1: WHO AM I?

Or more accurately, "What is my identity?" Each of us has an individual identity—an inner map of life and the world. This map is composed of our beliefs and experiences.

As NLP trainer Carl Buchheit says, *"Our inner maps of reality comprise most of what we deal with as human beings. These inner maps determine what is real and unreal, achievable and not achievable, believable and not believable for each of us. Understand another's map and you understand their world. Change the map and you change their world."*

Our maps, or our identities, enable us to make sense of our world and ourselves.

So often, we mistakenly assume our identities are static—fixed. But in reality, they are dynamic and vary, depending upon where you are, who you're with, what you do, and the feedback you receive from those around you.

As women, much of the identity we've adopted is based on appearance. For better or worse, many of us as women use our appearance as a measure of our value in society. Most of us have bought into the idea that a woman's value in society is related to her appearance. So appearance becomes the currency (or measure of value) for a woman. No one understands this better than women who have a weight problem.

For me, when I began my weight loss journey I had many identities—mother, manager, nurse, friend—but the identity that defined me most was that of a fat person. I want to mention here that I use the term *fat* because that was the exact term I used to describe myself. That identity described me and defined me, yet I simultaneously struggled and hated that identity with all my being.

More than anything, I wanted to rid myself of the excess weight. Even more so, unconsciously, I wanted *not* to see myself as fat. What I did not know at the time is that once we choose an identity, the identity chooses us.

WRIGHT

I can see how our identity shapes everything about us.

McDONALD

Yes it does, absolutely. Now I'd like to talk a little bit about how we experience our world and the part it plays in shaping us.

THE HUMAN EXPERIENCE:

The unconscious mind processes over two million pieces of information per second. Our conscious mind can *only* handle seven, plus or minus two chunks of information simultaneously. As human beings, we handle the discrepancy between our conscious and unconscious mind by using our ability to delete, distort, and generalize the information coming in.

The same processes of delete, distort, and generalize that enables us to make sense of all the sensory data that bombards our neurology is the same process that allows us to maintain our individual identities.

Once our individual identities are in place, they serve as filters for our experience and we tend to not even register information that is contrary to our identity.

Clients who come to me saying, "I am a depressed person" or "I am an unhappy person" must by definition not pay attention to the times when they are not depressed or are happy.

My identity was that of a miserable fat person. As a fat person I saw myself as fat. I thought about being fat. When I dressed, I dressed as a person who wanted to compensate for being overweight. When I chose relationships, I chose them wondering who was willing to be with a fat person. And when I ate, I ate as a fat person racked with guilt over every bite.

So from this unconscious space of identity, I would attempt to lose weight. And I would, but my very identity and ultimately my sense of safety meant I *had* to gain all the weight back. Why? Because when an identity has been formed from strong and powerful emotional experiences, our neurology will aggressively resist any changes to the identity. Our system responds as if our life is at stake.

My conscious mind wanted to lose weight and to be my perfect size, but my unconscious mind, driven by identity, acted like a thermostat and maintained the evidence of my life as a fat person.

> The biggest secret is that by defining our identity we define our life.
>
> —*Tony Robbins*

WRIGHT

So, how do people shift their identity?

McDONALD

Indeed, how do we shift our identity? How do we move from whatever identity we have now to an identity that supports our true desires?

The Perfect Size System teaches the answer.

Since the identity is composed of a series of beliefs about yourself and your world, when you shift your beliefs you shift your identity. This brings us to the next Logical Level—Belief.

WRIGHT

Very interesting, Gail. So tell us about the belief level, please.

McDONALD

Once my clients have an awareness of their identity and the impact that identity has on their lives, we then move to the next stepping stone in the Logical Level for Change—Beliefs.

POWER QUESTION 2: WHAT DO I BELIEVE ABOUT MYSELF?

What is a belief? Webster's dictionary defines a belief as, "A state or habit of mind in which trust or confidence is placed in some person or thing." Although that may be true, it doesn't begin to describe the impact our beliefs have on the quality of our lives. The beliefs we hold about the world and ourselves are the major determining factor in our lives.

The challenge for most of us, particularly women like me who have struggled with weight loss is the following:

- Our beliefs are often formed when we are very young.
- Our limiting beliefs are often created as a result of intense, painful, emotional experiences.
- Our beliefs by their very definition are assumed to be true.
- Beliefs rarely update on their own if at all.

In my work with clients (and on myself), I've uncovered a number of limiting and unexamined beliefs. These beliefs operate out of conscious awareness but they serve as filters in defining our experiences.

Some of these beliefs are:

- This is my cross to bear.
- Why start (losing weight) if you're just going to fail?
- I'll never reach my healthy weight goal.
- No matter what you do or how hard you try it won't work.
- My body will just not co-operate.
- I hate my body.
- Food = love.
- I'll never keep it off anyway.
- I'll feel deprived.
- It will be too hard to do.

> The thing always happens that you really believe in; and the belief in a thing makes it happen.
> — *Frank Lloyd Wright*

In many cases, the women with these beliefs were intelligent, beautiful, and sophisticated. Their conscious minds understood that their beliefs made no sense but their unconscious minds treated their beliefs as fact. And so the beliefs were logically false but emotionally true.

As I mentioned before, our beliefs operate under the radar. However, as we pointed out in the presuppositions of *The Perfect Size System*, "A current problem is actually a solution to a prior problem."

As humans, we struggle to give meaning to our experience. In the case of strongly held beliefs, the beliefs remove uncertainty and give us a way to provide meaning for our experience. Without beliefs to guide us and make sense, we may feel lost, confused, and unsafe.

As I mentioned previously, beliefs do not easily update, they may be grossly outdated, and they seldom change on their own. However, I have found that when we are able to acknowledge the "intended positive outcome" of the belief (like the nine-year-old girl I spoke of earlier who gained weight to avoid being too conceited), sometimes the belief will update, and the client is then able to access a more resourceful emotional state or make new choices. The idea of the intended positive outcome forms a major component of the Belief Revision Process.

The Belief Revision Process consists of a series of questions about the nature of clients' beliefs and seeks to uncover the intended positive outcome so clients are able to update the belief to a belief supportive of their new desired outcome.

What follows is an example of the Belief Revision Process from my work with a client, Helena, who had a belief that said she would always be a fat person.

Me: So what is your belief?

Helena: I'm always going to be a fat person.

Me: What lets you know it's true?

Helena: Because it's who I've been my entire life.

Me: When did you start believing that?

Helena: I don't know, I guess all my life.

Me: Was there ever a time when you didn't believe that?

Helena: (Pauses) Maybe, when I was a very young child.

Me: And what might have been going on for that young child when she adopted that belief?

Helena: I keep thinking about this memory when my mother took me to the doctor. The doctor told my mother that I was gaining too much weight and needed to stop eating so much.

Me: And how old was that young child?

Helena: Five.

Me: And so you've carried the belief of that five-year-old girl your entire life?

Helena: Yes.

Me: And why do you think that five-year-old girl adopted that belief?

Helena: I don't know, I guess she figured the doctor and my mom knew best.

Me: She thought they were right and knew best?

Helena: Yes, I guess so.

Me: Children tend to want their parents to be right because children love their parents. So by adopting that belief, what was that young child doing?

Helena: She was making them right. Oh my goodness, I've been making my mom right all these years!

Me: Yes you have. Many of us have spent our entire adult lives trying to either make our parents right or make them wrong.

Helena: Wow.

Me: Yes, and that little girl still lives inside you. Even after all these years, she is still, right now, trying to make her mother right. Here's what I want you to do: I want you to take a moment and go inside and thank her for her hard work.

Helena: Thank her?

Me: Yes, thank her because she did the best she could at the time.

Helena: (Closes her eyes. And then after a few moments opens them.) It's weird. I feel kind of sad and kind of happy at the same time.

Me: When we reconnect with ourselves in this way, we often feel mixtures of emotion.

Helena: Yes, and I actually feel somewhat lighter.

Me: So what was that belief you used to have?

Helena: (Hesitates) It was that I would always be a fat person. It's funny—it already doesn't feel as true.

Me: Now, what would happen if the belief wasn't true?

Helena: I think it already feels like it's not true.

Me: So what would happen if it wasn't true?

Helena: I guess it would mean I don't have to be a fat person. Wow! What a thought.

Me: Go on.

Helena: It's almost like being a fat person is one option among others .

Me: It's almost as if you can choose.

Helena: Yes, that's it exactly.

Helena and I worked again on several other beliefs. As we did so, she began strengthening her identity as a person who can choose her life.

Let me stress, clients gain the most value from the Belief Revision Process when working with a professional. However, many clients have been able to achieve excellent results working with a friend or alone with a notebook.

The process is as follows:

1. **ASK THE QUESTION:**

   "REGARDING MY WEIGHT, AND FITNESS GOAL, WHAT WOULD I LIKE?"

   ➤ Write down your answer in as much detail as possible.
   ➤ Note that what you want should be stated in the positive.
     EXAMPLE:
     I don't want to be fat = not stated in the positive.
     I want to lose twenty-five pounds = stated in the positive
   ➤ Describe what you would like in as much detail as possible.

2. **NOW ASK THE QUESTION: "WHAT STOPS ME?"**

   Note: Initially what will come to mind are things related to your environment.
   EXAMPLE:
   I want to lose weight, What stops you?

   - Not enough time to exercise.
   - Too busy.
   - Don't take time to eat.

   ➤ Write down all these factors
   ➤ Ask yourself again, *What would I like? What stops me?*

You want to continue the process until you uncover beliefs about yourself or the world. Beliefs involve statements about yourself and the world.

   EXAMPLES:

   - I'm not smart enough.
   - I don't know how.
   - I'm too old to have it be different.
   - I don't have enough willpower.
   - My fat keeps me safe.

It may feel uncomfortable to speak (or write) these things but I cannot stress enough the power of being able to speak the truth about what has been going on in your mind below the surface.

3. **NOTE THE BELIEFS ABOUT YOURSELF OR THE WORLD OR ABOUT WHAT IS POSSIBLE.**

4. **FOR EACH BELIEF, ANSWER THE FOLLOWING QUESTIONS:**

   ➤ What is the belief?
   ➤ What lets you know it's true?

> ➤ According to whom or what?
> ➤ When did you decide to start believing that?
> ➤ What would happen if it weren't true?
> ➤ Is that belief true in the world for everyone?
> ➤ Has there ever been a time when this belief hasn't been true?
> ➤ What would happen if the opposite were true?
> ➤ If the belief is true, then what does it mean about you, life, or the world?

5. **AS YOUR WRITE YOUR ANSWERS TO THESE QUESTIONS, NOTICE YOUR FEELINGS AROUND THE BELIEF.**

Many clients begin to notice a shift in the feelings of certainty that previously surrounded the belief.

6. **ASK YOURSELF THE QUESTION, "WHAT WOULD A PERSON NEED TO BELIEVE TO ACCOMPLISH THE GOAL I HAVE CHOSEN FOR MYSELF?"**

7. **IMAGINE YOURSELF WITH THAT BELIEF. SEE YOURSELF OPERATING WITH THAT NEW BELIEF WITH AS MUCH DETAIL AS POSSIBLE, AND NOTICE HOW YOU FEEL.**

After you finish step seven, go back and ask yourself about your original belief, and notice the changes you experience.

You may repeat this process as many times as you like. In so doing, you will begin to solidify new beliefs about yourself and release yourself from limiting beliefs.

After the Belief Revision Process, we then move on to our next steppingstone of Capabilities. Here we will begin work on the skills and strategies to support your new belief.

> Rule your mind or it will rule you.
> —*Horace*

WRIGHT

I can see why revising our identities and beliefs creates such powerful and dramatic changes.

McDONALD

Yes; they are the driving forces in all we do, think, and feel. This brings us to our next logical level of change, Capability. Capability refers to the skills and strategies we use.

POWER QUESTION 3: WHAT SKILLS AND STRATEGIES DO I NEED?

In the years prior to 2002, I had done what most of us who struggle with weight have done. I attempted to learn new strategies and new skills. I went to seminars, I read books, and I tried to learn the types of skills that would enable me to lose weight—and I failed, again, and again, and again. My fat person identity and my beliefs about being a fat person allowed me to start the food journal or the exercise plan or the new eating regime, but within a few weeks or a few months I would become too busy, too distracted, unmotivated, or in some other way unable to follow through.

But after the change in my belief and identify around being a fat person, I felt a renewed sense of energy and a new sense of belief about my ability to actually overcome this challenge.

The presenter at my NLP workshop stressed that upon leaving the workshop we *"Must, must* take immediate action" toward our weight loss goals! So as soon as I got home, I cleaned out my cabinets, dusted off the treadmill, and started exercising right away. I also started paying attention to what I ate and began eating a much healthier diet.

After forty-five days of working out and feeling hopeful, I got on the scale and discovered I had lost only five pounds. I was disappointed, yet because of the change in my belief structure instead of lapsing into despair, not only did I not gain the five pounds back, I realized, "Oh I get it—maybe I can't do this on my own. Maybe I need to find people who have been successful at this and do what they do."

What had begun to happen is that I knew I needed new Capabilities—new skills, new strategies. I joined Weight Watchers. Now, interestingly enough, I had been a Weight Watchers drop-out many times before. However, this time was different. I sensed that something profound had happened to me and I decided to embrace fully whatever the program offered. I actually followed the directions!

Individuals with a weight challenge tend to lack certain skills and eating strategies that those at their target weight take for granted. However, what I have noticed previously with myself and with my clients is a tendency to be self-critical and assume that the deficit in these skills is somehow an indication of fundamental shortcomings.

When you actually think about this, it is amusing. Proper eating habits are a skill—one that many of us (and most Americans) don't have. Each of us has skills we have spent years, in some cases decades, learning to acquire. For instance, carpentry skills, teaching skills, and professional skills all take time and practice. Yet we often brutally criticize ourselves when we discover there are certain weight management skills we lack.

WRIGHT

Explaining it that way, it does make perfect sense. It takes time to develop skills.

McDONALD

Yes, and it does require patience and perseverance!

WRIGHT

I imagine that there are other important skills one would need to develop.

McDONALD

Yes. One of the most important skills to be learned as part of *The Perfect Size System* is how to plan ahead.

Recently I read a profoundly validating account by Andrew Austin of the U.K. Mr. Austin is a clinical therapist who conducted an experiment to determine how individuals react to the need to plan their food. He wrote:

A few years ago, I tried an experiment. I booked a venue for a one-day weight loss seminar on a day when there would be no refreshments or catering facilities available. In addition, no nearby restaurants or shops. These seminars tend to attract both clients and therapists. Essentially, what I set up was an all-day situation whereby food and drink would not be readily available. I made this clear in the advertising and at the point of payment. I advised all attendees that they would need to bring their own packed lunch and drinks. And interestingly, what I predicted would happen did in fact happen. At the beginning of the seminar I asked for a show of hands of who had brought lunch or food and drink. Generally, as predicted, only the people in the room without weight issues raised their hands.

> It is impossible to behave consistently in a manner inconsistent with how we see ourselves.
>
> —*Unknown*

WRIGHT

What a fascinating experiment!

McDONALD

Yes, I was just like the non-planners in this experiment! Before I lost my weight, planning my food meant limiting myself. Planning my food meant I had to think about eating, and I liked to pretend I could avoid thinking about eating.

Weight Watchers taught me the value of planning my food, and so I teach my clients strategies on food planning.

Some of the additional skills we teach as part of *The Perfect Size System* are:

- How to specifically decide how you want to eat to lose weight
- How to establish a support network
- How to integrate exercise into a busy lifestyle
- How to stay focused on what you want
- How to deal with setbacks

 Information on these and other strategies can be found on my Web site: www.HeartOfYourSuccess.com

 However, let me stress again: *Strategies and skills alone are not the answer!*

The most significant work is done at the belief and identity level. However, after the work has been done at these levels, the new strategies and skills will help us to strengthen an identity that we can sustain and that will sustain us.

WRIGHT

Yes, I can see that, Gail. This is becoming so much clearer. I believe this brings us to the next logical level of behavior.

McDONALD

Yes. We now move to the next steppingstone in our Logical Level of Change–Behavior.

POWER QUESTION 4: WHAT NEW HABITS DO I NEED?

Let me pause for a moment and make the distinction between capability and behavior. In the logical level model, capability refers to your strategies and skills. Behavior refers to your action. I like to think of it like this:

CAPABILITY = the knowledge and skills

BEHAVIOR = habits

> We are what we repeatedly do.
> —*Aristotle*

In the case of weight loss, so many of us have read books or gone to seminars and learned skills. In many cases we learned them quite well. Yet it is only when those skills have been invested in action that we can reap the benefits. For me, in attending Weight Watchers the skills I learned have now become habits that are part of my life.

Our identity craves consistency with our behavior. As I mentioned earlier, it is impossible to act consistently in a manner inconsistent with how we see ourselves. Most of us who have worked on weight loss understand the challenge in developing new behaviors.

Without the identity level change work that is part of *The Perfect Size System,* developing new behaviors will be time-consuming and sometimes frustrating. However, here's the good news—if you follow *The Perfect Size System* and begin making the identity level changes, developing new behaviors may *still* be time-consuming, *but* this time you will have a belief structure that supports the change.

Clients will often ask me, *"So what are the right weight loss habits?"* My response is always the same: "That depends on you." With literally hundreds of thousands of systems, out there (a Google search of "weight loss systems" returned twenty-eight million hits), the better question is, what are the right behaviors *for you.* Modeling habits is one of the processes found in *The Perfect Size System.*

After we have begun to shift the beliefs that make up your identity, we then ask the question, what behaviors would someone who had that identity and that belief structure adopt?

Now, in many cases, we don't know the answer to that question. That's where the next question comes into play: Who can I model who already has the habits I need for my weight loss goal? Modeling enables us to collapse time and speed up our results. The process of modeling advocated by *The Perfect Size System* is a very simple process.

Modeling Successful Weight Loss Habits:

1. Determine the attribute or habit you wish to model.
2. Find someone who has that habit or attribute.
3. List the key criteria of that person.
4. Do what they do.

WRIGHT

Will you expand on these Gail?

McDONALD

Absolutely, let's go through these in detail.

1. Determine the attribute or habit you wish to model.

After you have gone through the prior step of looking at the skills you need to develop, you will notice that there are some areas where you feel confident and others where you feel significantly less so.

Sit down and make a list of the habits that would be consistent with your new identity. These may be habits such as meal planning or time management or even something as simple as food preparation when you have a busy and full life.

2. Find someone who has that habit or attribute.

The person you choose should be someone with whom you resonate. It needs to be someone you can relate to and you will be able to say to yourself, "If she or he can do it, so can I."

I often advise against using celebrities. We tend to think celebrities live a different life than we do, and so we unconsciously assume their life is different from our own. For example, "Well, if I had a chef and personal trainer, I could drop thirty pounds with no problem."

The choice of who to model can have a profound impact. Kellie had struggled with her weight for years. After we had worked

> Perseverance is not a long race; it is many short races one after the other.
> —Walter Elliot

with her beliefs, she then began looking for a person to model. She found it in her close friend, Janet, who had recently taken up power walking and dropped twenty pounds. Now they power walk together. Kellie says, "I realized if she could make the time, I could make the time."

3. List the key criteria of the person.

How does that person do what he or she does? If possible ask, "How do you do that? What steps specifically do you take?"

When I joined Weight Watchers, I was working to develop the habit of tracking my food (an essential component of the program). It was a new habit and I wanted to find the best and most successful way to do it. So I asked my program leader and several other members how they were able to be so diligent. They said they kept notebooks and pens in their car and purse at all times. They all tended to write down their food before they ate it or immediately afterward, instead of at night before going to sleep. That detail helped me to model them and become more diligent.

4. Do what they do.

Marie wanted to work out regularly but she felt overwhelmed with three kids and working full-time. And being sixty pounds overweight, she was intimidated by gyms. She found a model in Sarah who had six kids but who worked out every day without fail. She asked her how she did that. Sarah said, "I set myself up to win. I told myself that all I had to do was work out for ten minutes for it to count, and wake up before the kids do. Now sometimes I work out for a half hour or even an hour, but I always get at least ten minutes. It may not seem like much, but I realized ten minutes is better than nothing."

Finding out that Sarah had ten-minute workouts freed Marie to begin trying something similar for herself. She felt a little silly working out for ten minutes when she had so much weight to lose but she realized Sarah was right. By making ten minutes the goal, not only did she set herself up to win she noticed she's going longer!

WRIGHT

Great! I can see that you must have modeled some successful behaviors that have enabled you to achieve and maintain your results! I am sure the road, like life in general, is not always smooth. How does *The Perfect Size System* advise someone on how to handle setbacks?

McDONALD

That is a great question! One of the important parts of this process is how you handle the setbacks.

Here's the reality that everyone who has lost weight and kept it off for years knows: you will have setbacks, and you will have disappointments, and you will sometimes feel as if it's not going to work; and that is all simply part of the process.

All of us who have become excellent at any task, whether raising children or managing a business or building a healthy relationship, know that you will have setbacks. With a stronger identity in place, those setbacks don't define you. The failure is no longer failure—it's feedback that what you're doing now may need to be refined.

As I so often tell my clients, it's not always going to be easy, but it will always be worth it.

> Yesterday I dared to struggle. Today I dared to win.
> — Bernadette Devlin

WRIGHT

Yes, that is so true of anything worth being, doing, or having. Where are we now in our logical levels of change?

McDONALD

We now move to the last steppingstone of the Logical Levels—Environment.

POWER QUESTION 5: WHAT CHANGES CAN I MAKE IN MY ENVIRONMENT?

Environment can be one of the easiest to shift and can serve to strengthen both behavior and identity. Simultaneously, environmental changes can be the easiest to overlook.

Environment involves the following key components revolving around:
> Who is in my environment?
> What are the emotional triggers in the environment?

When I work with clients, after we have made the changes regarding identity and belief structure and they have learned new capabilities and behaviors, we then sit down and begin to assess how their external environment supports or hinders the achievement of their weight loss goals.

The challenge for many of us is that who we spend our time with is often beyond our control. Part of the answer involves proper planning and negotiation.

Susan worked at a small computer advertising company. Once a month, the management would celebrate by taking the team out for pizza and beer. Susan had recently begun *The Perfect Size System* and had already lost twelve pounds. She was using Weight Watchers as part of her ongoing support system and knew the pizza and beer would not support her goal. So she took for her what was a bold step and brought small containers of grilled vegetables and chicken with her to the pizza party. As her coworkers ate pizza, she ate her own food. "Initially I felt a little uncomfortable, but after a while everyone was completely supportive and several of the women told me what a great idea it was."

Michelle's environmental challenge was her husband who loved ice cream. "Despite my protests, he would have three or four different pints of ice cream in the freezer. Finally, I said to him, 'I'm doing this so that I can be as sexy as possible for you.' He stopped buying the ice cream."

Environmental triggers are another component we address as part of the system. When working with clients, we assess when they tend to overeat and we then assess how we can shift that.

In my own case, I tended to overeat at nighttime. I would come home from a long day at work and both reward and numb myself with food. Typically, there would be no plan. Since I didn't think about food until I was hungry, I ate whatever was in the refrigerator.

After I had my breakthrough regarding my beliefs, I began planning my meals and snacks. In the morning, before going to work or the night before, I would prepare food that would be ready for me when I came home. I would have something there that was both tasty and accessible. I still enjoyed my nighttime snacks. The more I did this the easier it became.

Wanda's challenge was travel. She traveled for a living and spent large amounts of time on the road and in hotels. Rushing through airports, she found her options limited. "There are a lot more McDonald's than there are organic produce

> It is your human environment that makes climate.
> —Mark Twain

stores," she said with a smile. After she had begun using *The Perfect Size System* and shifted her beliefs, she found ways to have her environment support her change. "Now, whenever I travel to a new city, I get on the Internet and find the nearest grocery store to my hotel. I only stay at hotels where I have a refrigerator. I also purchased a larger purse and keep it full of energy bars and raw nuts. If it's a long flight, I may even have a few ziplock bags of grilled chicken!"

The Perfect Size System teaches that as you change your environment, the environment will help change you.

Yes, *The Perfect Size System* changes lives. My entire family has had a complete identity shift over the course of these many years. As a family, we have lost over two hundred pounds! Our behaviors, environment, and, of course, our bodies of today do not even resemble our previous selves. We live our lives fully and in a balanced, fun, and satisfying way!

In conclusion, I am reminded of one of the great movies of all time, *The Wizard of Oz*. This movie reminds us about life, learning, and the possibilities existing within ourselves in a sometimes confusing and frustrating world. While Dorothy struggles to find her way home, she discovers new experiences and a completely new way of looking at life.

I will leave our readers with the memorable words the good witch Glenda ultimately tells Dorothy: **You've always had the power!**

ABOUT THE AUTHOR

As a Success Coach, Gail Fallon McDonald has over thirty years of experience in the delivery and study of Behavioral Change Services and Systems. Gail has provided extensive executive level leadership and teambuilding to multiple wellness and recovery programs in Northern California.

As a certified Masters level NLP Practitioner, Coach, Master Time Line Therapy Practitioner, certified Hypnotherapist, and Registered Nurse, Gail applies these pragmatic accelerated learning and change techniques to assist her personal and business clients, both nationally and internationally, to be the architect of their own success.

As the creator of the Heart of Success Perfect Size System Gail has taken her own personal experience with weight loss strategies and combined this with her experience as a trainer, consultant and speaker and designed a unique practice that encompasses a sound system for success. The Heart of Success Perfect Size System is designed not only to clarify what has prevented you from achieving and maintaining your perfect size goals in the past, but to also provide a direct means to attain that.

Gail brings her front-line experience in personal change, leadership, and teambuilding, combined with her high energy and bold delivery to inform and delight audiences through her workshops, radio interviews, speaking, consulting, and coaching.

Gail outlines her original Heart of Success System in the book, GPS for Success where she is contributing author with Stephen Covey, John Gray, and Les Brown.

Gail is the proud mother of two daughters and lives in the San Francisco Bay Area where she leads a fulfilling and active lifestyle.

GAIL FALLON MCDONALD

735 Hickey Blvd., Suite 260
Pacifica, CA 94044
800-680-2137
gail@gailfallonmcdonald.com
www.heartofyoursuccess.com

CHAPTER TWENTY

God Has Your Plan: Understanding the Temporary Inconveniences of Life

An Interview with . . . **Hank Van Joslin**

DAVID WRIGHT (WRIGHT)

I am sitting here with Hank Van Joslin of the prestigious Van Joslin Real Estate Company in The Woodlands, Texas. Today we are talking about "God Has Your Plan: Understanding the Temporary Inconveniences of Life."

Hank, no doubt you have done very well in the Real Estate brokerage business, however, there is more to you than what most people realize. You have quite a story of "overcoming" that is truly inspiring and is exactly why we wanted to include your story in *Stepping Stones to Success*.

HANK VAN JOSLIN (VAN JOSLIN)

Yes, thank you. And yes, we do a very good business in The Woodlands, Texas; Cap Cana, Dominican Republic; and in the Mexican Rivera, Mexico. We enjoy what we do and love meeting the interesting people who seek our services.

However, there is more to life than just earning a living. And every day this is what we bring to the table, so to speak. Our clients are our friends. We know buying a home is the single largest investment for most people. Moreover, we also know we are dealing with human beings. We know each family has their own issues, their own goals and challenges. We take each client, each family, and each couple and try our best to serve them holistically. We engage with them.

WRIGHT

You seem to have a greater depth of compassion than what I think most Real Estate brokers have, Hank. Is this due in part to the traumatic events you have conquered in your life?

VAN JOSLIN

I believe most successful businesspeople have one thing in common—they care. But to be great at what you do, you must also understand people and be compassionate about their issues and concerns. Right now we are living through interesting times. People are having financial difficulties. Some are having to scale back, some are declaring bankruptcy or have done so in the past, yet they need to be invested in a home and move on with their life. Some people feel stuck in life. I know a little something about feeling stuck, not being able to move! And, well, I can identify with the pain and suffering of the people I work with.

WRIGHT

Knowing your story, Hank, I would say so. You can identify with the pain and suffering of others. You have overcome great obstacles in your life and encountered those at the pinnacle of your career at the time. Some might have felt that God was a cruel God, but you have a different approach to adversity.

VAN JOSLIN

To say I know a little something of adversity is an understatement, but there are people who have gone through far worse things than I have physically, spiritually, and/or emotionally. They have experienced far greater trauma than I. I happen to be the one speaking to you right now, but there are so many others who have conquered great odds. What we all have in common is that God created each one of us. We all have a divine blueprint for our lives. God has a plan for everyone. So no matter the adversity, one must believe that somehow it, too, was written on their blueprint.

It is true—at the height of my youthful "career" I incurred an injury that left me paralyzed for almost two years. I don't wish that experience on anyone, but I am grateful for that experience today. When I see that someone is stuck in life (and I'm speaking to issues greater than a home-buying decision), I can empathize with how he or she is feeling mentally.

I know and hold fast to the belief that God has a plan and if that person is in front of me, then I know God has sent that person to me for encouragement and hope. I have a lot of those kinds of moments.

Many people are looking for explanations as to why certain things have happened to them. Sometimes there simply isn't an explanation, but I do know that God means everything for good. Just knowing that and accepting that truth can lift a person up from having a victim mentality to having a victorious mentality. The circumstances physically are the same, but the shift in one's mind and heart can make all the difference in the world when it comes to overcoming and moving beyond adversity.

It is a trap to look at things and say, "Is this ever going to end?" or "Why is this happening to me?"

I was very fortunate that thirty-eight years ago, during my time of extreme physical suffering, the message came down to me that this was a temporary inconvenience; this was something that would pass. If I was lying on the floor taking a class or hobbling to move about or unable to do something seemingly simple, there were still other things I could benefit from. That's what I would draw from.

There is always an opportunity to see the larger landscape if a person will break out of the confinement of his or her limited thinking. There is always something good out there for us.

WRIGHT

So what you are saying is that everything happens for a reason?

VAN JOSLIN

Yes, but sometimes we don't know it at the time. Take, for instance, a bad day. You might think yesterday was a bad day, but then realize because of the events of yesterday, you were moved to a more compelling place today. In essence, yesterday was a good day because you learned something new or were moved to a different place in your mind. That's just it—we have no idea what today really means. All we have to do is live today to the absolute fullest. Let each experience become a teaching moment. Just go for it! Three months from now you might realize that what you did today paved the way for something grand to happen in your life. And I do believe that is how life works. We are set up for grand things to happen. Then when something terrible happens, we focus on that and hold people, places, or even God accountable for our misery. I'm here to tell you that misery is optional. If you live every day as an exclamation instead of an explanation, then you are going to have some superior "Wow, I can't believe that just happened" days in front of you!

The truth is, there are times in our life that we are expected to wait. To everything there is a season. So, while in college, I actually resigned myself to the fact that my timing was to wait. I can remember everyone around me living his or her life and that didn't bother me. I didn't feel cheated or slighted. I found great significance in waiting. It was a positive thing. And just because I was waiting didn't mean things weren't happening. Like the farmer who plants the seed. Just because he doesn't see the seed in the ground doesn't mean that something isn't happening. But when that seed sprouts, grows, and becomes the crop he has planted, he then realizes that there was a necessary time to wait.

I would talk to my body and use the time wisely while waiting. I wanted to make sure I was planting good seeds. Like the farmer, if he plants corn he doesn't expect potatoes to grow. Likewise, if I am talking positively to myself, I am expecting positive results. The seeds I planted and cultivated were for my vertebrae to fuse together, giving me back my strong and stable back. And yes, it did happen!

Do I feel that we draw those bad things to us? No. Do I think God is going to use these situations for our good? Yes! This is the amazing power of God. And I don't mean to get preachy and I hope you don't perceive that I am, but I think this fact gives people a great sense of relief to know that no matter what is going on in their life, God sees it and He will use it to make a difference in our lives.

I can only share from my personal experience, but what I am communicating is that if God can turn things around for me, He can for you, too. I went from being paralyzed to competing successfully in all facets of my life. I couldn't have done that just drawing on my own strength because at one time I was physically weak, but in faith I was strong.

WRIGHT

Tell me about that kind of faith. It seems extraordinary to me. What do you have to believe about yourself and about God to have turned your life around?

VAN JOSLIN

I had to believe all situations can be temporary inconveniences. Now, defining "temporary" can be a challenge since today we all seem to be looking for immediate gratification. Remember, it is not like the movies!

For me, "temporary" meant lying on the floor and being in pain for many years. Years later I was able to run, jump (two- to three-inch vertical heights only, but it is still jumping!) and have much less pain.

I was sixteen and the only American competing in the Dominican Republic National Motocross. I had no fear! I had a formidable will to win! Such is the optimism of youth. The next day, after winning that race, everything was great. The morning newspaper featured a photo of me leading the pack. I felt victorious and was back on my motorcycle riding to school thinking it was a good time to be me.

Suddenly, without obeying a stop sign, a truck pulled out in front of me and I broadsided the truck. I could actually hear and feel my back go "crunch." My bike and I were thrown three lanes over and I landed on my head. Although I had my helmet on, my head cracked just above both my eyes. There I was, sprawled in the road, blood gushing from my head, when a classmate and his father discovered me. They put me in their truck and rushed me to the hospital.

The operating neurosurgeon was world-renown; I was in the best of care. During the operation, the physician made an eight-inch incision and pulled out all the pieces of vertebrae and discs shattered in the accident. They felt they had gotten everything. They also thought I was going to lose my left eye. It was horrible, to say the least. It was certainly not the worst accident, compared to what others have gone through, but for my family and me, this was very traumatic.

After the operation, I was on an IV drip and was strapped down to my bed so I wouldn't try to get up. I just didn't realize then the severity of the situation. I remember telling my friends who came to visit me that I just needed to fix my bike and I'd be back in time for basketball season, which was just beginning. They just looked at me with amazement thinking, "There is *no way!*"

I had a broken back, a concussion, and I had myriad more maladies; however, when I woke up I was still "me." That was the blessing. I woke up and I was still me. There was no brain damage. Not only did I not see myself as a victim, but I did not want special treatment. I was not an invalid. I was just suffering a temporary inconvenience. In all the time I was on paraplegic crunches, I never used a handicap sticker or handicap parking. And I don't do so now, either. I always felt that these privileges were for those with greater challenges than mine.

Though the doctors' consensus was that I was paralyzed and would never walk, my dad had another vision. Ultimately, we left the hospital very late one night, long before the doctors were willing to release me. We had our own plan—God's plan—for my recovery. What I would later find to be one of my biggest challenges was that of asking others for assistance. Today I feel it is a noble thing to ask for help, as it gives others great joy to be of service.

I was to have played football for the University of Tampa. Again, it would have been easy to slip into that "victim mentality," but why? What purpose would it have served? Even at registration I "stood" (actually laid), in line for eight hours. I was told that there was a handicap line for registration that I should have used. I did not because that was not for me. I did not consider myself handicapped, but rather, temporarily inconvenienced. While at the University of Tampa I ate meals with a girl who was born with deformed arms, not only could she use a knife and fork with her feet, she sewed a colorful (back then it was called psychedelic) trim on the bottom of a pair of my jeans, which she did with her sewing machine using her feet. This just shows that just when you think you have all the challenges, look around; you will see someone else who has it worse.

And, I share all this to say that if you knew you could have it all someday, would you be patient and do what you could today? Of course you would. This is what you must believe—the challenge will ultimately pass, but the joy will be found in the good seeds you've planted while patiently waiting.

You have to believe that you are still who you are regardless of whether you are temporarily on crutches or walking around just fine; whether you are happily married or newly divorced. The fact is, you are still you! Whether you've just suffered the greatest loss in your life or the greatest glory, you're still who you are. Don't give up because God never will. Allow good things to happen in your life despite what is going on in the environment that surrounds you.

In essence, you have to believe that not only are you capable of having, doing, and being what you want, but also that you are worth it. You are worth living a great life. God instilled that in all of us on purpose! To you reading this right now: *you* are worthy of living a great life!

WRIGHT

Yours is a fantastic story, Hank, of overcoming. I do not think you could have achieved this without a firm resolution in God, as you have talked about. Did you always have a strong faith or did you find that faith as you went through the process of overcoming your "temporary inconvenience"? What I am asking is, which came first?

VAN JOSLIN

The first thing is to believe in God. If you listen carefully, you will realize that He is offering guidance all the time. Listen to the messages. You must know that just as things can change and become a mess overnight, so can they change and become a miracle overnight. You must trust that all messes can be cleaned up as long as you have patience and perseverance. You must believe that you, too, have the ability to overcome. Decide to think of your messes as temporary inconveniences. Once you decide this, then be patient and allow yourself time to figure out what you need to do to clean up the mess. Take this in steps—don't think you must tackle it all at once.

Once you believe it is a temporary inconvenience, you are on your way to getting out or over it.

It is easy for me to believe that God has a plan for me because of my background with overwhelming struggle. However, mine could be considered slight compared to what others have gone through. Anyone who has conquered any great feat knows that the hand of God was involved. I don't believe we can fully overcome great challenges on our own.

My upbringing was that of a God-fearing and God-respecting family. I think those beliefs have created hope in me. I've become even more faithful as the years go on because I have become so much more aware of the blessings given to me and what I'm now capable of offering to others in my own small way. Yet, for me, this is huge because I can see it and feel it in a manner that, I guess, as a youngster I just didn't realize was there, yet it was happening all around me.

Like the story of the man who was fired from a home decorating center. He was crushed. He had founded this business with his partners and was ousted. But then God did a new thing. He increased this man's confidence and compelled him to start his own do-it-yourself center. The man created a catchy name for his enterprise—Home Depot. To think that such a successful business was born out of being fired. I'm sure he thought being fired was the worst day of his life, but in reality, it turned out to be a really great day!

And what I believe is that God doesn't have that kind of story for just a few, He has this divine and prosperous blueprint for all of us!

WRIGHT

It's as though you are saying that when people have a life-changing moment, they must either recreate their life or die?

VAN JOSLIN

Yes, for me it was thirteen days after my 1972 accident. I had been conscious for several days and my friends were coming in and out of my hospital room visiting me; however, no one stayed very long, not because of doctors orders, but because I would tell them to not worry. I would tell them I would be on the basketball court before the season started and would be in the next motocross race. It became obvious to me that none of these people believed what I believed. No one believed that I would ever function normally. So one afternoon, right after my motocross teammates had left the hospital room with teary-eyed faces, I suddenly just stopped thinking of moving and getting well. I laid there staring at the ceiling.

That evening my father came to see me as he did every day after work. He walked over, lowered the railings on the bed, and told me to put my arms around his neck. I was not to be moved and was still on intravenous drip. My dad was a retired Marine Corps Colonel, stood six feet, five inches, and was a strapping marine even in his 50s. I dangled from his neck, feeling nervous that I could not feel anything in my legs.

With me hanging from his neck, he took three steps from the bed, grabbed hold of me with the tubes containing my nourishment and medicines dragging behind me, and assured me that I would walk. It was as if our bodies were connected at the torso. Looking straight into his eyes, he firmly told me, "You will walk." He took several steps back to the bedside and carefully, but with force, placed me back in the bed. He looked me in the eye with his piercing blue eyes and I knew then that I *would* walk and have a normal life.

In many cases it takes a big jolt for most of us to realize what it is we need, to realize it's time, and the opportunity has come to move on, to better ourselves, or to draw from that which God has planned for us.

These are those self-defining moments that spur on the motivation to succeed and thrive in life. Not everyone has a support group around him or her. I realize that there are many others going through challenging times. They feel they are sinking and they have no support group there to cheer them on. That is precisely why I am writing this chapter. If you don't have a support group around you, then consider me your support group. I want to encourage you just as I was encouraged.

WRIGHT

I look at you and hear your story and then feel heartache for those who have gone through similar experiences, but can't seem to dig themselves out. What is the difference between those who can rise above and those who sink down?

VAN JOSLIN

The defining moment for me was that I did not try to rely solely on my own power. There was no way for me to do so. I had to rely by faith on a greater power to lift me up. So for those who are able to rise above situations when others can't, they, too, are relying on something greater than themselves. For some it is God and for some it is the belief that there is meaning and purpose to their life. I do not think a person can single-handedly conquer great challenges on their own, *neither do I believe that we were meant to handle great challenges on our own.*

For others, there is always a reason "not to overcome." For me, there were only reasons why I should. Tiny steps make the overall change, to be sure. The thing is, if one is compelled to do something, then do it! Furthermore, do it because you know you're supposed to! That is how I felt. I was compelled to walk again because I knew I was supposed to. Today I walk only aided by a foot drop brace on my right leg. I also run, not very fast, but it is such a joy just to have my legs moving me in a direction I choose, just like God continues to move my life on the course He has set for me. And the message is now for me to share with others what God has planned for each one of us through my upcoming book series, *God has Your Plan.*

WRIGHT

What I like about what you have to say is that people don't have to be perfect, pedigreed, or otherwise acclaimed to achieve greatness. Greatness is available to everyone, isn't that what you are saying?

VAN JOSLIN

Yes. Why would God create anything less than "greatness" in us all? Fortunately for all of us, we are endowed with talents and gifts, and that is the good news. What is so wonderful is knowing that no one person has more of that divine spark than someone else. Again, it is what we do with what we have, both negatively and positively. Our gifts might be different, but we all have that endowment, so to speak.

WRIGHT

You also talk about how a person must decide who and what he or she is. So this is more than just ideas on goal-setting. This is about redefining who a person is and what he or she stands for, isn't it?

VAN JOSLIN

When going through a difficult time, the question is not "what am I going to do?" but, rather, "who am I going to be?" When we decide who we are going to be through an experience, then we almost immediately get creative and push through.

Some decide that they want to be a victim. Well, if that is the decision, they are not going to get very far. But if people decide that they are going to be conquerors, then they have already moved that mountain through their intention.

You are what you think about. Deep down inside, each of us knows what we want to be. However, some need a little encouragement and support to help them realize that dream.

WRIGHT

Do you ever stop to think about the gift you are giving to people to live lives greater than what they thought possible?

VAN JOSLIN

I believe the gift is already in them. What I want to share by telling my story of adversity is that there is nothing too big for God and there is no plan too awesome for your life.

Yes, I sell real estate, but I don't just sell real estate. What I do is meet people every single day of my life. And I decide who I am going to be to that person and what I am going to model. If I decide that I am going to be the face of God to that person and to model to that person the benevolence of God, then that person is going to have an awesome experience with me. God is going to make sure of that. Does it mean that everyone is going to buy a home from me? No. Neither is that the expectation.

Not only do I rely on God for my strength and courage, but I also rely on God as my source and for my sustenance. I know that "God has a plan" and that God may send me someone who just needs encouragement, a friendly face, a smile, or simply someone to listen. God is going to give me my provision; I have no worry about that. So every person who comes into my office is not a prospect or a suspect, but a real, live, human being.

WRIGHT

What do you believe about people, Hank, to want to reach out to them in this way with your book, your message?

VAN JOSLIN

I believe that God has done an outstanding job in His creation. And when someone crosses my threshold, I thank God for giving me the opportunity to interface with one of His creations. It's just that simple, really. And honestly, what would the world look like today—what would business look like today—if everyone adopted that spirit and the heart of God? I don't think we would have a lot of the financial heartache that so many are experiencing from the greed of others.

Practical application of my beliefs, though, is that every day I try to center myself around "who do I want to be today" and respond to my adversities, my successes, my triumphs, and learning lessons around that. Somehow it keeps me in check!

I believe there is good in all of us. There is a plan for all of us and it is goodness, and it is service, and it is to be kind and helpful and to be caring and considerate. We are all striving for success, but success in what, I ask? I feel successful in life. By not making our primary focus that of striving strictly for success in business, but to simply succeed in life, the business will come as a tremendous by-product.

Where I feel I have succeeded in life is that I know how to love and to appreciate others. This is how I define success. I know and appreciate God. If that is how one can define success, I would say one would experience success far more often than if we defined success as a monetary figure or a number of widgets one had to sell.

WRIGHT

What is the ultimate for you, Hank? What needs to happen for you to feel you have succeeded in life?

VAN JOSLIN

In all ways I am blessed. This is not to say that I don't have my challenges, but fortunately I have been able to turn around many areas of my life. To be an example doesn't mean that I have it all figured out. Who knows what tomorrow may bring. What I can be, though, is a resource for hope and an example of faith. This is very important to me.

Life is a continuing journey and with God's grace, my journey will continue. My future goals are to simply appreciate more, to love more, to care more, to be more considerate, to find the kindest side of me, and to be able to share that with others.

WRIGHT

Thank you, Hank, what a great conversation. I really appreciate all this time you've taken to talk with me and answer all these questions today. I've sure learned a lot about overcoming adversity and who is really in charge.

VAN JOSLIN

David, thank you so much for including me in *Stepping Stones to Success*. I want to wish you and everyone in your organization the very best. I think that what you do to help get these messages out is something that is extremely important.

WRIGHT

Today I've been talking with Hank Van Joslin, of the Van Joslin Real Estate Company in The Woodlands, Texas. Hank is a man who has overcome tragic and traumatic events in his life and has decided to help others by writing the book series *God has Your Plan*. I think he's got Someone on his side who is probably more powerful than he is, at least he thinks he does and so do I. I hope our readers will see this, too.

Hank, thank you so much for being with us today on *Stepping Stones to Success*.

VAN JOSLIN

Thank you, David, and God bless you.

ABOUT THE AUTHOR

Hank Van Joslin is founder of Van Joslin Real Estate specializing in luxury properties in The Woodlands, Texas, USA; Cap Cana, Dominican Republic; and in the Mexican Rivera, Mexico. Hank shares his inspirational story of "overcoming" focusing on his book series, *God Has Your Plan,* of which this chapter is an excerpt titled, "Understanding the Temporary Inconveniences of Life." (For more information, go to www.GodHasYourPlan.com.)

From the beginning of his career as a licensed Texas Real Estate broker thirty years ago on through today, Hank has been honored with some of the most prestigious awards given by national builders, major developers, and building/Real Estate trade associations as the top sales and marketing agent/agency, nationally and regionally. He is a Certified International Property Specialist, Accredited Luxury Home Specialist, Certified Real Estate Auctioneer, Personal Property Appraiser, and a member of Who's Who in Luxury Real Estate.

Hank is a graduate of the University of Tampa with degrees in Finance and Business Management. A tireless entrepreneur, Hank founded and built a $100 million food company that he and his partners took public in 1994. In 2009, he became a founding master retailer for CieAura, cutting-edge non-transdermal holographic chips used for relieving discomfort, helping with focus/clarity/energy, and deeper rest.

Prior to Real Estate, Hank was an accomplished actor and model, featured in major Latin American publications, including Cosmopolitan's Latin America's bachelor of the month, and television while reaching stardom on the big screen in Mexico as Carlos Rivera, his stage name.

A proud father of three wonderful children, and his first granddaughter, Hank and his wife, Lori, are, as they put it: "living the time of life that God has made us for" as they nurture and help their children develop while continuing to grow in their own faith.

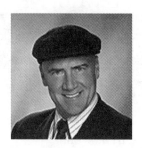

HANK VAN JOSLIN
9595 Six Pines Drive, Suite 8210
The Woodlands, TX 77380
(713) 823-3600
(832) 631-6093
Fax: (832) 631-6095
www.VanJoslinRealEstate.com
www.GodHasYourPlan.com
www.HankVanJoslin.CieAura.com

CHAPTER TWENTY-ONE

Driving Success with a Goal-Focused Image

An Interview with . . . **Patty Buccellato**

WRIGHT (WRIGHT)

We're talking today with Patty Buccellato. Patty is internationally recognized as a Certified Image Professional and founder of Refined Images, specializing in image management coaching for professional men and women. A member of the Association of Image Consultants International (AICI), Patty finds joy in helping clients discover their authentic visual presence. She works with corporate employee groups and in private consult with individual clients, defining the appearance that supports their goals.

Patty has worked with organizations ranging from CPA firms, manufacturing companies, and credit unions, to higher educational institutions and professional associations like NAWBO (National Association of Women Business Owners) and Fashion Group International. A recreational SCUBA diver, she views her work with clients as yet another opportunity to dive below the surface and uncover the uniqueness and wonder inherent in all beings.

Welcome to *Stepping Stones to Success*, Patty.

PATTY BUCCELLATO (BUCCELLATO)

Thank you, David. It's a pleasure to share in the discussion.

WRIGHT

Patty, with *Stepping Stones,* we're helping our readers to be better, live better, and be more fulfilled. As an image consultant, you probably have some ideas about how one's personal image can influence success. Let's begin with why you think image, or personal appearance, plays a role in success.

BUCCELLATO

My pleasure, David. More compelling than my personal opinion, though, is the research on image and first impressions. Did you know, for example, that the human eye draws conclusions and sends non-verbal messages to the cerebral cortex in one-twelfth of a second? That is much, much faster than the brain's interpretation of the spoken words we use to communicate our character or competencies. "First Impressions" really are formatted in a split second, and they play a significant part in our business dealings and interpersonal relations.

WRIGHT

So this is important to career success then?

BUCCELLATO

Not only career success, but success in any area of our lives—whenever we are interacting with other human beings! We often place a focus on career success since it's the area where we earn a living to create the kind of life we desire. And, irrespective of the amount of money one earns, the degree of satisfaction from doing what we desire often depends on being selected, hired, promoted, or contracted by someone who reacts to judgments he or she has formed about us.

WRIGHT

So people are discriminating in their choices based on their impressions of us?

BUCCELLATO

To a degree, yes. It's an innate and primal tool, really. Before we had spoken language to relay our thoughts and feelings, we trusted what we interpreted through nonverbal communication—our *body language.* These were our first communication skills, so we continue to rely on them, particularly when there is a discrepancy between a delivered verbal message and the nonverbal cues. If we sense incongruence, we fall back to trust the long-standing interpretive skills of our nonverbal communication experiences.

For example, I'll often do an exercise in my workshops where I shake hands with someone seated in the audience as if we were being introduced to one another. I'll make contact with the hands, but my eyes are moving around the room at other people and objects as I speak the words, "It's a pleasure to meet you [name]." My body's center—the core of my torso—is not directly facing the person, and my handshake is limp. When I ask them what message he or she received from the encounter, the response is not related at all to the "nice to meet you" verbal message that was heard. The impression received was that I couldn't have cared less to be in the same room, much less pleased to be engaging in conversation!

We often underestimate the power of our nonverbal communication. If we're aware and intentional in self-projection, we have the ability to choose an accurate and positive message about who we are at the onset of interaction. This route is far more productive than backpedaling to overcome a negative first impression.

WRIGHT

So what are some of the impressions people give that are counterproductive and what might be some undesirable consequences?

BUCCELLATO

On a very elemental level, people who fail to make adequate eye contact are often perceived as untrustworthy or "shifty." In some cases, we may interpret that their lack of eye contact is due to an extremely shy nature, rather than deceptive motives. In that case, we might lack respect or confidence in their ability to accomplish professional or personal goals.

In the area of physical appearance, namely dress and grooming, people draw some of the strongest, and sometimes harshest, conclusions. For example, when we notice a person dressed in outdated clothing, we might be led to believe that the person's thought processes and ideas are outdated as well. This would have a direct influence on assumptions about his or her work processes, and could negatively affect a decision about doing business with that individual.

Fortunately, this is an area where people have the most potential to make conscious and positive choices. The key is in knowing what message or "personal brand" you want to relay. Where a hereditary spinal condition that you have little or no control of may prevent you from standing tall in posture,

313

the color of your clothing and your daily grooming habits are choices you can make with intention each day of your life.

WRIGHT

That's a term we're hearing a lot of these days. What *is* a "personal brand," Patty? Do I have one? Do I need one?

BUCCELLATO

Yes, David. You have a personal brand; we all possess a personal brand. You might know it by the word "reputation," which, in essence, is the summary to others of what we stand for—what people think of when they hear our name. Often the distinction between reputation and personal brand is *intention*. My reputation may come by default as others have encounters with me and draw conclusions about who I am. My personal brand, though, will result from careful attention to consistently projecting an accurate message in all areas of my life. If I do this well, there will be no confusion about what I stand for.

People who create an intentional brand do so by choosing a consistent message based on their goals, values, and strengths. Personal appearance is one element in communicating the personal brand statement.

WRIGHT

So the visual element of the personal brand is what your work involves? How does this come into play for regular women and men?

BUCCELLATO

I work with clients in defining and projecting an accurate picture of who they are. That visual picture is critical in first impressions for good reason. As human beings, we draw nonverbal conclusions about those we meet. The early-life nonverbal communication skills that we mentioned earlier are held in the ancient area of our brains. To this day, they are our most reliable connection to the truth of others, so we continue to call on these skills, often below our conscious awareness.

When we meet people, we make judgments about their marital status, occupation, education, or economic status—often based simply on what we see. It's not that we intend to be judgmental, but since visual messages make it to the brain faster than any verbal message can be delivered, we're at a disadvantage if we don't send an immediate, positive visual statement right from the start.

WRIGHT

Is that positive visual statement the same for everyone? I would imagine there are some unique circumstances you encounter with your clients.

BUCCELLATO

Each of us are unique, David. Yet there are general paths to follow based on what one's life looks like. And certainly, there are cultural expectations for particular career fields, especially when it comes to professional fields of work.

The best visual brand is one that represents the individual on all levels. Once a client I'm working with is clear on the elements of values, goals, and lifestyle priorities, we can design an appropriate visual expression for them.

One key in developing the decided visual representation of a personal brand is maintaining consistency. If you're an architect, for example, and you want to project the image of being a creative, outside-the-box thinker, you'll want to attire yourself a bit left of center on the conventional continuum. Chances are, if you're living an authentic life and doing what you love, this is easily achieved. Perhaps your eyewear is bold and striking, your clothing more fashionable than average, and your haircut is on-trend. This is only credible as a creative statement, however, if we see you this way every day. The best-case scenario for working professionals is that their career truly suits them. If their everyday work and environment is in harmony with their personal values, then it's a natural extension for them to "match" the look of a given field of work.

WRIGHT

Is that important—to match what others look like in work?

BUCCELLATO

For those working in professional fields, it can be beneficial to match expectations that the public has for someone in that role. If gaining the faith and confidence of a prospective client is a factor in the success of the business (and when isn't it?), then it's beneficial for the service provider to match that particular vision.

For example, we don't expect our CPAs to be dressed like rock stars. We feel comforted to know that their attention is on staying abreast of financial trends and our business, not on the latest fashion trends. At the same time, we like to see that they are polished and reasonably current in their attire. It sends the message that they are attentive to detail and receptive to change.

Consider how you might react to a lawyer if he or she greeted you in frayed jeans and a hoodie. Despite it being a very familiar look, it's not the one you expect to see on your attorney, and although it may be comfortable, the look doesn't scream competence. In fact, it says the opposite. If this same attorney met you wearing an impeccable blue suit, and a crisp white shirt, you would have fewer initial reservations about hiring him or her than you would if wearing a hoodie and jeans.

We have come to expect that certain professionals look a particular way. When they do, we concentrate on assessing their talent and business acumen without distraction of inappropriate attire. A conservatively dressed, well-groomed lawyer is one we assume will take as much care with our legal matters as with his or her appearance.

This theory holds true for more casual work environments as well. Consider the advertising executive who greets you in an unadorned, black business suit, looking more like a banker than an ad man. Your first thought might be, "How creative will my campaign be if I hire this guy?" In an industry that thrives on knowing and anticipating what will be hip, trendy, and fascinating to the sixteen- to thirty-year-old demographic, the adjectives "funky, cool, and hip" should come to mind when you see an advertising professional. You'll feel more comfortable putting your company's brand in the hands of a chic, modern executive who will surely put forth as much creative effort on your campaign as he or she did on attire. As a customer, that first impression can reinforce a great portfolio by effectively proclaiming a candidate's competency in areas important to your industry.

Casual work environments aren't exempt from the benefits of a powerful professional image. E-commerce companies are well known for having more casual dress policies and an informal working environment. Upon meeting a Web designer who will potentially launch your company's next e-commerce venture, what image would impress you? A Web designer in faded shorts, a stained tee shirt, and a serious case of bed-head, or the Web designer in a clean polo shirt and jeans with a Lego-brand watch, funky sneakers, and (if male) a neatly trimmed beard? The first designer would tend to make you wonder if he or she would be able to meet deadlines or even understand what is key to your online business. The second designer presents himself (or herself) as a career-oriented professional with a creative, innovative personality that would put those qualities to work for your company. While both may design fabulous Web sites, the customer feels drawn to trust the talents and priorities of the person who presents himself or herself as goal-oriented and thoughtful.

Wardrobe and grooming are instrumental to an individual's career image, but it's important to remember that it isn't just the clothing that matters.

Details such as color also convey a message. Certain colors, for example, evoke very particular feelings. A red tie indicates power and success. A blue suit says "conservative and professional." Yellow wardrobe pieces instill happiness. It's surely no accident that UPS chose brown as their corporate color. Browns and greens indicate earthiness and friendliness—the perfect attitude for a company that moves and delivers your precious packages, be they corporate shipments or your granddaughter's birthday gift.

Even if people aren't considering the affect of their appearance on client/customer relations, chances are that their employers are. A national survey of Fortune 500 executives showed that more than 50 percent of them feel that how people dress influences their daily behaviors. Not only is the expectation-match helpful in gaining clients, it can be critical in hiring and promotion decisions as well. One study has shown that "plain" people earn 5 to 10 percent less than people of average looks, and that those earners in turn make 3 to 8 percent less than people who are deemed good-looking.

The good news is that anyone can increase his or her attractiveness. Simple actions make a difference. When people maintain good eye contact, behave in an upbeat manner, and dress well, they influence the "good looking" assessments of others.

WRIGHT

The earnings statistics probably get many people's attention if nothing else does. What about people who have zero interest in fashion trends? Does that pose a problem for them in their personal branding?

BUCCELLATO

Lack of fashion interest doesn't have to be an obstacle and shouldn't preclude someone from projecting a positive, powerful brand image. It's a common reason for hiring an image consultant. Many women and men I work with recognize the value that a polished, professional appearance brings to their professional skill set. They may prefer not to take their time, however, to learn about and identify their best choices in clothing, hairstyle, or color. That's where an image professional comes in. A skilled image consultant advises on appropriate styles (clothing and hair), color, and other elements of attire like eyewear and other accessories.

I work with many professionals in technical or analytic-based careers. They've dedicated much time and energy to becoming highly competent in work that calls on the strengths of left-brain oriented skill sets. For many of them, the creative abilities of the right brain hemisphere are underdeveloped. Since it's the "right-brained" competencies that rule in clothing and other visual appearance choices, these individuals find great value in having a professional to turn to.

In one situation, I worked with a CPA who was in contention for a high-level leadership position in a very creative industry. For this client to be perceived as qualified to lead in an innovative culture, an inspired visual message was necessary. Fashion-forward wardrobe elements incorporated into his usual business dress accomplished this. We used artistic accessories and interesting fabrics to present subtle but visible changes to a previously conservative dressing style. The visual changes made a statement about his understanding of the creative aspects of the business. This is a direct example of visual brand image as a tool for success.

WRIGHT

This is a fascinating area of coaching that is unfamiliar to many of our readers. What are the factors you consider when doing a wardrobe or image consultation?

BUCCELLATO

I like to know about my clients as individuals. Who are they? What do they believe in? Their lifestyle is important—including and beyond what they do for a living. If I'm going to work effectively with them, I need to know and honor the financial budget they're comfortable with in terms of clothing and other personal items. And, aside from what their life looks like at the moment, it's important that we consider where they want to be in the future. Specific career goals are obvious factors to be considered in building a personalized appearance strategy. Other life events and experiences are important, though, and can prompt a person to consult with an image coach.

I've worked with many clients as they are re-entering the dating world following divorce or death of their spouse. Maybe they've gone through a period where they haven't devoted much time to personal appearance and care, and they desire the extra boost of a professional to get "back in shape." In those cases, I'm a bit like their personal trainer—we have to start with the basics and build up to the new image. Other life transitions, like becoming a new parent or a first-time empty-nester, are prompts for image coaching—and essential knowledge for the consultant to possess.

WRIGHT

Patty, what inspired you to create an image consulting company?

BUCCELLATO

It's the perfect blend of a number of my strengths and passions, David. I've always had an attraction to color and style, and the power they have as wardrobe tools. They have the potential to enhance the appearance and experience of the wearer. I've been fortunate to find an outlet for these interests, combined with a desire to help and coach others.

I didn't always see image consulting as a career option, though. As a college student, I'd often find myself helping others select attire for a date or party event, sometimes to the detriment of my own timeliness in dressing! My undergraduate degree was in fashion merchandising, and upon completing it, I accepted a position working in advertising and marketing for a women's fashion retailer. Before I knew it, I had landed an unintended career in advertising. You might think that makes sense in terms of working in an industry that facilitates creative expression. Unfortunately, I was working as a media planner and buyer. (For those unfamiliar, that's a numbers-based role.) *Not* the best match for a right-brain-dominant woman!

One quiet evening during that phase in my life, I took out a yellow legal pad and drafted the structure for an in-home closet audit and wardrobe consultation. I envisioned a service I'd offer as a part-time hobby to make side cash and feed my fashion passion. That was more than twenty years ago. Recently, I found those yellow pages of notes in a box of old books and papers. It was stunning to see how similar that outline was to the services I provide today. It brought to light that it is indeed possible to form a career doing what one truly loves.

WRIGHT

Speaking of people who are doing what they love, how important is that to success and how has living your passion changed your own life, personally, and professionally?

BUCCELLATO

When we do something we love, our passion propels us to excel and to enjoy time spent on that activity. Of course, one can be accomplished in an area of work without passion. I was acknowledged and promoted for my work in advertising media without the presence of that passion. But when we choose a career field that we feel an affinity with, and it capitalizes on our innate strengths and interests, we naturally experience more joy. We put heart and soul—a piece of ourselves—into what we do. If we're working directly with others, they catch the fire of our excitement, and we have a positive energy of reciprocity.

I find my business personally rewarding. I enjoy the clients I work with, I appreciate making a difference in their lives, and their feedback fuels me further. A client recently sent a note sharing the results of her enhanced personal image and the positive feedback she was getting from others. In her mail she said, "Thanks for these opportunities for me to 'walk tall.'" *That's* what brings me satisfaction! As cliché as it may sound, when doing something of passion, it's difficult to name it "work." Of course there are necessary pieces of my business that I don't absolutely love. I have learned to get outside help in those areas that don't coincide with my personal strengths. One day, *all* of those pieces will be outsourced. It's a work in process, just like life in general.

In the meanwhile, I see others accomplishing goals and having a different life experience as a result of my work with them. A Central Michigan University study showed that image consulting services gave clients more than just a "superficial boost." Sixty-three percent of people who were interviewed before and after their image services felt they had more self-esteem after working with their consultant. That's something I wasn't able to do as a media planner.

WRIGHT

How does one go about choosing an image consultant?

BUCCELLATO

Image consulting goes beyond fashion styling or personal shopping, so knowing that the consultant is well-trained is important. For the image coach, dressing a client isn't about the clothes or creating a trendy fashion look—it's about the individual person. The clothing, color, body language, voice, and etiquette skills are the tools that develop the visual image as a brand statement.

Skilled consultants are trained in color theory, the psychology of color, and color's relationship with the personal characteristics of a client. They understand design elements of line, shape, and texture. They consider the subtleties of nonverbal communications and the paralanguage of voice, and they often coach on etiquette skills as well. If working with corporate leadership or employee groups, they'll have an understanding of the business environment and they'll possess strong communication skills.

A certification program has been established by the Association of Image Consultants International (AICI) to help clients discern a consultant's experience level. Clients can get this information at www.aici.org. Also important is the communication style and professionalism of the consultant.

The client-consultant arrangement develops into a unique relationship, so comfort and ease in relations is important.

I encourage those considering hiring a consultant to look at all of these factors as they relate to the desired image service.

WRIGHT

What would you say is the biggest contribution to your own professional success, Patty?

BUCCELLATO

I'd have to say tenacity and flexibility. The two are a valuable contradiction. I won't say I've always possessed both as innate qualities, although tenacity comes easy for one born under the sign of Taurus, the bull, as I am! As a self-employed business owner, it's been critical to remain committed to my own aspirations. There's no supervisor outlining my career path or "next step," much less a weekly or daily work plan for me. No formal office structure or lines of command exist, so sticking to a goal plan and enduring through challenging times is up to me.

I've learned to be flexible during the years of building and maintaining a business. The business and economic environment is constantly changing. What's valuable in the marketplace today may not be in demand tomorrow. In 1993, when I established Refined Images, workplace casual dress policies were new in the business world. My work focused, at that time, on helping organizations establish effective appearance policies and training their staff groups on maintaining professionalism in casual environments.

Then came a phase where corporate training budgets were disappearing in my geographic market due to the local economy. At the time, as an alternative to traveling nationally, My focus shifted to working one-on-one with private clients. My business services have changed with the market's changing needs. Today, Refined Images serves corporations, professional service firms, educational institutions, and private clients across North America.

WRIGHT

What is the message you want people to hear so that they can learn from your experience?

BUCCELLATO

Know who you are and what you want out of your life. Seek out self-assessment tools to help define this if necessary, so that you're living a life that brings satisfaction and feeds your soul. Then choose your actions with conscious intention. Allow your visual brand statement to support you on the course of confidently living an authentic life.

WRIGHT

Patty, it's been a pleasure visiting with you. I know our readers will enjoy your perspective. Thank you for sharing.

BUCCELLATO

Thank you, David. The pleasure has been mine!

ABOUT THE AUTHOR

Patty Buccellato is internationally recognized as a Certified Image Professional. She is founder of Refined Images, and specializes in image management for professional service firms and individual men and women. A member of the Association of Image Consultants International (AICI), Patty finds joy in helping clients discover their authentic, goal-focused visual presence. Patty founded Refined Images in 1993 at the dawn of "business casual." Since that time, countless organizations have used Refined Images staff training programs to uphold professionalism in their new, less formal environments. Clients range from CPA firms, manufacturing companies, and credit unions, to higher educational institutions and professional associations like NAWBO (National Association of Women Business Owners) and Fashion Group International.

Today, Refined Images provides coaching to employee groups whose firms recognize that productive business development efforts begin with effective brand ambassadors. Services include: staff training in image and personal brand management, visual assessments, professional wardrobe planning, and digital brand management. A recreational SCUBA diver, Patty views her work with clients as yet another opportunity to dive below the surface to uncover the uniqueness and wonder inherent in all beings.

PATTY BUCCELLATO
Refined Images, LLC
Rochester Hills, MI
(248) 650-2916
www.RefinedImages.net
www.facebook.com/RefinedImages

CHAPTER TWENTY-TWO

The 7 C's and E's of a
Compelling and Effective Speaker

An Interview with . . . **Jordana Tiger**

DAVID WRIGHT (WRIGHT)

Today we are talking with Jordana Tiger, an award-winning speaker who once ran away from any type of public speaking opportunity due to her nervousness and shyness. She now runs a company, Making Speaking Easy, whereby she coaches others to overcome their nervousness as well as trains them how to deliver dynamic and memorable presentations. Transforming fear of public speaking to freedom and fun in speaking is where her passion lies. Jordana also works as a life coach and marriage/family therapist inspiring others to live their amazing life. She believes all and anything is possible.

Jordana, welcome to *Stepping Stones to Success.*

What motivated you to want to help others overcome their fear of public speaking?

JORDANA TIGER (TIGER)

When I was a kid, my biggest fear in life was talking to more than one person at a time. I was extremely shy. If I was standing around with a group of

325

friends, I wouldn't say anything if there was more than one friend present. I was so afraid they wouldn't like what I said or they would disagree with me or, worst of all, make fun and laugh at me. I felt so uncomfortable—always. It was the worst feeling in my life at the time.

I had that same awful feeling while giving speeches in class, and after I was an adult, my fear continued. I was always competent in talking one-on-one while providing therapy and facilitating change for others, yet I didn't enjoy putting on the workshops.

I have definitely changed over the years. Now I love putting on workshops and being a motivational speaker. Speaking comfortably in front of large groups is my proudest accomplishment. I truly didn't think that was ever possible, and now I absolutely love speaking in front of thousands of people. The more the merrier, I say. I have a passion for it, and I want people to know and see that it is completely possible for anyone to transition from fear to freedom to fun in public speaking. I truly believe that if I can do it, anyone can!

My passion is in helping others accomplish this tremendous and exciting journey, not to mention inspiring them to have fun at the same time. I believe that if you are having a good time learning something, it will be easier to learn. I get so excited helping others overcome their fear and it is a beautiful sight to see someone transform right before your very eyes.

The fear of public speaking keeps people from doing things they love. I want to change that. Once you conquer the unfamiliar territory, it feels great to march through it.

My father and grandfather were amazing public speakers, and now I have followed in their footsteps; this is also a proud moment in time for me.

WRIGHT

How did you overcome this fear?

TIGER

It was definitely a combination of tools that helped me over the years. For example, my own personal therapy, trying to speak up at Al-Anon meetings, continuing to put on therapy and coaching workshops, and finally going to Toastmasters International.

I have a funny story to tell you about getting to Toastmasters. I had wanted to check out the organization since my father was a member when I was young. So I called the main office at Toastmasters and asked what I needed to know about attending a meeting. The woman on the phone said that as a guest, all I would need to do was to stand up and say my name and how I found out about

Toastmasters. It wasn't until twelve years later that I had the courage to show up. People who know me now and hear me speak can't believe that story. Let me tell you something; it is absolutely true. I have completely changed.

The main thing that got me over the hump was practice, practice, and more practice. And even more so than the practice was my passion for the topics I was speaking on. I longed to get my message across, to add value, and make a difference in people's lives. By putting on workshops and doing speaking engagements, I was able to take myself out of the fear and instead focus on the value I was giving the audience. It is something so special and important for me to take something that is a universal problem or issue and present my topic in such a way that it affects the audience, leaving them inspired to change something they are doing in their life in order to make something better for them and/or better for the people in their lives. My passion for my speeches and workshops was the focus I needed to overcome my fear. Making a difference for others is the bigger and better picture. After all, how can I be a motivational speaker if I'm afraid to speak? I had no choice but to change.

WRIGHT

What are some of the topics you speak on?

TIGER

There are several topics I like to speak on, and they are all somehow related. I will tell you about three of them.

The first one is on "living authentically with *no* regrets." In my therapy practice, I used to work with people who were in the process of dying. They all had things they regretted doing in their life, as I believe we all have; however, the things that stood out for them were the regrets of things they didn't end up doing. There are so many reasons we hold back, yet at the end of our lives we wished we hadn't.

I talk about the main reasons we hold back (fear of authenticity, fear of trying new things, and fear of not wanting to hurt others). At the end of your life, why should you have wished for something that you had a choice and chance to do something about but didn't do it because you were afraid? I talk about not leaving anything on the table. This is your life. You have so many choices and for me, hearing so many people talk about the things they wished they did and didn't do is sad. I say go out and be yourself; go for your dreams.

I also speak about "being authentically present for people"—to look people in their eyes while speaking with them. Too many people are distracted and not focused when speaking with one another. Feelings get hurt and connections are lost. I say we need to "Listen with Love."

I also speak on the "Five Avenues of Awesome Living." So many individuals are living by rote. They just go on with their "automatic pilot" day and miss opportunities. I work with others on finding out what they truly value and love and assist them in setting concrete goals for meeting these desires.

The other thing I do is run a "Speakers Training Camp®." I help people overcome their fears as well as teach practical techniques to being an effective speaker.

WRIGHT

What are the benefits of taking your *Speakers Training Camp®*?

TIGER

There are many wonderful benefits for taking this one- or two-day workshop. Participants will learn to handle their nervousness and be more confident as well as learn innovative techniques that help deliver a powerful and memorable presentation, whether it is corporate or motivational in style.

Participants will be given the tools that will connect and engage them with their audiences. They will also learn how to influence audiences with a compelling opening, organized body, and lasting conclusion. We go over the use of humor along with identifying personal strengths and challenges and how to overcome the challenges. I give individualized coaching and a money-back guarantee if those who attend are not satisfied with the workshop.

Many people need to make presentations for work and are terrified. This workshop will help them get over their fear. In my camp, participants will get valuable and honest, specific feedback along with a lot of encouragement. And of course, it's a camp—it's fun!

WRIGHT

I heard that you make a video of your participants' presentations. Tell me why this technique is useful in polishing one's speaking skills?

TIGER

Yes, I make a personalized video recording of everyone in the workshop. This is the most effective and efficient way for people to see what they look like when they speak and how they come across visually. They see all their gestures, facial expressions, body language, and hear their voice.

Most people are afraid and dislike seeing themselves on a recording; however, if you are looking for the best way for constructive feedback, this is it. It is amazing how many participants end up liking this method of feedback after having experienced it. Don't worry, everyone only takes home his or her own personalized video—no one else will see yours!

I give them their own personalized DVD to keep at the end of the workshop for their own personal review and use. They then can watch it in the privacy of their home as often as they like. My feedback on their presentation is also on the DVD. By reviewing the recording and listening to it, they get to see their strengths and challenges right before their own eyes. It is right there in front of them. There is no assumption; the picture is worth everything.

Their non-verbal communication stands out and that is one of the most important parts to notice and work on when refining speaking skills. Body movements, eye contact, gestures, and facial expressions are right there in view along with the little twitches and habits that could be distracting to an audience. The message beyond the words pop out and it is apparent if the powerful message being sent is matched together with their body and words.

By watching the recording, transformation can occur faster than if someone verbally tells you what you need to work on. Self-learning is always a powerful tool.

WRIGHT

Who attends your workshops?

TIGER

Many kinds of people attend the workshops. The people who come usually need to make presentations or speak in a group at their place of work. It can be anyone including executives, sales managers, presenters, speakers, trainers, teachers, attorneys, small business owners, therapists, and so on. Sometimes people come simply because they want to improve their personal communication skills, learn how to handle their nervousness, and they want to refine their speaking skills in general.

WRIGHT

So tell me, Jordana, what are the "7 C's & E's of a Compelling and Effective Speaker"?

TIGER

There are many qualities that will have you stand out as a top notch speaker. I believe these seven are crucial for a powerful presentation or speech.

1. CONTAGIOUS ENTHUSIASM

There have been studies done on audiences that measure what people are looking for when listening to a speaker. Enthusiasm comes up as being number one. If you are not captivating and engaging the audience with your presence, you will lose them. When you have enthusiasm, it is also contagious. They will catch the wave that keeps them listening to your every word. They are definitely more interested and curious to see what you are going to say—what message you want to convey.

2. EMOTIONAL CONNECTION

This is very important. You need to have passion, authenticity, and sincerity for your topic as well as having those qualities for your audience. They go hand in hand. The audience wants to see your excitement about what you are talking about. Being emotionally connected with them keeps them listening to you just like your contagious enthusiasm does.

Put your personality into the presentation. They want to see the real deal—the real you. This is the part of you that is authentic and sincere. They will relate to you and feel moved to listen, even if they don't necessarily agree with what you are saying. Be conversational in nature. This has a big affect on your connection with them. In order to "sell" an idea or have them "believe" in you, the emotional connection needs to be there first. Emotionally moving and touching your audience is a key ingredient to keeping them focused, engaged, and wanting more.

3. EFFECTIVE AND CLEAR CONTENT

The content needs to be well thought out and organized. Having an organized opening, body, and conclusion shows respect for your audience, letting them know you value their time. The flow is important because you don't want your audience to have to work hard to piece together your material; that is your job.

To have clarity, you first want to develop a need in them, present the issue or problem you are going to solve, solve it by giving three to five details with poignant personal stories, examples, or facts, and then tie it all up with a meaningful conclusion. Stories creatively woven together illustrate the message and main point you want to convey. Clarity, purpose, and timing of your stories and humor are also important.

You want to remember not to put too much information in your presentation, otherwise you run the risk of losing your audience. Keep in tight and say what you want to say.

Involving and including your audience whenever you can is also extremely valuable. Use individuals' names during your talk if you have the opportunity and use the word "you" when speaking to them. Making it personal for them helps them stay connected and interested.

Using dialogue to stress a point is also very effective in keeping them "in" the speech. Putting them in the scene such as saying, "Have you ever—" has them paying attention and thinking of their actual response. This is an invaluable technique to use. You can also have them raise their hands, shout out things when you invite them to, and definitely have a call to action at the end.

4. CREATIVE OPENING AND CLOSING

One of the most important parts of your presentation is the *Opening*. It needs to "Wow 'em!" It needs to be an attention-getter that makes a profound effect, yet puts the audience at ease so they are ready for the rest of your talk. Be compelling.

There are a few good ways to do this. You can ask a question, quote someone, tell a story, or give an unusual fact. If you ask a question, try to bring it back around toward the conclusion so the speech comes full circle. If you use the story approach, make it personal if possible and just jump right into it to capture them at the beginning. You can also "call back" your story later on to keep them engaged and connected with the speech in its entirety. Referencing your stories in general keeps them connected and makes your point succinct. Your connection with them at the beginning of your talk can definitely make or break your presentation.

The next thing you need to do is to let them know what they will be listening for. An audience always feels more comfortable if they know where both of you are going. Let them know the benefit and value they will receive in listening to you. Tell them what you plan to tell them, then tell them, then tell them what you just told them.

Influence them with your powerful and memorable *Closing*. You want to "Wow 'em!" with it so they remember your message. A call to action is a great thing to do. (I will talk more about that later on.) Make sure the

Opening and *Closing* tie in the body and your message. Very often the *Opening* and *Closing* are what they will remember the most. Make them count.

5. CONFIDENT AND ENGAGING COMMUNICATION STYLE

In your speaking style there are many things to pay attention to.

GESTURES:

Must be natural and fit what you are saying. Some speakers try to plan out their gestures; however, it can come across as unnatural and the audience might lose interest in you. I would recommend not practicing your gestures; instead, notice them when you practice and make sure they fit. Be authentic in your gestures.

BODY MOVEMENT:

A part of gestures is Body Movement. You want to learn to use your body effectively. Being poised and relaxed are two ways to set the audience at ease. Your physical body sends non-verbal messages all throughout your speech; therefore, purposeful movement is important. This helps create your environment.

When people are nervous they tend to fidget, rock back and forth, sway, or put their hands in their pockets. This is very distracting to the audience, which in turn makes them tune out to your message.

A few ideas for movement are as follows: If you are going to be speaking in chronological order, it is a good idea to move from the audiences left to right while making your point because they are used to reading from left to right; therefore, your material will sink in more.

Be careful not to move as you are in the middle of delivering your strong point; make the movement occur right before you speak your highlighted point. If you move while you are giving pertinent information, it will get lost in your movement. You can also step forward to make important points, back up when you want them to digest some material, and move from side to side during a transition to a new point in your presentation.

Your hand gestures should be at shoulder level and your hands should be held in an open fashion. Your gestures are your punctuation. Use them wisely.

FACIAL EXPRESSIONS:

Another important part of gesturing is your Facial Expressions. Smiling is huge. When you smile at an audience they feel more connected, comfortable, and they will listen more attentively to your message. And, as I said before, it is your job and goal to make your audience comfortable.

Your audience will decide in the first few moments of your presentation if they like you or not. When nerves get in the way, awkward facial expressions may come through. Practicing in a mirror and watching your DVD recording is a great tool to help you see what you look like. Be sure your face matches what you are saying.

EYE CONTACT:

Is another important feature as far as style. Speaking directly to each member of your audience is a wonderful way to make direct personal contact with them. They will feel valued and you also come across as more credible, interesting, and sincere. This definitely helps them remember your presentation.

Try to look at different people throughout your speech and keep your focus on each person for at least three to five seconds. At first this will feel uncomfortable, yet with practice you can do this. It will definitely enhance your presentation and you will receive positive feedback from your audience.

VOICE:

The last point I want to cover about style has to do with your voice. There is a lot to know about your voice. It should be natural, dynamic, pleasant, and expressive.

Rate of Speed is one of the qualities to pay attention to. Speaking too fast is a common practice among beginning or nervous speakers. It can create confusion in your audience and you may lose them.

This is something I did often when I was first speaking. I was nervous and just wanted to be done with it. Now I do it sometimes because I am so excited about what I am saying. I still have to watch myself.

Along with everything else, practice is the key to improvement.

Volume and *variety with inflections* is also important. They should change as you move through your presentation. You can be louder or softer to make or point or set a mood as well as have a *variety of inflections* in your voice depending on what you are talking about. Very often audiences report the speaker was boring because he or she spoke in a monotone voice. You would be surprised how many people speak this way during their presentations. Make your best effort to engage your audience with variety in your voice.

The *tone* and way you say something is also important. You want to have energy and sincerity all at the same time. And, as I stated before, you want to be conversational as though you are talking to a friend. Make it all fit the message. You can tell a lot about your *rate of speed, volume, variety of inflections, and tone* from making an audio recording of yourself while practicing your speech. Of course, if you want to watch your gestures as well, a video is best.

Gestures, body language, facial expressions, eye contact, and voice are all important features in having a confident and engaging communication style. These styling qualities can make or break your speech.

1. CAPTIVATING, CHARISMATIC ENERGY:

Many times, when you are coming to the end of your speech, a lull can exist. It is important to keep up your energy throughout the entire speech. Keep on top of your game by punching it up with some more exciting and touching stories and/or humor to keep your audience from getting restless. Keep up that captivating and charismatic energy that makes your presentation memorable and unforgettable.

2. COMPELLING CHALLENGE CALL/CREATING A COMPELLING SHIFT:

This is something you want to accomplish at the end of your presentation. This is where you get the audience to make a positive shift in the way they are thinking or feeling. It is in this feeling they will make a decision to take actions in their life that will make a difference for them or someone else. It can be a lifelong lasting shift. If they are still thinking about your speech days later, you can be assured that you had a huge effect on them. This is the value you gave them and it's the best result you can ever ask for.

As far as the challenge goes, if your audience is personally invited to do something, it does several things: 1) it makes them feel even more connected to you, 2) it helps them remember your message, and most of all, 3) it inspires them to take the action that will bring rewards into their lives. This is our mission and purpose as a speaker, isn't it? To have an effect on audiences in such a powerful way that we move them to a better position in their lives is the gift we provide. At least, this is the dream I have.

WRIGHT

What are the advantages of being a more proficient speaker?

TIGER

Many corporations and companies are looking for individuals who can sell whatever their product or idea is. It takes a polished speaker to bring in business for a company. It is actually stressful these days to not be a good speaker. The stress can lead to poor work habits and more importantly, poor health. Some people are held back from promotions or lose their job simply because they are too afraid to speak for the company or they are just not very good speakers.

I know of some people who were passed over for promotions because they did not know how to present the material they knew in their head. How frustrating for them. There is nothing worse than being qualified for the actual job yet not get it because you were hesitant to stretch yourself. However, if you "put on a new pair of glasses" and speak through those confidence-building "lenses," you will be a changed person—professional and personally. The world will be yours to step into whenever you choose when you cross that line from fear to freedom to fun.

WRIGHT

What are the personal advantages to stepping up to the plate in speaking?

TIGER

You will have taken a huge step for yourself in your confidence to conquer whatever you challenge and will have a new found respect for yourself. In the process, you will also develop acceptance, compassion, and patience for yourself.

We spend so much time in our lives inside our own body (our whole life, actually) that I think it's worth feeling comfortable speaking in any situation. You will realize a benefit from this ability in more situations than in just a job where presentation skills are needed. You will feel more comfortable wherever speaking is necessary. It could be with your family, friends, or co-workers. It could be at the bank, the grocery store, or in any sticky situation you may find yourself. Once you develop the confidence and skills to speak, you can take your speaking anywhere.

WRIGHT

What do audiences want from a speaker?

TIGER

They want "the 3 E's." The 3 E's are: to be Energized, Enlightened, and most of all Entertained. You can provide them with these through your enthusiasm, great stories, organized content, and humor.

Audiences like speakers who: know their topic and are prepared, have a clear and organized message, get to the point, tell poignant and funny stories, and leave them with something. They want to relate to you, they want real examples, they want you to be interesting, and they want you to be enthusiastic, confident, sincere, passionate, and dynamic.

Most of all, the audience wants you to succeed. They also want to be comfortable. If they notice you are nervous and are having trouble up there they will feel uneasy. It is part of your job to be prepared so the audience feels relaxed. If you are prepared, poised, and polished, they will listen with ease, feel relaxed, and they will want to hear you again.

WRIGHT

What are some of your final thoughts about speaking?

TIGER

Speaking is an adventure. It is a fun and exciting way to send and deliver a message. Speaking gives you opportunities you didn't know were possible. The unexpected opportunity to speak is always lurking somewhere. If you are confident, then you are ready for anything.

Speaking effectively is a growth and personal challenge for so many people. I always say people feel awesome about themselves when they are prepared for anything. Step up to the challenge. Be unforgettable. Be in the moment.

Speaking also helps your listening skills since being a powerful speaker entails powerfully listening to the reaction of your audience. If you want to improve your listening skills, being a compelling and effective speaker definitely can assist you in that area.

The main thing is to go out there and have fun while speaking. I hope this chapter has helped you in some way to transform your fear to one of fun.

ABOUT THE AUTHOR

JORDANA TIGER is an award-winning speaker who is described by others as "riveting," "engaging," and "inspiring." She is the President and owner of Making Speaking Easy, a company specializing in coaching and training others to give compelling, dynamic, and powerful presentations. Along with giving you a variety of strategies that make your presentations unforgettable, she teaches you how to connect and engage with your audience. It is her passion and love of helping people feel comfortable engaging in the number one fear—public speaking—that sets her apart from other trainers. As a catalyst for change, she believes everyone can enjoy speaking and have fun doing so. Her dedication to excellence and personal service make her invaluable. She is also a life coach and marriage/family therapist.

JORDANA TIGER MFT, CPCC
Making Speaking Easy
11856 Balboa Blvd., Ste. 234
Granada Hills, CA
818.519.9080
Jordana@MakingSpeakingEasy.com
www.MakingSpeakingEasy.com

REFLECTIONS